Sacred Tarot

– Course 6 –

Sacred Tarot

The Art of Card Reading and the Underlying Spiritual Science

C. C. Zain

The Church of Light
Los Angeles

Published in the United States in 1994 by
The Church of Light
2341 Coral Street, Los Angeles, CA 90031-2916

Library of Congress Cataloging-in-Publication Data
Zain, C. C. (Elbert Benjamine), 1881–1951.
  Sacred tarot : the art of card reading and the
  underlying spiritual science / C.C. Zain. —Rev. 2nd ed.
  (Course 6)
      p.   cm.   — (The Brotherhood of Light : course 6)
  Originally published: [S. 6.] : E. Benjamine, 1936.
  Includes index.
  ISBN 0-87887-376-7 (alk. paper) : $14.95
  1. Tarot. 2. Kabala. 3. Numerology 4. Occultism I. Title.
II. Series.
BF1879.T2Z35 1994   94-22401
133.3'2424—dc20   CIP

Sacred Tarot may be obtained through your local bookstore
or you may order it from The Church of Light, 2341 Coral Street,
Los Angeles, CA 90031-2916, (213)226-0453.

Contents

List of Major & Minor Arcana and Tarot Spreads

Major Arcana

Minor Arcana

Court Cards

Tarot Spreads

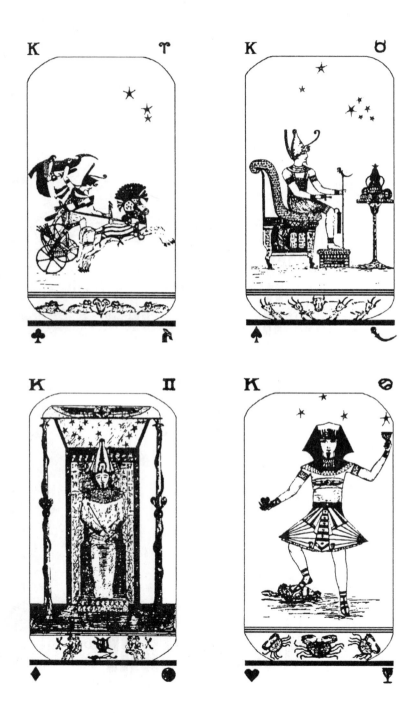

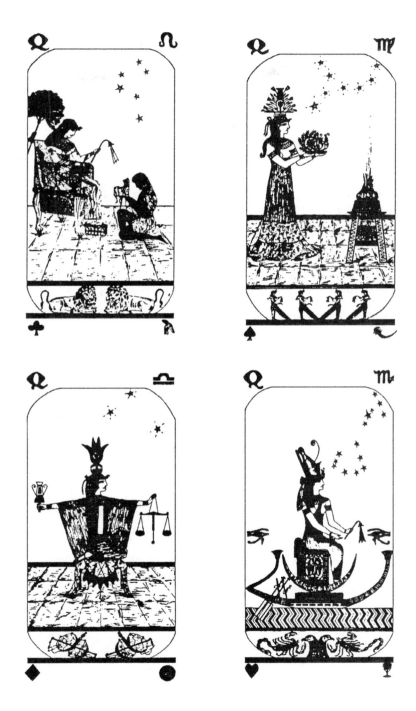

ix

Table of Correspondences

Number	Hebrew Letter	Hebrew Character	English Letter	Astrological Correspondence	Color	Gem or Metal	Divinatory Significance
1	Aleph	א	A	Mercury	Violet	Quicksilver	Dexterity Will
2	Beth	ב	B	Virgo	Darker Violet	Jasper	Science
3	Gimel	ג	G	Libra	Lighter Yellow	Diamond	Action Marriage
4	Daleth	ד	D	Scorpio	Darker Red	Topaz	Realization
5	He	ה	E	Jupiter	Purple or Indigo	Tin	Religion Law
6	Vau	ו	V–U–W	Venus	Yellow	Copper	Temptation
7	Zain	ז	Z	Sagittarius	Lighter Purple	Red Garnet	Victory
8	Cheth	ח	H–CH	Capricorn	Darker Blue	Onyx or Sardonyx	Justice Equilibrium
9	Teth	ט	TH	Aquarius	Lighter Blue	Blue Saphire	Wisdom Prudence
10	Jod	י	I–Y–J	Uranus	Dazzling White	Uranium	Change of Fortune
11	Caph	כ	C–K	Neptune	Iridescence	Neptunium	Force Spiritual Power
12	Lamed	ל	L	Pisces	Darker Purple	Peridot	Sacrifice Expiation
13	Mem	מ	M	Aries	Lighter Red	Amethyst	Transformation Death
14	Nun	נ	N	Taurus	Darker Yellow	Agate	Regeneration Temperance
15	Samek	ס	X	Saturn	Blue	Lead	Fatality Black Magic
16	Ayin	ע	O	Mars	Red	Iron	Accident Catastrophe
17	Pe	פ	F–P–PH	Gemini	Lighter Violet	Beryl	Truth Hope Faith
18	Tzaddi	צ	SH–TS–TZC	Cancer	Lighter Green	Emerald	Deception False Friends
19	Quoph	ק	Q	Leo	Lighter Orange	Ruby	Happiness
20	Resh	ר	R	Moon	Green	Silver	Awakening Resurrection
21	Shin	ש	S	Sun	Orange	Gold	Success Attainment
22 0	Tau	ת	T ⊥	Earth Pluto	Black Ultraviolet	Clay Plutonium	Failure Folly Spirituality

Chapter 1

Doctrine of Kabalism

THE word Kabala signifies traditional knowledge. It thus refers to the Oral Law, as handed down from antiquity; and embraces the occult traditions of all lands and all peoples.

Often it is used merely as referring to the esoteric doctrines of the Jews; but in its broader sense it includes also the secret doctrine of other races. This secret doctrine, common to many lands, was jealously guarded from the profane, and was never permitted to pass into writing except in such ambiguous terms as to baffle the uninitiated as to its true purport.

In this sense the sacred books of the world, including the Avesta, the Vedas and the Bible are largely kabalistical; for they set forth traditions that are capable of an inner, or esoteric, interpretation. In fact, there are usually several interpretations possible, each more inner version revealing a deeper truth to those who have advanced along the path far enough to comprehend it.

The Kabala has two divisions; the Written Kabala and the Unwritten Kabala.

Of the unwritten Kabala, S. L. MacGregor Mathers, in his *Kabbala Unveiled* says: "The term 'Unwritten Qbalah' is applied to certain knowledge which is never entrusted to writing, but communicated orally. I may say no more on this point, not even whether I myself have or have not received it."

The author of these lessons is not so modest about his acquaintance with the unwritten kabala. He has received it fully, and has also investigated the written traditions of the Jews and of all other peoples having had much influence in shaping the world's thought. And this seems the proper place to point out that the unwritten

1

kabala, like the written kabala, is set forth in symbolical language, with purposeful blinds and subterfuges to confuse the uninitiated; so that of the few who undoubtedly exist at the present day who have received it, most remain in as much ignorance of its true interpretation as the majority of students do after studying the more accessible written kabala.

This unwritten kabala has been transmitted only through certain secret schools. Those receiving it well merit what is given to them. They are left to their own devices in the matter of interpretation. And because the real keys to its interpretation—astrology and the tarot—have been largely ignored, or distorted, they have floundered sadly in arriving at its meaning. Whether written or unwritten, the kabala is a philosophy correlated to esoteric astrology as exemplified by the tarot; and it can only be comprehended fully by those who perceive the true relation between astrological energies and their pictured tarot exemplification.

The Kabala of The Jews

Because the Jewish kabala has been the source of inspiration to so many alchemists, metaphysicians, occultists and mystics, it deserves special attention, and the remainder of the lesson will largely be devoted to it. It has three main divisions: A. The Practical Kabala. B. The Literal Kabala. C. The Dogmatic Kabala.

A. The practical kabala treats of ceremonial magic, and includes the making of magic circles, wands, swords and pentacles, and the use of inscriptions and symbols for performing wonders. It deals with necromancy, sorcery, exorcisms, sigils, enchantments and communications with angels and devils.

Accessible books treating of this subject are: The Sixth and Seventh Book of Moses, The Greater Keys of Solomon the King, and The Lesser Keys of Solomon. Needless to say, as set forth in detail in Chapter 3 of Course 18, *Imponderable Forces*, these books and all such practices are highly dangerous, and innocence is no protection to those who dabble in such matters.

B. The literal kabala is so written that the letters and numbers and words must be transposed to perceive the meaning. It is a work really written in code, and must be systematically decoded to have any value. And the code in which it is written, and which must be used to decipher it, takes three different forms as follows:

are renowned.

Before the last cataclysm, in the Bible referred to as the flood of Noah, when the last of these two older continents sank, the Priests of Stellar Wisdom, perceiving through astrological cycles the approach of such a disaster, had encouraged the establishment of colonies in what later were to become the seven ancient centers of civilization—Egypt, India, Crete, Peru, Mexico, China and Chaldea. And to these colonies then established, that the ancient spiritual wisdom might not perish from the earth, they sent those to reside who were familiar with it.

Just when the colonists from Atlantis or Mu reached their various outposts is not clearly defined. But in Egypt, Moses, educated by the priesthood, came directly in contact with their teachings, and in his wilderness wanderings received further communications from higher intelligences; all of which became a part of the doctrine held by the Jewish priests, and handed down to later times in the form of abstruse allegories.

It seems certain that none of what now is known as the Jewish Kabala was written until after the commencement of the Christian era. The first to place any of this traditional knowledge in writing is reputed to have been Ben-Ha-Kanah, about 70 A.D. Rabbi Ismael be Elisha wrote about 121 A.D. And Simon be Jochai, another Talmudist, the supposed writer of the Zohar, appeared about 150 A.D.

However as a matter of historical research, it is found that the Kabala first put in an external appearance in the seventh century, apparently through Neo-Platonist and Neo-Pythagorean channels. The main body of the Zohar seems to have been unknown, except in the secret schools, until the thirteenth century of our era.

The early writings on the Kabala include a work called Palaces, describing God's throne and His angelic household, a work of The Dimensions of Deity, and the Alphabet of Rabbi Akiba. In this letter each Hebrew letter is taken to represent a primordial spiritual idea.

The Sephir Yetzirah

In the eighth century the Sephir Yetzirah put in an external appearance. It is a complete philosophical system, divided into 33 brief sections, each in reality based upon one of the 12 zodiacal signs, one of the 10 planets, one of the 10 numerals, or the seal of the earth.

The work opens with the statement that there are 32 paths of secret wisdom. These are further elaborated in a commentary, called the 32 Paths of Wisdom, written in 32 brief sections.

Sephir Yetzirah signifies The Book of Formation, and is supposed to have been dictated by Abraham. The key to its meaning is the manner in which it is divided into chapters. As in all there are 6 chapters, the formation of the universe is to be explained through a study of the number 6. This number, as reference to Arcanum VI indicates, has for divinatory significance the word Temptation, and in numbers indicates the oscillation of unequilibriated forces in their action and reaction. Astrologically, it corresponds to Venus, the planet of love. Therefore, according to the system upon which the Sephir Yetzirah is to be interpreted, the idea is conveyed that the Infinite was Tempted into expression through the desire to love. The Supernal Mind, that it might enjoy love, brought forth the manifested universe.

Of these 6 chapters, the first contains 12 sections, which, of course, correspond to 12 zodiacal signs.

The second chapter has 5 sections and the third chapter has 5 sections. Thus these two chapters represent the universal man divided as male and female; the number of man being 5 and the number of woman being 5; and together these numbers embracing the 10 numerals of the decade.

The fourth chapter has 4 sections, each representing one of the formative attributes of the septenary, corresponding to the 4 negative planets: Saturn, Venus, Moon and Mercury.

The fifth chapter has 3 sections, each representing one of the 3 active principles of the septenary, corresponding to Sun, Mars and Jupiter.

The sixth chapter contains the remaining four sections each representing one of the three remaining planets of the chain, Uranus, Neptune, Pluto, and the seal of the earth which synthesizes these 32 numbers and astrological forces into a single grand unity.

Masonry and the tarot are both founded upon 33 universal principles. These are rather unsatisfactorily set forth in kabalistical code in the Sephir Yetzirah. They bear a correspondence in human anatomy to the 24 vertebrae plus the 9 ankylosed bones that form the base of the spine. In the widest sense Deity is the 33, or unifying principle. Thus we have the doctrine set forth kabalistically that Deity, all-potential and alone, was Tempted into an expression of his Love, and this formative power became diversified into the 32 principles through which His love is Realized.

The Letters. In the kabalistical system each Hebrew letter is not only a number but in addition represents an idea. Just what the idea is which is thus associated with each letter it is a function of the Tarot to reveal.

The Hebrew alphabet as a whole contains 22 letters. These are divided by kabalists into three groups. The first group contains the three mother letters, representing certain general principles, from which the other letters and their corresponding principles were formed. Then there are seven double letters, and finally twelve single letters.

The three mother letters are Aleph, Mem, and Shin. Aleph represents the plane of spirit, Mem relates to the astral world, and Shin to the physical where all is given form. Thus do the three mother letters correspond to ego, Soul and Body of the Universal Man.

Certain other letters are sometimes aspirated and sometimes not, and are thus called double letters. As there are seven planets and seven active attributes in nature so are there seven double letters; Beth, Gimel, Daleth, Caph, Pe, Resh, and Tau. And as there are 12 zodiacal signs, so there are 12 single letters, although in detail they do not correspond to them: He, Vau, Zain, Cheth, Teth, Jod, Lamed, Nun, Sameck, Ayin, Tzaddi, and Quoph.

And now we arrive at a point which may easily prove somewhat confusing to the student. It is the numerical equivalence of the Hebrew letters, and of the corresponding English letters.

The Hebrew and the Chaldean square-formed letters are identical, and the square-formed Egyptian letters are very similar. These letters were originally hieroglyphics for the spiritual ideas represented by the corresponding Major Arcanum of the tarot, these, in turn, being correlated spiritually to astrology. Each letter, thus, expressed a number—some number from 1 to 22—which had the same thought-vibratory rate as one of the 22 astrological influences.

But these letters coming into use by those uninitiated in this spiritual and vibratory relation naturally were subject to conventionalizing influences. And furthermore, those who sought to make translations from Hebrew into the English language had no knowledge of the vibratory rate of a letter, and no care for its spiritual correspondence. Consequently, translators have made use of equivalents which, although convenient for them, are not of the same vibratory rate.

Therefore, to preserve the true numerical value of each square-formed letter, occult students have continued to use their original numerical significance rather than those established by later conventional use. And in deriving the English equivalent of a square-formed ancient letter, in those cases where translators have substituted an English letter with a different thought-vibratory rate, occult students use a true vibratory equivalent. Thus the Hebrew Tau, which means the sign of the cross, is translated conventionally as Th; and Teth, which means serpent, is translated conventionally as T. But not only is T in the form of the Tau cross used in many lands, but with its point down thus represents the creative energy diverted to earthly ends, and as such it has the significance of 22 and not 9; and 9 has the vibration of Th, the serpent, the spiral of life, being the Deific number.

This translation of T and Th is the outstanding difference between conventional translators and occult students. But it should be understood by those who study the kabala and the tarot, that in such studies the real vibratory rate of a letter is the important thing in determining its correspondence in another language; and that the English equivalent of each square-formed letter has been tested out on this basis.

The correct numerical and English equivalent of each square-formed ancient letter will be found in a table at the front of this booklet. And that the student may also have the conventional, and therefore exoteric, significance, a list here follows:

1. Aleph, A, means ox. 2. Beth, B, means house. 3. Gimel, G, means camel. 4. Daleth, D, means door. 5. He, H, means window. 6. Vau, V, means nail. 7. Zain, Z, means weapon. 8. Cheth, Ch, means fence. 9. Teth, T, means serpent. 10. Jod, J, means hand. 20. Caph, K, means palm of hand. 30. Lamed, L, means ox-goad. 40. Mem, M, means water. 50. Nun, N, means fish. 60. Samek, S, means support. 70. Ayin, O, means eye. 80. Pe, P, means mouth. 90. Tzaddi, Tz, means fishing-hook. 100. Quoph, Q, means back of head. 200. Resh, R, means head. 300. Shin, Sh, means tooth. 400. Tau, Th, means sign of the cross.

Sephir Sephiroth

The Sephir Sephiroth is also called the Book of Emanations. It treats of the numerical expansion of the undifferentiated state of evolution. That is, it explains that creation, as it later came into existence, was first in the Divine Mind. Then to give this mental conception a more external form it was projected into an evolutionary system, by means of definite impulses, each of which bears a relation to a certain number. The universe is thus shown to have been created according to a definite plan, the parts of this plan bearing numerical relations to each other. This plan calls for a continuous expansion of possibilities, whereby an infinitely diverse number of forms move perpetually forward toward greater perfection.

The work, as written, is highly mystical; for it considers these impulses from the Divine Mind, by which the universe is brought into existence, as bearing the same relation to each other as do certain numbers. These numbers are thus the representatives of universal principles.

The student, therefore, who would read the Sephir Sephiroth understandingly must be well versed both in the Hermetic System of Numbers, and the Doctrine of Signatures; for the Doctrine of Signatures reveals in full concrete details the action of those principles which are but abstractions when merely considered as numerical relations.

Asch Metzareph

Asch Metzareph, or Purifying Fire, treats of alchemy. To comprehend the allegories in which it is written the student must have a thorough knowledge of chemistry, of astrology, and of the tarot. The action of substance upon substance, as set forth in this treatise in the language of universal symbolism, depends upon the inner nature of each; upon that quality which we now recognize as its vibratory rate.

The Zohar

The most studied of the Jewish kabalistical works is the Zohar, or Book of Splendor. It is generally supposed to have been written by Simon be Jochai, about 150 A.D. Moses de Leon made it accessible to the public in the thirteenth century.

It embraces The Book of Concealed Mystery, The Greater Holy Assembly, The Lesser Holy Assembly, The Aged Man, The Book of Clear Light, The Faithful Shepherd, The Palaces, The Secret of The Law, The Concealed Treatise, Mysteries of Mysteries, Song of Songs, Come and See, The Youth, Illustrations of The Law, The Early Work, and certain fragments.

The aim is to reveal to the worthy the nature of the Supreme Being, the equilibrium of contrarities, cosmogony, the symbolism of numerals, the nature of man and angels, the law as revealed, the nature and destiny of the soul, and much about angels, elementals, demons and other occult intelligences.

The most essential and most emphasized of all kabalistical doctrines is expressed in translations of the Jewish work as "Quod Superius, Quod Inferius," which means, that which is above is as that which is below, the Macroposopus, the universal man, is to be understood by a study of Microposopus, the finite man. God is thus related to the natural universe as the ego is related to the body of man. Consequently, we find Deity commonly referred to as The Ancient One, The Vast Countenance, Illimitable One, The Concealed of the Concealed, Adam Kadmon (the Archetypal Man), etc.

Next in kabalistical importance comes the doctrine of the Ten Emanations of the Sephiroth, by which the universe was created. Sephiroth means numerical emanation, and the kabala teaches that all manifestation is accomplished in definite numerical proportions through actions and reactions in the One Primeval undifferentiated substance.

Prior to creation there was Ain Soph Aur, meaning limitless light, or non-differentiated substance. The first emanation, or numerical impulse is known as Kether, meaning Crown, and symbolizing Motion or Life.

Instantly, upon motion being transmitted to the non-polarized, universal, all-diffusive spirit, it becomes polarized into two attributes, positive and negative, masculine and feminine, action and reaction; for life or motion is impossible apart from sex, or polarity. It is impossible to have action without reaction, positive polarity without negative polarity, motion without something moving, something moving without form. Consequently, springing into existence simultaneously with Kether, or Life, are two other emanations called Chocmah and Binah. These usually are translated as Wisdom and Intelligence by theological kabalists who try to dethrone anything feminine from the Deific Trinity. But all initiates are aware that they mean Love and Light; for Love is the highest and truest Wisdom.

However large the orbit of the student's investigations, or however recondite the plane of its action, he will find that it must start with, and finally end in, this kabalistical trinity of Life, Light and Love. From this primitive trinity of positive, negative and union the universe became differentiated into Seven specific attributes through seven additional emanations.

The Ten Emanations of the Sephiroth are, therefore, the Seven Active Principles of Nature springing from a central source of Life, Light and Love—from a triune God-head, or Spiritual Sun—just as we receive magnetism, light and heat from the physical sun.

Although it has been well known that there is a strict correspondence between astrological principles and the 10 Emanations of the Sephiroth, the Emanations really manifesting as astrological forces, this correspondence has heretofore been carefully concealed as part of the Greater Mysteries. Also, as the universe is divided into positive, negative and union, kabalists have divided the 10 Emanations into three pillars, or Trees. The tree on the right is the Biblical tree of Good, the Masonic pillar Jachin, kabalistically known as the Father, or Pillar of Mercy. The tree on the left is the biblical tree of Evil, the Masonic pillar Boaz, kabalistically known as the Mother, or Pillar of Justice. Centrally between these two trees of the knowledge of good and evil stands the tree of Life, conferring Immortality. It is the place of union of Jachin and Boaz, kabalistically known as the Shekinah.

But early kabalists, to conceal their knowledge from the profane, in illustrating the trees in the form of a diagram, gave it incorrectly, knowing the spiritually enlightened in the course of their initiation would discover the error. It would thus point to the truth without actually revealing it, which by their oath they were bound not to do. In all current works upon the kabala, therefore, being copied from older works, we find emanation 2-4-7 constituting the Tree of Good, 3-5-8 the Tree of Evil, and 1-6-9-10 the Tree of Life, the Shekinah, or Pillar of Mildness. The correct diagram is given on page 130 in chapter 6, where it will be seen that as should be, the even, or esoteric, numbers 2-4-8 constitute the right-hand Pillar of Goodness, and the exoteric numbers 3-5-7 constitute the left-hand Pillar of Evil. Also it will be seen that the necessary planetary correspondences to each of the emanations when arranged in the latter manner will place benefic planets on the Tree of Good and malefic planets on the Tree of Evil.

The First emanation is called Kether, meaning Crown, and symbolizing Life or Motion. It corresponds to the planet Pluto. It belongs at the head of the Tree of Life, containing latent within itself both male and female potencies.

The Second emanation is Chocmah, meaning Wisdom, and symbolizing Love. It corresponds to the planet Neptune, the head of the Tree of Good, in a spiritual sense being positive to Uranus, though not so from the material plane.

The Third emanation is Binah, meaning Intelligence, and symbolizing Light. It corresponds to the planet Uranus, being the head of the Tree of Evil, being external to, and therefore more gross and spiritually negative than Neptune, and also commonly much more malefic.

The Fourth emanation is Chesed, meaning Mercy, and symbolizing Beneficence. It corresponds to the planet Jupiter, being the middle of the Tree of Good, and positive to the Saturn principle of Evil.

The Fifth emanation is Geburah, meaning Severity, and symbolizing Affliction. It corresponds to the planet Saturn, the middle of the Tree of Evil, and is negative to the principle of Good.

The Sixth emanation is Tippereth, meaning Beauty, symbolizing Attraction. It corresponds to the planet Venus, the middle of the Tree of Life, where all influences join in a common harmonious Union.

The Seventh emanation is Netzach, meaning Victory and symbolizing Conflict. It corresponds to the planet Mars, the foot of the Tree of Evil, and is negative to Mercury even as blind force is ever subject to intelligence.

The Eighth emanation is Hod, meaning Splendor, and symbolizing Knowledge. It corresponds to the planet Mercury, the foot of the Tree of Good, and is positive to the instincts and impulses of Mars.

The Ninth emanation is Yesod, meaning Foundation and symbolizing Formation. It corresponds to the Moon, next to the foot of the Tree of Life, the enfolding, formative power that gives external expression to Tippereth.

The Tenth emanation is Malkuth, symbolizing Vitality. It corresponds to the Sun, at the foot of the Tree of Life, wherein the Spiritual Ideals of Kether, having been attracted by Tippereth, and having undergone formative gestation of Yesod, are brought forth in full Virility of expression, becoming in man Self-Conscious-Immortality.

These three trees have been the great mystery of the kabala, and volumes of abstruse reasoning and mystical allegories have been written in the attempt to throw light upon it; for kabalists have all perceived that the Tree of Life, or the four emanations 1-6-9-10, constitutes the secret of Immortality. But just what this signifies in human life only a few have discovered, and others have blundered along blindly for want of proper keys, which astrology and the tarot alone afford. But the moment any kabalist is shown that Venus is Tippereth he immediately perceives the truth.

The head of the Tree of Life is the planet Pluto, symbolizing the separation of the sexes, the place where soul-mates part on their downward journey and the place where they must again unite on their upward path. But the Tree of Life itself is formed by the union of the Tree of Good with the Tree of Evil—three positive forces and three negative forces meeting at a common point called Tippereth. Thus what Venus is to the human body, by the law of correspondence, Tippereth must be to the Tree of Life.

Now Venus rules the seed and union, and kabalists are well aware that the Shekinah, or Tree of Life, is some kind of union. But what they usually fail to recognize is that in man there is a spiritual seed as well as one physical, and that union, as indicated by the four vibratory levels, or stations, represented by the four emanations within the Tree of Life, can take place on the plane of degeneration, on the level of generation, in the realm of regeneration, or in the exalted state of the reunion of soul-mates.

Yet Venus, the planet of love, is the key to this revelation. For those who recognize that Tippereth is a seed endowed with life during union, giving formative expression in the womb of Yesod, and brought forth into life and action by Malkuth, even as daily this is known to happen in the generation and birth of children, should easily recognize that the same principle applies to the evolution of Immortality. But, of course, as in bringing forth life in the domain of Malkuth, at the foot of the tree, the energies are directed toward the earth, and as immortality is not of earth but of the highest spheres, the energies must be directed toward the highest level of union, toward the exalted and permanent exchange of spiritual energies which corresponds to Pluto when that planet is represented by the letter T with its point up, instead of down toward Malkuth, as commonly written.

A few kabalists have perceived the truth of this matter. One, for instance, who was also a great alchemist, states in his writings that he was acquainted with the mystery of transmutation but had never proceeded to the practice because he had not found a woman who could help him in the work.

Also Mr. A. E. Waite, the eminent kabalist, in speaking of the Shekinah says: "I have said there are intimations of this state in eastern teachings, by which, I mean India, but that—so far as I am aware—they have not passed into writing." And he further concludes, after an exhaustive study of kabalistical literature: "We shall come to recognize only one secret doctrine of Jewry, which is the secret concerning sex."

Reincarnation

This seems to be the place to mention that the Jewish Kabala teaches reincarnation, but only for those who fail to finish their work, and never more than three times. And even in these instances, more often than not, more than one soul occupies the same body to gain strength. Thus the teachings of the Zohar contradict the teachings of reincarnation as commonly taught in the East. It sets forth the impossibility of numerous reincarnations, and really seems to be a confused notion regarding the attachment of a discarnate soul to one in the flesh for some definite gaining of experience or the performance of some unusual purpose.

Soul-Mates

The doctrine of soul-mates is quite distinctly taught in the Zohar, it being stated that those who abide by the laws of the Lord will meet and marry their true soul-mates; but that those who pervert the law will be denied such union. Impurity keeps soul-mates apart, but purity and a moral life bring them together, and when so united there also will be a permanent heavenly union after death.

God, Himself, is both Father and Mother. The word Elohim, translated in Genesis as God, is Feminine plural; but the translators of the Bible, not wishing women to share in anything Divine, have rendered it throughout in the Masculine singular. There is, however, an inadvertent admission of the Father-Mother principle when Adam is said to have been made in the image of "Elohim, Male and Female made He them." Hebrew scholars say that "Eloh" is feminine singular, and that the ending "im," is a termination of the masculine plural, the two being used together to indicate a feminine potency united to a masculine idea.

Throughout the Kabala "The Ancient of Days" is considered both Male and Female, and the Ten Emanations are divided into 5 positive and 5 negative attributes.

The Four Realms

The Ten Emanations of the Sephiroth are divided into groups having affinity with the four worlds; but at the same time the ten emanations also each manifest in these four realms. The four kabalistical worlds are:

1. Atziluth, meaning Emanation and symbolizing the celestial realm and the element fire.
2. Briah, meaning Creation and symbolizing the spiritual realm and the element air.
3. Yetzirah, meaning Formation and symbolizing the astral realm and the element water.
4. Assiah, meaning Action and symbolizing the physical realm and the element earth.

The first 3 emanations relate particularly to Celestial realms, the place of ideals, even as Pluto, Neptune and Uranus have an influence over the highest ideals of man.

The second 3 emanations pertain specifically to Spiritual realms, to the creative regions, even as Jupiter, Saturn and Venus have an influence over man's moral nature, his reflective powers and his affections.

The third 3 emanations relate more closely to the formative regions, to the Astral realms, even as Mercury, Mars and the Moon image, construct and mold the products of man's genius.

And the final emanation belongs to the Physical world, to the realm of practical action, even as the Sun vitalizes and brings forth from the soil innumerable forms of life.

Interpreting the Kabala

The great kabalistical student, Eliphas Levi, asserts that the kabala is a sealed book to anyone unfamiliar with the tarot. Not only is this true, but the tarot, as here presented, will be found a key to unlock all other sacred books as well. To the discriminating student the most difficult kabalistical phrases will yield their inner meaning when the tarot methods are applied.

Very briefly to illustrate, we find The Book of Concealed Mystery opens thus:

1. The Book of Concealed Mystery is the Book of the equilibrium of balance." The balance here referred to is Polarity, as exemplified by the Second Major Arcanum of the tarot.
2. For before there was equilibrium, countenance beheld not countenance." That is, consciousness was not possible before this duality.
3. And the Kings of ancient times were dead, and their crowns

were found no more: and the earth was desolate." These kings of the tarot being in ancient times, indicates a previous round of evolution; being dead refers to the cosmic sleep of nirvana. Kether, or Crown, means activity; therefore, intelligence of the Divine Mind was inactive, and there was no differentiation in progress.

4. Until that head, desired by all desires, appeared and communicated the vestments of honor." Arcanum I, Deific Intelligence, awakens and sends the first Divine thought-wave throbbing throughout the unmanifested void of Ain Soph Aur.

5. This equilibrium hangeth in that region which is negatively existent in "The Ancient One." Arcanum II, Isis, where polarity first manifests, is negative, or feminine.

Such explanations might be carried out in regard to every Kabalistical statement.

Summary

As the Jewish Kabala is mostly written in code, and all of it in the form of allegories, it takes much effort for the student to form a clear idea of its chief tenets. I will, therefore, here sum them up in unequivocal language:

1. God and the Universe are the Ego and Body of the Grand Man, or Macrocosm; and finite man, or the microcosm, is a miniature copy of the Grand Man, corresponding to Him in all details.

2. The universe sprang into differentiated existence in conformity to the law of numbers. These ten emanations from Deity manifest on every plane as 3 general and 7 specific attributes. In their interaction with one another they form, by a principle similar to that giving musical overtones, 22 less abstract and more specialized influences, or astrological qualities. These, manifesting as the 12 zodiacal signs and 10 planets of the chain, together with the 10 original numbers, form the 32 paths of evolution, which really are the 32 factors of all manifested existence. Yet at any given time all these 32 influences converge at every point in the universe. That is, in some quantity they are everywhere present. And the

specific point where they thus manifest—the earth, for instance—being a synthesis of their influence, constitutes a
33rd factor.

3. Great importance is attached to sex, it being taught that man
   can reach the feminine principle above only through union.
   The Shekinah is perfect union; and it is taught that mankind
   approaches God only through Shekinah. Those of impure
   mind and gross passions can not partake of Shekinah, for
   Shekinah is the Tree of Life, partaking of the fruits of which
   mankind is brought face to face with Adonai; entering thus
   into Divine Consciousness.

4. Souls are differentiated in pairs, have an existence before
   material birth, are separated before incarnation; and it is this
   separation which constitutes the original transgression. But
   through living a pure and spiritual life on earth they ultimately are attracted to each other and may even meet on earth. This
   meeting is the Shekinah, and in time permanently reunites
   them in heaven.

5. As exemplifying these four doctrines and their numerous
   offshoots, there is the mystery of the pronunciation of the
   name of Deity, which in the Bible is translated Jehovah, and
   in Hebrew is a word of four letters, IEVE, or Jod-He-Vau-He.

Jewish tradition holds that, "He who can rightly pronounce it,
causeth heaven and earth to tremble, for it is the name which rusheth
through the universe."

The real significance of this venerated word is that it stands as
representing the four universal principles; and therefore he who
understands these four letters is also able to comprehend all power
and all manifestation; and he who is able to pronounce it—or utilize
his knowledge—is able to live in complete harmony with the Divine
Law and thus partakes also of Divine power. It really signifies that
nothing is impossible to one who unites himself to the Cosmic Will.

Because it is composed of four letters the name is called the
Tetragrammaton. These four letters, which are symbols of positive,
negative, union and vibration, can be transposed in 12 different
ways, all conveying the same meaning, just as nature manifests
through the 12 zodiacal signs, yet in essence remains the same.

These twelve ways of expressing the Deific name are called the
12 banners. These banners are spelled thus: IEVE—IEEV—IVEE—
EVEI—EVIE—EEIV—VEEI—VIEE—VEIE—EIEV—EIVE—EEVI.

The Tarot Cards Utilize Both
Extra-Sensory Perception and Extra-Physical Powers

A vast amount of experimentation by universities in America and in England since the discovery of Pluto in 1930 not only proves that man possesses the power to gain, through extra-sensory perception, information not accessible to reason and the physical senses, but that this perception extends into both the past and the future.

On the inner plane consciousness can be extended unhindered by physical distance, and extended backwards and forwards in physical time. Even as to gain knowledge on the physical plane, so on the inner plane the attention must be focused on the information desired. The tarot cards, through their universal symbols, are designed, among other things, to assist in extending the inner-plane consciousness and focusing it on the information desired.

All mental processes are governed by the LAW OF ASSOCIA-TION. What has been perceived on the inner plane through extra-sensory perception resides in the unconscious mind as a memory. To remember it—to bring it up into objective consciousness—there must be a line of association between what is in objective conscious-ness and this memory. The symbols on the tarot cards are the most effective means known of forming the associations that enable what was perceived through extra-sensory perception to be recognized by objective consciousness.

The university experimenters have also demonstrated that physical objects can be influenced without the aid of any physical contact with them. This result of using extra-physical power they call the PK (Psychokinetic) Effect. The unconscious mind, or soul, uses this power to cause the tarot cards in a spread to become so placed as to reveal information obtained through extra-sensory perception.

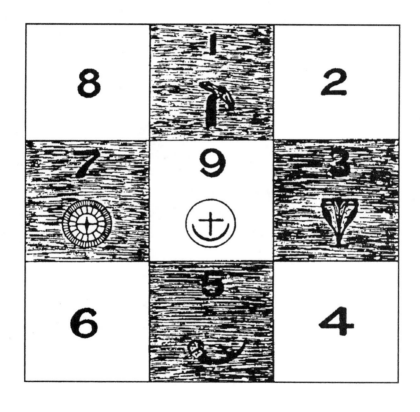

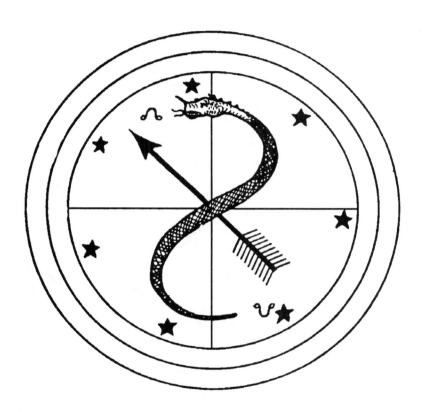

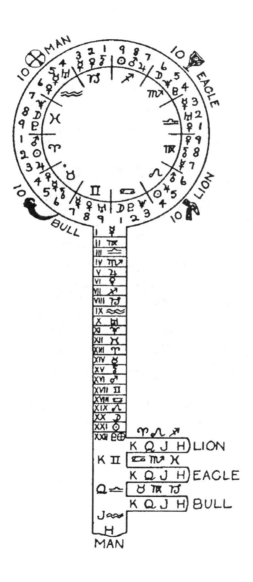

Chapter 2

Foundation of the Science

I T HAS BEEN said by that eminent kabalist, Eliphas Levi, that four signs express the absolute, and in turn are explained by a fifth. And we find this very true, both as applied to astrology and to the tarot. In each, the fifth term, by which the four fundamental elements are explained, is the language of universal symbolism. Therefore, the student may expect, in his study of the wide range of symbols employed in the tarot, to be made thoroughly conversant with a language which has been employed by learned men in all ages and all climes to impart the most profound truths, a language which, because of its wide appeal does not essentially vary with the passage of time, which is imperishable, and can be read by the intelligent members of any race. The tarot is the ONE standard text-book on the meaning of universal symbols.

Now these four signs, which are explained by universal symbolism, as applied to the Grand Man of the universe, are represented by the four quadrants of the heavens. These, in turn, of course, correspond in function to the four letters of the Deific Word, Jod-He-Vau-He. And because the sacred tarot pictures and explains this Grand Man from the feminine, or esoteric standpoint, it also has, in addition to being a text-book of the most ancient of languages, four distinct functions to perform.

Therefore, even before explaining the source from which the sacred tarot is derived, I feel that these four distinct and important functions should be set forth, and that those who teach this Hermetic System should insist that their students should at all times keep these four functions in separate compartments of their minds, without confusing one with another; for each is a distinct and clear-cut

23

system in itself.

Two of these systems—as must be true if they correspond to the Divine Jod-He-Vau-He—are positive. They are really sciences. And the other two are feminine and negative. They are systems of divination, each accurately corresponding to one of the four corners of the universe.

Corresponding to the Leo quarter of the zodiac there is a Science of Vibration, to which numbers furnish the key. Corresponding to the Scorpio section of the firmament there is a system of Divination by means of Cards. Corresponding to the Taurus quadrant of the sky there is a system of Numerology, or Divination by means of Numbers. And Corresponding to the Aquarius region of the heavens there is a Spiritual Science, which forms the basis of a complete philosophy of life.

The Science of Vibration

Right here it should be emphasized, so that later no confusion may arise, that the Hermetic System of Vibration as determined through using numbers is quite unrelated to any system of numerology. Numerology, new systems of which are being devised each year, is a method of divination. And as divination by numbers is one of the four functions of the tarot, nothing here is said in disparagement of numerology. In fact, I set forth such a system in chapter 8 of this course.

But the vibratory science here explained, although dependent upon numbers for the determination of effects, is not numerology. It is a positive science, as precise in its results, and as independent of psychic matters, as any physical science. Through it, as the physicist determines by means of numbers the vibratory frequency of different colors, or as by means of numbers he determines the vibratory frequency of any selected musical tone, so also by means of numbers, can the vibratory key of any thought be determined.

The great Caruso, in demonstrating the power of his voice, also well illustrated the importance of the vibratory key. When he went into a cafe, at times he would call for a wine glass. Tapping the glass to get the key, he would request the waiter to place the glass on a table in a distant part of the room. And then, by singing the tone to which he had found the glass keyed, by the powerful vibrations of his voice reaching it across the room, the glass would be shattered.

Thoughts, like vocal tones, are vibratory rates; but they are definite vibrations in astral substance. Nevertheless, like Caruso's voice, they have the power to travel across space and bring about physical changes. And like his voice, also, it is their vibratory key, as well as their volume which determines their effect.

The key to which thoughts are tuned often can be determined by their subject matter. But other thoughts, which also have powerful vibratory rates, are abstract in quality. That is, they merely designate some thing or quality. Such are names, and such are numbers.

It is not the physical sound of a name or a number that is its potent influence; it is the thought-vibration of the one thinking it, which radiates outward from his mind to the person or thing thought about. This vibration reaching a person thought about influences him according to the key of the thought. Different names and different numbers vibrate in different keys. Different vibratory keys produce different effects upon the objects or persons they contact, even as do different sounds. And, wholly apart from any process of divination, it is the object of the Science of Vibration as set forth in these studies to determine the key to which names and numbers vibrate, and how they affect the things and people with which they become associated.

Divination by Numbers

Because, as I have already pointed out, there are an increasing number of methods of using numbers in divination, little need be said about this phase of the subject here other than to point out that all these systems of Numerology, as well as the Hermetic System of Divination by Numbers, are really methods of divination. As such they possess a legitimate function. Many of them other than the Hermetic System give quite accurate results. But in no case should they be considered as a Science of Vibration; for such a science is based upon the observed effect of thought vibratory-rates, and is something entirely apart from any kind of divination.

Divination by Cards

Nor is any system of laying out the cards strictly a scientific and positive process. Like numerology, the methods of card reading set forth in this Hermetic System, as well as all other card-reading methods, are useful; but they essentially are systems of divination.

Spiritual Science

Now, however, when we come to that function which sets forth a spiritual science as a basis for a complete philosophy of life, we are again back on positive and scientific footing.

It is true that in perfecting this science there is recourse to the law of correspondences. Nevertheless, the philosophy of life derived from this science is based upon the strict observation, by those throughout the past ages who were most competent to ascertain them by experimental methods, of spiritual facts. Every noteworthy spiritual fact that has been uncovered by the researches of the most exalted minds since the world began, and checked as to accuracy by subsequent illuminated ones, is set forth in the language of universal symbolism in the sacred tarot. That is why we who delve deeply into it call it Sacred. But while the spiritual facts are thus clearly set forth, except for certain guiding lines each is left free to draw from them such conclusions as his state of evolvement will permit. The facts are there, but to us is given the task of giving them an adequate detailed interpretation. But after all, of what particular use is a spiritual philosophy?

Because the vibrations of people thinking our name, or our telephone number, reach us and conduce, through stimulating harmonious or inharmonious conditions within ourselves, to our health and happiness, or to our failure and misery, it is easy to see that a science of vibration which enables us to regulate such matters is important. And, in so far as divination gives us valuable and reliable information, it is not difficult to understand the prevalent interest in numerology and in card reading. But of what value is a spiritual science, or the philosophy derived from it?

Well, to give a proper perspective to this one of the four chief functions of the tarot, we must make a brief examination of life in general, and of man in particular.

Man, for instance, like all other living entities, possesses a strong desire to live. But the life of any organism continues only so long as it makes successful adaptation to its environment. Part of man's environment consists of countless other forms of life, toward which it is essential he should observe a proper code of conduct. He must obey the impulse of the moment seldom, but instead, consider the effect of his action as influencing his future welfare.

Especially is it important that he shall conduct himself properly toward others of his kind, otherwise conflict, or wanton depletion of food supplies, may cause all to perish. His chances of survival are greatly heightened when he can obtain, not the antagonism, but the cooperation, of some of his fellows.

Such cooperation, however, is only made possible by an understanding as to mutual aims. When such mutual aims have been established a single tribe becomes better equipped to attain them than any individual, and a nation becomes superior to a tribe. Yet members of any cooperative group who have variant aims weaken the effectiveness of the whole. Thus for mutual advantages, and to prevent disaster befalling, there must come to be a recognized standard of conduct.

Such a code has for purpose those actions which will confer the greatest advantages on the whole group, and thus also confer them upon the individual members. And the advantages striven for are determined by the knowledge of the people. But whether those prescribed in the standard of conduct actually contribute to the welfare of the group or not, and to what extent, depends entirely upon how correctly they have interpreted the true relation of one life-form to another, and the true relation of the individual to the group. This interpretation, because actions are based upon it, is the most dominant factor in shaping the lives of a people. It is called their ethical standard.

Now in national life those things are advocated which are believed to add to the richness of people's lives, and those things considered destructive are prohibited. Yet people have not found a means by which physical dissolution can be postponed more than a few short years.

After-Death Survival

Not being able to make the continuous adaptation to a physical environment which would enable them to continue living upon earth, it was quite natural that some should investigate the possibility of a life in a region after physical death. And our foremost scientific men, by means of careful experiments, have confirmed their findings that man does live beyond the tomb.

Yet wherever life is found, its survival and the fullness of its existence depend upon successful adaptation to environment. This same law must apply to the after-life of man. That is, to the extent he is able to make perfect and continuous adaptations in that future realm, will his life there prove satisfactory. Furthermore, as he has found knowledge to be the most essential factor in his adaptation on earth, he has a right to assume that the more knowledge he has concerning the conditions to be encountered, and about how difficulties are to be met and overcome, the better he will get along in the life after physical death.

Many as yet are content with mere surmise as to the conditions that there obtain. And all through the dark ages man was content merely to surmise how matter behaved under different circumstances. Yet the progress man has made in material ways, the attainment of numerous comforts, and all of what we call modern civilization, was brought about by those who were not content with surmise, but who set about gathering accurate knowledge about physical things.

Furthermore, ancient ruins give testimony of considerable scientific achievement even before history began. We have surpassed the ancients in these matters, it is true, and we may be able to surpass them in that other field to which tradition and ruins alike bear testimony, that is, in the field of spiritual science. But if we are able to do so we must discard surmise and substitute accurately observed phenomena.

Upon the accuracy of the Chaldeans in calculating certain celestial phenomena, modern astronomers are forced to place considerable reliance, and to base some of their own findings. And as to the knowledge of astrology these same Chaldeans possessed, anyone who will take the pains to learn to erect a birthchart can soon prove to himself that they had accurate knowledge which is scoffed at by the abysmal ignorance of parrot-taught scholars.

Instead of taking the rules laid down by the ancients, and testing them by the approved methods of experimental science, conventional intolerance does battle with them by appealing to prejudice. And the same dogmatic assertions are used to discredit and block the path of anyone who makes a candid investigation of spiritual science.

It is true that mystical folly runs rampant under the guise of occultism; but for that matter less than three centuries ago material science was no less a medley of confused notions and dogmatic opinions. And it became necessary, in order to build a sound structure for material science, to discard all that had gone before, and build on the solid foundation of observed facts. Upon such an unyielding foundation the framework of scientific thought has been reared, each timber being fitted to its proper place by the methods of deductive thought. And so erected, it constitutes a shelter which protects man from a thousand and one dangers which threaten his physical survival.

But it has been unable to prolong the physical life indefinitely, and man as of yore, looks beyond the earth-plane to another existence after the tomb. About this after-life much is said, but little is commonly known. Yet all seem to agree that some kind of preparation for the new condition is necessary, or at least desirable. That is, they feel that as effort is necessary to enable one to adapt himself to physical life, some kind of effort must be necessary to make successful adaptation to any life in the future. But men do not agree of what this preparation should consist.

The very yearning of the human soul, therefore, demands that there shall come into existence a spiritual science, a science which shall inform man definitely about the life he will be called upon to live after he leaves the physical plane; and that will direct him as to the preparations which should be made, while still on the physical plane, that will enable him the more successfully to adapt himself in the realms of the future. Thus do the necessities of man demand a spiritual science. But such a spiritual science can be soundly constructed only on the plan which so successfully has been used in the construction of material science. Notions must be cleared away, surmise must be swept to one side, and a foundation laid of indisputable facts quarried from the lode of critically observed phenomena. Then upon this foundation a framework should be erected according to the strictest methods of logic. And if the work thus done has been thorough there should result a shelter which is effective in protecting us from the inclemencies encountered in any life on any plane.

In gathering this information for the foundation, we can use the reports of the physical senses somewhat; because they have been found to give rather accurate information as checked by practical affairs. But they also, at times, have been found unreliable; and thus they should be checked by those other senses, the senses of the astral, the psychic senses. These psychic senses also, in so far as practical experience proves them to be accurate, should be used to gather information. But because they also sometimes report falsely, their findings should be checked as to accuracy by the physical senses. Information should be quarried wherever it can be found, and by whatever method can be used; but before entering into the foundation of a spiritual science it should be tested by every known means.

Now as to these psychic senses, about which some people may be skeptical, bear in mind that because a man can not track a hare by scent does not imply that a hound can not do so. And because many hounds fail to follow some particularly cold trail does not prove that some other hound may not be able to do so. The limits of one hound's ability is not the measure of the ability of another hound, and whether a particular man can do something that another man can not should not be made a matter of surmise, but subjected to experimental proof.

And thus in the application of the psychic senses; just how reliable their reports are must be experimentally determined for each individual, by subjecting their reports to subsequent proof. Yet when used judiciously, and in conjunction with his physical senses and common sense, they are found to be extraordinarily valuable aids to spiritual knowledge.

In using the physical senses to gather material to be included in the foundation of a spiritual science, we find that there is a sympathetic relation between objects and events upon the earth and the heavenly bodies and their movements. No psychic faculties are needed to prove this, as it comes directly under the methods of physical experiment. Yet the science of astrology, which sets forth in mathematical terms, the relation of the heavenly bodies to things on earth, has mostly been handed down to us from the ancient magi. Not that we merely accept what they have stated; but, using statistical methods upon observed results, we have found their statements and interpretations amazingly accurate.

The same magi specialized, generation after generation, for thousands of years, in just two things: they specialized in astrology, and they specialized in gaining information concerning the soul of man.

In the acquisition of information on these two subjects they developed their psychic senses to a high degree, and they kept laborious records of experiments, day after day, year after year, generation after generation.

And, in so much as the vast amount of information which has come down to us from them concerning astrology has been proved by experimental methods and modern research to be highly accurate, we are justified, I think, in placing some confidence in their findings where their other specialty is concerned. All the more so, because they linked their spiritual findings to astrology. Astrology, to them, was not merely character-reading, and a means of predicting events. It was also the science of the soul and the key to all spiritual possibilities. It had an exoteric side, which was applicable to the physical affairs of life; but it also had a more important esoteric side, which revealed the nature of the soul and to what conditions it would be subjected in the future.

Thus these men of an olden day formulated just such a spiritual science as that for which we search. They scanned the universe with highly trained psychic vision, they checked the information gained in one manner by information gained in another manner; and when, as time went by, they became convinced they had some spiritual treasure, by means of correspondence, which they understood so well, they traced this spiritual fact as a constellation in the sky.

Still further applying this principle of correspondences, they attached each to a number, so that spiritual ideas might be combined and handled mathematically, even as by means of numbers we solve the more humble problem of the family budget. And that they might thus be handled with facility, even as in algebra we use x, y, z, to represent more complex things, they used symbols to represent the spiritual verities that were being considered.

For convenience in handling, these symbols, which stood for definite spiritual ideas, were engraved on plates. And thus it came about that each plate contained, in the language of universal symbolism, the explanation of some important spiritual fact. It explained in more detail than the pictured constellation or the symbol of the planet, just what these men of old had discovered. It was an esoteric interpretation of the spiritual truths associated with some planet or zodiacal sign. And attached to the plate was its corresponding number, so that through combining numbers having the same value as definite spiritual ideas, spiritual ideas could be handled mathematically. By combining their numerical equivalents a number could be thus obtained which would represent the correct resulting spiritual idea.

Now, of course, we should not accept the spiritual findings of these ancients until they have been subjected to rigorous tests. We should not accept the findings of either moderns or ancients as conclusive. But because in those things where rigid tests have been applied these men of old have proved to have had such amazingly accurate and comprehensive knowledge, if we were to overlook their work it would, no doubt, make our own research far more laborious. Let us approach the spiritual ideas they have left us, not as conclusively proved, but in the same manner as we approached exoteric astrology. Let us take them, one at a time, and subject them to proof. And if the knowledge they left us concerning spiritual things compares in accuracy with the knowledge they left us concerning astrology, our labors in establishing a true spiritual science will surely be lightened.

Origin of the Tarot Cards

Those plates upon which, in the language of universal symbolism, the ancients inscribed their knowledge of spiritual things and the attainments possible to the human soul, were called by the Egyptians, The Royal Path of Life.

In Egyptian, Tar means path, and Ro means royal, and thus, even at this day, the plates are known to us as the tarot.

As a part of the mysteries divulged to candidates only after passing hazardous trials and hardships, they have largely remained the property of secret schools of occultism and jealously guarded by them. What has filtered through to the public has been rather unsatisfactory and vague, although occult students the world over have recognized their importance.

The magical wheel discovered in the thirteenth century by Raymond Lully, which was to solve all problems, was the tarot. In the sixteenth century, William Postel wrote concerning it as, The Genesis of Enoch, in a book entitled, *The Key of Things Kept Secret From the Foundation of the World.* He believed it antedated the Bible. Count de Gebelin wrote concerning it, and St. Martin studied it. Eliphas Levi wrote his masterpiece, *The Dogma and Ritual of Transcendental Magic,* from studies of it, and S. L. MacGregor Mathers, Papus, and A. E. Waite have contributed works about it.

From this it might be concluded that little is left to be said about the tarot. But unfortunately for the general public the secret schools have had no intention of permitting real knowledge concerning it to escape from their midst. Consequently, much that has been written about the tarot has been, not for the purpose of making clear its real significance, but to reveal what had clandestinely escaped from the secret schools. Even so fearless a writer as Eliphas Levi admits this, and the few mistakes he makes in his own writings are so glaring, and yet so near the truth, that they can be ascribed neither to carelessness nor ignorance.

One of the most conscientious of mystical writers, Mr. A. E. Waite, explains the matter thus:

There is no extant ritual, as there can be no doctrine, which contains, or can possibly contain, the secret of mystical procedure or the essence of mystical doctrine. The reason is not because there is, or can reasonably be, any indictable secret, but because the knowledge in question is in the custody of those who have taken effectual measures for its protection; and though from time to time, some secrets of initiation have filtered through printed books into the world at large, the real mysteries have never escaped.

In the *Pictorial Key to The Tarot*, he further comments:

There is a secret tradition concerning the tarot, as well as a Secret Doctrine contained therein; I have followed some part of it without exceeding the limits which are drawn about matters of this kind and belong to the Laws of Honor. This tradition has two parts, and as one of them has passed into writing it seems to follow that it may be betrayed at any moment, which will not signify, because the second, as I have intimated has not passed at present and is held by very few indeed. The purveyors of spurious copy and traffickers in stolen goods may take notice of this point, if they please.

Men who follow science as a profession have a very different code of honor. The truly scientific man does not hold what he discovers, or what others have discovered, merely to benefit a chosen few. It is the code of science to give whatever information is discovered to the public that not one select clique may have an advantage, but that the whole human race may be the gainer. And it has always seemed to me a colossal piece of selfishness for any group of men, if they really possessed information that might be beneficial to all mankind, to hoard it for themselves alone.

I hold, therefore, that secrecy in any matter that will aid the soul in gaining knowledge of its true relations to the universe, or that will assist in making life happier, or the attainment of spirituality easier, is not a virtue. Consequently, departing from the custom of many other writers on this subject, I am introducing no blinds and no subterfuges into these lessons. As to traffickers in stolen goods, what I present, in its essentials, has been in the custody of The Brotherhood of Light for ages. But even were it otherwise, I would not hesitate to present any information that I deem might in some manner assist human progress and happiness, from whatever source it might be gleaned.

The time has ceased, I trust, when a few shall possess a monopoly on the truths regarding spiritual things. The reader will find here all that is necessary for him to know about the tarot and its Secret Doctrine to put him on the right path, and he could hope for no more even within the most exclusive circles; for attainment is not vicarious.

As to the methods of mystical procedure so carefully guarded, supposed never to have been committed to writing, possessed by so very few, whose mysteries have never escaped to the world at large; I take pleasure in pointing out that it is the method by which man reaches God directly. It may be mentioned also that it is not the exclusive possession of the Occident, but is known as well to initiates of the Orient. To give the western version might be deemed trafficking in stolen goods. Therefore, as the eastern interpretation is fully as valuable and accurate I will state where it may be found:

The original work is exceedingly ancient and rare, is inscribed on palm leaves, and found only in the remotest parts of India and Tartary. It is called, The Atma Bodha, or Book of Soul Knowledge. It is divided into three books, the second being a commentary on the first. The third book contains but seven statements which form a brief summary of the whole subject. The work, translated into English was possessed by members of The Hermetic Brotherhood of Luxor (long since closed), and is fully as lucid in explaining mystical atonement as are the teachings on this subject of any western order. Lack of space prevents the giving of more than the summary, the key to the whole matter; but this meditated upon in connection with the tarot will prove quite sufficient for anyone whose spirituality is such as to permit illumination; which is all that any outside help can give, although the whole work is of utmost value.

BOOK III
The Aphoresmata of The Logos

I.   Whatever exists, exists as a Whole, as God, or is a part, or emanation from God.

II. In the Whole as an angel, unconscious of the Whole, is an undescended spirit.

III. Parted from the Whole, yet a portion of the Whole, and unconscious of the Whole, is the Law of Differentation.

IV. Parted from the Whole, with the Whole, yet external to the

Whole, is a descended or fallen spirit.

V. Parted from the Whole, with the Whole, yet conscious of the Whole and knowing it has fallen away from, and that it should, and can, return to the Whole, is the Law of Reascension.

VI. That which is parted from the Whole, turns again to the Whole, is the Law of True Repentance.

VII. That which was parted from the Whole, and has again returned to the Whole, is a part of the Whole, remains so forever as a blest spirit, and is the Law of Perfect Atonement.

Tarot Correspondences

Of the plates on which the ancients pictured the facts they ascertained regarding spiritual science and universal law, which have been handed down to us in the form of the tarot cards, 22 are more important than the rest. They correspond to the 12 zodiacal signs and the 10 planets in the chain. And the ideas thus pictorially expressed in universal symbolism later came further to be condensed as conventional and easily written hieroglyphics, and this is the origin of the square-formed letter of the Hebrew and Egyptian alphabets. And, because there were no separate characters for numbers, each such square-formed letter also became the number expressing the spiritual idea embodied in the pictured plate.

Then to still further express the numerical interaction of forces and ideas between the four kingdoms of fire, earth, air and water; a scale of ten numerals was added, and repeated in association with the emblem of a kingdom, giving a total of 40 additional plates, or suitcards. Each according to its number, of course, corresponds to some astrological subdivision of the original 22 conceptions.

All these forces, however, have an influence upon man. He is the point where they come to a focus. But men are not all the same, and this difference in type is best expressed by the sign of the zodiac under which each is born. So we have 12 plates, or cards, picturing people born under each of the zodiacal signs. To express the family relation they are represented as Father, Mother and Son, pictured more commonly as King, Queen and Youth (Jack). The temperaments of these people are further shown by the suits; for the fiery signs of the zodiac represent the sanguine temperament, the watery signs the lymphatic temperament, the earthly signs the bilious temperament, and the airy signs the nervous temperament. Thus the suit denotes the temperament.

In addition to cosmic and other influences there is another thing of importance. People have thoughts. They are probably the most potent of all forces. Consequently, it was essential to have them represented. And to show their source of origin they should be associated with people. Therefore, to depict them, the ancients had recourse to a horseman; for the Twins, ruling the house of private thoughts in a natural birth-chart, were often represented on horses; and Sagittarius, ruling the house of publically expressed thought in a natural birth-chart; is a horseman. The complete set of the tarot plates, or cards, therefore consists of 22 Major Arcana, 40 Minor Arcana, and 16 Court Cards; a total of 78.

Just why each Major Arcanum is a pictorial representation of the spiritual associations of the planet or zodiacal sign with which it is given will be made plain as we make a study of each.

The four members of each suit of court cards represent, in their wider application, the Hebrew name of Deity—Jod-He-Vau-He; signifying masculine, feminine, union, and the product. And they also throw light upon the origin of the Holy Trinity worshiped by Christianity.

In Egypt, Osiris the Father, Isis the Mother, and Horus the Issue, were popularly worshiped; and in addition there was a fourth deity which included the three others, and overshadowed them, as do the thoughts of a family, called the Holy Ghost.

So when Athenasis came from Egypt to the Holy Council of Nice to assist in settling of what the orthodox Trinity consisted, he introduced the Holy Ghost. Most contemporaneous nations, other than the Egyptians, held merely to the Trinity of Father, Mother and Issue. But the Holy Ghost came to Christianity at an opportune time; for due to the teachings of Paul, and the fanatic asceticism that was developing, it was becoming quite certain that woman could have no part in anything divine.

The monks who retired to monastic life looked upon woman as an instrument of evil, a tempting agent of the devil, strictly to be avoided. They characteristically shifted the blame for all the ills of humanity to her shoulders by teaching that the fall of Adam was due to the guile of Eve. So, while the Church still retained the Virgin Isis—which as the sign Virgo, has from time immemorial been pictured as a virgin with a crescent Moon in her arms to symbolize the immaculate conception—as the Mother Mary, and venerated her accordingly; they felt compelled to cut her from the Holy Trinity. In her stead they substituted the Holy Ghost.

Yet while cutting woman from the Holy Trinity, they were powerless to efface her from nature; and in the common playing cards as in the tarot, she holds her rightful place as Queen, joint ruler with the King. But the fourth court card, still retained in the tarot, even as the spirit of rectitude and justice which in its wider application it represents, has departed from our midst.

Origin of the Suits

As to the emblems by which the four suits are recognized, they were derived as universal symbols from the most important of natural phenomena, the passing of the seasons.

Even as heralded in the verses of Omar, the spring is signaled by the rose. In certain older cards the rose is sometimes found. The spring is the period of renewed life, and thus the rose, as representing it, in some mystical orders, is the symbol of a renewed life. Spring brought a new food supply, which nourished life. But this food supply, by which life might be sustained also might be purchased. And thus we have the pieces of money, the coins of the tarot. But in later days a more commercial age decided that for sustaining life through trade, diamonds were even more precious than money. So in modern cards we have the suit of diamonds.

The summer brought the trefoil, or three-leaf clover, which was important for forage to the flocks of a pastoral people. So the clover became associated with the heat of summer. A similar heat could be produced with wood. And thus scepters came to be the symbol of summer heat, and are so represented in the tarot. Moderns, however, continue to picture the clover, but refer to the wood still, calling it the suit of clubs.

The autumn, when the wine was pressed from the grape, came to be the season of festivities, of dancing and of marriage. To represent the emotions then engendered, the cup, from which the wine was quaffed, came to be used, and thus is still one of the suits of the tarot. But moderns, associating the emotions of joy, and those that result in marriage, with the heart, have preferred to use them in picturing the corresponding suit of playing cards.

The winter was a time of dearth and want. To provide for this period when no food could be garnered, it was customary to work hard to gather and hoard a supply sufficient to last through until spring. And it was observed that the oak also thus provided a food supply which was similarly stored by the squirrels. Thus the acorn came to be used as the symbol of winter. But, in time, the afflictions of winter, and the struggle to sustain life, especially as it often led to strife among peoples, came to be depicted by the emblem of strife, the sword. Yet a still later people looked upon the unfruitful season as the cause of their unceasing toil; and to depict this, used the modern emblem of toil, the shovel, or spade as it is called in modern playing cards.

Thus the balmy air of spring is represented by coins, the fire of summer by scepters, the bibulous festivities of autumn by cups, and the hardships of winter by swords. Therefore, we must consider that coins correspond to the airy signs, scepters to the fiery signs, cups to the watery signs, and swords to the earthy signs, of the zodiac.

Making the Spread

When the unconscious mind has its attention focused on obtaining certain information, the psychic senses are active to obtain that information. And because of the vastly wider scope of their power, due to the properties of inner-plane existence where they function, they are able to acquire information quite inaccessible without their aid. This information then resides in the astral brain as a memory. That is, it is a memory of what has been gathered astrally.

The tarot cards afford both a means by which the attention of the soul is directed to acquiring such information, and a means by which this information, which then exists as a memory in the astral brain, can be raised into the region of objective consciousness.

One who has experience with the tarot cards will become convinced that there is some power present, not merely that directs how they shall be read, but that actually directs their distribution so that they will give a correct reading. Extra-sensory perception is able to observe their positions in the pack as shuffled. And extra-physical power (now demonstrated in our universities as the Psychokinetic Effect) in cooperation with the unconscious muscular activities of the shuffler, tends to arrange the cards in shuffling, and so to cut the pack, that when dealt they shall fall in positions to give the information desired. Full details of this process are set forth in Chapters 1, 2 and 3 in the Course 11, *Divination*.

The first essential of a reading is that there shall be a strong and unprejudiced desire to know something. If other strong desires or preconceived opinions intrude during the shuffling and reading of the cards, they will warp the reading from the truth. The mind should be concentrated on obtaining a correct answer.

While the mind is so occupied, the cards should be shuffled in such a manner as not merely to rearrange them in the deck, but to reverse the ends of some. They should then be cut into three piles and gathered again into a pack. This shuffling and cutting should be repeated three times; and then the cards dealt, face downward. They are turned over from top to bottom, but turned over only one at a time, as read.

Yes or No?

To answer a question Yes or No, five cards are dealt in a single row, from right to left. The middle card counts 2 and the other cards each count 1. A majority of the counts right end up is an affirmative answer. A majority of the counts wrong way up is a negative answer. If the right way up and the wrong way up are evenly divided, it is a draw, and the answer is undecided.

Seven cards dealt in a row in this manner, from right to left, will answer a question briefly, and nine so arranged will give greater detail. The present of the matter is revealed by the middle card. The conditions or events leading up to it are signified by the cards commencing at the right. The cards commencing at the left of the middle and moving to the last one on the left, show the conditions and events pertaining to the matter in the future.

THE PYRAMID SPREAD

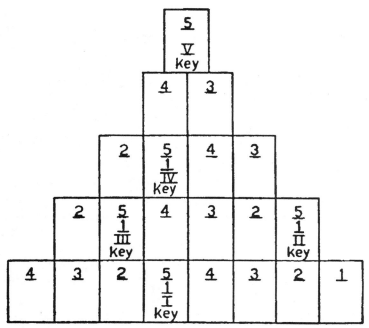

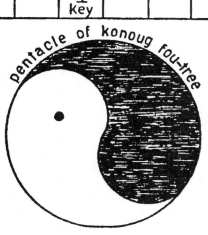

pentacle of konoug fou-tree

Chapter 3

Scope and Use of the Tarot

I AMBLICHUS, a Neo-platonist of the fourth century and an initiate of The Brotherhood of Light, has left us an important document entitled, "An Egyptian Initiation".

It contains an account of the trials of initiation, and of certain information given to the neophyte while passing these tests, in the Mysteries of Ancient Egypt. The different steps in this initiation as thus described, and what each step signifies, are set forth in full detail in Chapter 9 of Course 2, *Astrological Signatures*.

At one point in his journey the candidate is stopped before 22 frescoed paintings which picture the 22 Major Arcana of the tarot, and it becomes his duty to commit to memory these pictures, as well as their symbolism, which is then explained to him. As these pictures, together with such of their symbolism as is then explained to the neophyte, are fully described by Iamblichus, his work affords an accurate description of the Egyptian Tarot.

"An Egyptian Initiation" was translated from the original MS. into French by P. Christian, and those who have written much of value concerning the tarot have drawn heavily upon his translation. In 1901 it was translated into English, for private circulation, by my friend Genevieve Stebbins. And I am indebted to her for permission to use her translation of the description of the Egyptian Tarot.

In these lessons I have faithfully followed the description of the plates, the meaning of the symbols found upon the Major Arcana, and the interpretation of the Arcana in each of the three worlds, just as given in the translation of Genevieve Stebbins; and also the admonition after each Arcanum which runs, "Remember, then, son of earth," etc.

The Admonition

As to this admonition, although it probably will be used seldom by tarot students, I have thought it better not merely to include it, but to preserve it without change. It is a part of the old initiation ceremony, and may serve a more important function in the future than can now be discerned.

Modern translators of the old square-formed alphabet have changed the numerical value of some letters, and have transposed some letters. And modern astronomers, thinking to be more scientific, have sought to abolish the pictured constellations in the sky, using areas not identical in space and bounded by straight lines. Yet the original connotation of each letter revealed its vibratory significance and astrological relationship; and the original picture which each constellation presented revealed, as fully set forth in Course 7, *Spiritual Astrology*, the spiritual teaching it was designed to convey to later generations. Obeying an old Masonic command to "Alter not the ancient landmarks," The Brotherhood of Light has preserved the original vibratory significance of the letters, and here faithfully reproduces the Egyptian Tarot, including the admonition associated with each Major Arcanum.

This admonition has a practical application both in card-reading and in astrology. Usually in a tarot spread, there is one card which is the key to the situation, or which indicates the individual for whom the reading is being given, or, perhaps, what this individual should do. And in a birth-chart, or in a horary figure, some sign or planet usually indicates the person for whom the reading is being given. When, therefore, it is desired to give an admonition to this person, the admonition given below the Arcanum which is the key influence in the spread, or indicates the person, may be used. And the admonition given below the Arcanum which corresponds to the dominant sign or planet in an astrological chart may be used in a like manner.

Correspondences

The corresponding letter and number are a part of the translation of "An Egyptian Initiation." But in order to handle the cards in the solution of any conceivable problem, as wide a range of accurate correspondences to the principles depicted by the Major Arcana as possible should be at hand. I have, therefore, given the astrological correspondence of each Major Arcanum. In the past this has been attempted in a desultory manner by one or two others, but those who attempted this were quite ignorant of astrology. My own familiarity with astrology dates from the year 1900, and by virtue of teaching it for years in class-work and writing courses of lessons on its various branches, which have become standard works upon the subject, I feel that I can speak in this matter with some authority. In these lessons the astrological correspondences of the tarot cards are given correctly in writing for the first time.

In addition, I have added the corresponding color, corresponding musical tone, corresponding occult science, corresponding human function, corresponding natural remedy and corresponding mineral, to each Arcanum.

The System of Presentation

In order that the student shall have at hand concrete explanations of the application of the tarot, examples which he can use as models to follow in his own researches, after each Major Arcanum I have given some application of the principle which the arcanum represents in ten different domains as follows:

1. *Number:* The numerical significance of the principle is stated.
2. *Astrology:* It is shown why the principle pictured by the arcanum inevitably corresponds to a certain planet or zodiacal sign.
3. *Human Function:* It is pointed out which one of man's various forms and activities are expressions of the principle.
4. *Alchemy:* How this principle, indicated by the arcanum, operates in alchemical procedure.
5. *Bible:* As an aid to Bible studies, and the interpretation of allegories by means of the tarot, Bible passages are quoted which are exemplifications of the principle pictured in the arcanum.
6. *Masonry:* To aid the Masonic student to use the tarot to gain the esoteric meaning of his rituals, it is shown what Masonic teaching is conveyed by the arcanum.
7. *Magic:* In magic, also, the tarot is a valuable aid; and some magical principle corresponding to the arcanum being considered is set forth.
8. *Initiation:* If I were to omit examples of the use of the tarot in pointing out the steps in the soul's pilgrimage, it would be

        sadly remiss. This most valuable application is illustrated in connection with each arcanum.

9. *Occult Science:* For those who desire to use the tarot in special occult studies, the correspondence to some occult science is given under each arcanum.

10. *Minor Arcana and Court Arcana:* As a transition function, it is shown why the exoteric divinatory significance of the Minor Arcana are derived from their numerical relation to the Major Arcana, and how their esoteric and more spiritual significance derives from a corresponding decanate-division of the zodiac; also how the Court Arcana acquire their significance from the zodiacal signs.

And in addition to these examples of the use of the tarot, the lessons give instructions in the science of vibration, in divination by numbers, and after each second Major Arcanum there is given a different method of spreading and reading the cards.

If, however, the student goes no further than what is explained in these lessons, he has merely learned the fundamentals of the use of the tarot; for in the treatment here the attempt is to give accurate information, and to set forth examples, to the end of establishing proper methods of procedure which the student can apply at greater length in his own researches.

Different Tarot Packs

The Egyptian Tarot pictures illustrated and described in these lessons, teach in still greater detail the same spiritual ideas that are taught by the constellations. Both constellations in the sky—the stars of which usually offer not the slightest suggestion of the design pictured—and the Tarot pictures adorning the walls of the ancient Egyptian initiation chamber, make use of primitive symbolical pictograph writing to convey the most important things the ancient wise ones had found out about the human soul. The Egyptian Tarot, then, portrays the spiritual conceptions of the Egyptian initiates, as derived from a still more remote past. There is a peculiar sympathy, however, between the thoughts of man and actions for which he finds no rational motive. That is, the same sympathy that exists between the happenings on earth and the positions of the planets in the sky also manifests through the unconscious mind.

If we but analyze our dreams we shall find that symbolism is the common language of the unconscious mind. And the successful use of the tarot cards as instruments of divination depends upon their sympathetic response to invisible factors of intelligence. So it would be indeed strange if they responded merely in the transitory laying of the spread, and not also in their symbolism to the minds of those who handle them.

When, therefore, the Tarot cards came into the hands of a people with a different conception of life, it would be remarkable if, at least in those tenets wherein they felt most strongly, the pictures on the cards were not changed sufficiently to portray these intense convictions.

Gypsy fortune-telling cards differ markedly from the Egyptian Tarot pack, but I am sure their symbolism is more correct in portraying the Gypsy philosophy and the Gypsy mode of life.

English, German, Italian and French packs differ from each other, because of national characteristics, and from the Egyptian and Gypsy cards because Christianity has made its impress upon them. But each pack, through that sympathetic response to the minds of those who use it, more correctly than the others, portrays in symbolical pictograph the deeper convictions of those who have thus somewhat altered its designs.

Even the playing cards, which are derived from the Tarot, show variations from the Tarot quite characteristic of their constant use as instruments of gambling.

To indicate more clearly what I mean, consider that in one of the best English packs the knight (horseman) of swords is an armored crusader, dashing across the frontier into another's domain in the well-known effort to spread enlightenment by means of the sword. The picture suggests instantly the conquest of far-flung empires and the forceful dissemination of Christian creeds among the benighted heathens thus conquered.

Variations of quite as important significance are to be found on almost every card in the different tarot packs; but I shall be content with indicating one more, which is, perhaps, the most striking of all.

The Egyptian Initiates believed justice to be the operation of an undeviating natural law. The number 8, by its two loops, is a symbolical pictograph of the two pans of the scales. The number 8 also represents an equal division; two realizations (4's) in equilibrium. In the Egyptian pack, the number 8 is attached to the Major Arcanum picturing the Goddess of Justice holding the balances in her hand, and, even as in the picture adorning the front of our court houses, Justice is pictured blindfolded, to signify that she is unprejudiced and not subject to bribery.

The Jews, however, believed that they were a chosen people; that Jehovah was a God of favoritism who could be cajoled into granting unmerited rewards to those who gained His good graces. Christianity inherited the same idea. In many Christian packs, therefore, we find Justice, although holding the balances, not associated with 8, but with 11. Because the scale of digits is complete with 9; and 10, by adding the circle of spirit, commences a new gamut on a higher plane, we have no difficulty in conceiving 11 as a force operating from the spiritual plane. But as the digits of 11 can never be equally divided, rewards, according to this Christian conception, are never exactly according to merit. They are meted out from above, not according to the Egyptian belief in an undeviating and blind law, but according to the whim of some higher power.

To make this conception of Divine Justice even more obvious, which seems to be patterned after the kind prevalent in some courts of earth, in these various Christian packs the eyes of Justice are not blindfolded, but wide open to prejudice.

It is not that one pack is better or worse than another, but that each pack of tarot cards has been unconsciously modified by the philosophy of life of those who designed it.

The Magus—Arcanum I

Letter: Egyptian, Athoim; Hebrew, Aleph; English, A. Number I. Astrologically, the planet Mercury. Color, violet. Tone, B. Occult science, esoteric psychology. Human function, the spiritual body. Natural remedy, mental treatments. Mineral, the metal mercury.

A—I expresses in the spiritual world, Absolute Being, which contains, and from which emanates, the infinity of possibilities.

In the intellectual world, unity, principle and synthesis of numbers, and the will principle of acts.

In the physical world, man the highest placed of relative being, who is called upon to raise himself by a perpetual expansion of his faculties in the concentric spheres of the Absolute.

Remember, then, son of earth, that man should, like God, act without ceasing. To will nothing and do nothing is more fatal than to will and do ill. If the Magus should appear in the prophetic signs of thy horoscope, it announces that a firm will and faith in yourself, guided by reason and a love of justice will conduct you to the end that you wish to attain and will preserve you from the perils of the way.

In Divination, **Arcanum I** may be read briefly as **Will** or **Dexterity**.

Arcanum I is pictured by a Magus, type of the perfect man, that is to say, in full possession of his moral and physical faculties. He is represented standing; it is the attitude of will which precedes action. His robe is white, image of purity, original or regained. A serpent biting its own tail serves him for a girdle; it is the symbol of eternity which alone circumscribes his endeavors. His forehead is girt with a circle of gold. Gold signifies light, and the circle expresses the universal circumference in which gravitate all created things.

The right hand of the Magus holds a scepter of gold, surmounted by a circle representing spirit; symbol of the authority conferred by spiritual attainment. He raises it toward heaven in the sign of aspiration to science, wisdom and force.

Above is a four-pointed star, its rays extending heavenward; it is the over-shadowing genius of his spiritual master directing his efforts and counseling him in his upward struggles. The left hand extends the index finger to the earth to show that the mission of the perfect man is to reign over the material world. This double gesture also expresses that the human will should reflect the Divine Will in order to procure good and prevent evil.

Before the Magus, upon a cubic stone, are placed a cup, a sword, and a piece of gold money in the center of which is engraved a cross. The cup signifies the mixture of the passions which contribute to happiness and unhappiness according as we are their masters or their slaves. The sword signifies the work, the struggle which traverses obstacles, and the trials which sorrow submits us to. The coin, sign of determined value, is the symbol of realized aspirations, of work accomplished; and shows the sun of power conquered by the perseverance and efficacy of the will. The cross, seal of the infinite, by which the coin is marked, announces the ascension of that power in the spheres of the future. The cube upon which these symbols rest typifies the physical world; and has graven on its side an ibis, to indicate that eternal vigilance is a necessity if physical limitations are to be surmounted.

Number

Numerically, I expresses the absolute. It is also the starting point of all measurements, and suggests infinite possibilities. All that is proceeds from one cosmos, which contains all, and to which all ultimately must return.

One is a synthesis, for nothing can be thought of without parts. It is the universal principle of existence, the creative intelligence of Deity, the motive force of the universe, which in man becomes will. In the macrocosm it stands for unlimited potentiality, and in man for relative potency. It expresses the law of the conservation of energy and the indestructibility of matter.

Astrology

The commencement of all work is its formulation, and this is a mental activity. Before the universe became manifest it was conceived within the spaces of the Divine Mind, from whence it was launched into objective evolution by the power of creative thought. Thus does mental activity correspond to number I.

A Magus is one skilled in magic. And magic is performed chiefly through the creation and vitalization of mental images. The Magus, therefore, is one in whom the power of the mind has been highly developed, and as in astrology mental ability comes under the rulership of the planet Mercury, this planet must correspond to both I and the Magus of Arcanum I.

Thus does Arcanum I represent the creative energy being directed intelligently, in distinction to the 2nd decave of I, which is pictured by Arcanum X, the planet Uranus, representing the one universal force unrestrained. It also differs markedly from the 3rd decave of I, pictured by Arcanum XIX, corresponding to the zodiacal sign Leo, representing the application of this energy to the attainment of happiness and the elaboration of domestic bliss.

In these three Arcana, each picturing the one universal virile force being used on a different plane, we have a complete commentary on the necessity of using the creative energies properly if any high degree of spirituality is to be attained. Without virility, without an abundance of creative power, nothing of importance can be accomplished in any field. Yet if this creative energy is generated in abundance and is permitted to act without proper guidance, it brings many abrupt changes in fortune, and through instability prevents little worth while being accomplished. If it is directed into mental channels alone it yields intellectual power. But when diverted into refined emotions such as true love and holy aspirations, it furnishes a power which attracts to the soul the highest spiritual bliss.

Human Function

The spiritual body of man is constructed by states of consciousness having intensity enough to affect spiritual substance. Man does not possess a spiritual body merely by virtue of being man. He possesses it when, through the refinement of his thoughts and aspirations he has provided energy of a proper quality to build it. And only when the creative energies are active is there generated enough power, if it can be directed by ecstatic emotions, quickly to build anything on any plane. By a proper mental attitude toward them, all experiences may be made to contribute to this finer form. But to build anything on any plane quickly, there must be an abundance of the proper kind of energy, and this applies to the building of a spiritual body as well as to more material things.

Alchemy

In alchemy, Arcanum I represents the most important of all discoveries, the philosopher's stone. Tradition informs us that any object touched with this stone is converted into gold.

This touchstone of alchemy is Truth; for when truth is pressed against anything its eternal principles are revealed, and these all-enduring qualities thus obtained constitute the gold of their underlying nature. Truth is correct knowledge, and this correct knowledge, if comprehensive, embraces the proper relation of souls and things to all other entities and forces. Thus truth is a freeing and transmuting power, a feeling as well as an intellectual perception. And when fully realized it results in deep aspiration, and in an unutterable longing and determination for a more perfect life.

Bible

Even as Arcanum I is the opening page of The Book of Thoth, as the Egyptians sometimes called the tarot, so the Bible also opens with the principle of creative activity: Gen. I:I; "In the beginning God created the heaven and the earth."

It is a principle especially revered by the Jews, constantly referred to throughout the Bible. Nor has it been entirely ignored in the New Testament, for the last chapter of the last book contains a clear, even if brief, exposition of Arcanum I.

Rev. 22:13; "I am the Alpha and Omega, the beginning and the end, the first and the last."

Masonry

The E.A. degree of Masonry is founded upon Arcanum I. This Arcanum represents the candidate who has been admitted into the Lodge, presented with the Masonic implements, and prepared to undergo initiation.

Magic

Arcanum I indicates the importance of thorough preparation before any feat of magic is attempted. Every principle involved, and every implement used, should also be fully understood. The chief implements, including the magic wand, are depicted. The scepter indicates that the virility of some intelligence, either on this plane or another, is back of all magical phenomena. The star indicates the participation of an intelligence from another plane in the work.

In magic there are four operations, which are here symbolized by the four implements; the first operation, that of formulation, which means building the thing clearly in the mind, is also represented by the arcanum as a whole.

Initiation

In the soul's pilgrimage Arcanum I represents the stage in which manhood has been attained and self-consciousness realized. He has learned the transitory and illusive nature of physical possessions, and has placed his feet once for all upon the road leading ultimately to adeptship. He realizes that success depends entirely upon his own efforts. In his aspirations he has raised his vibrations so that he tunes in on an intelligence of the spiritual plane, as signified by the star, and at critical times asks and receives guidance from this source. He moves forward henceforth with supreme confidence and sustained by an unwavering determination.

Occult Science

The science of esoteric psychology embraces the complete field of mental activity; not merely on the physical plane, but on all planes where intelligence has expression.

The ancients placed so great importance upon the development of will power that they formulated a science of the will, the various phases of which each have a correspondence to one of the Major Arcana of the tarot. In expressing this, the name of each major card is taken as the emblem of some special principle involved. This science of the will, as given in "An Egyptian Initiation", is as follows:

> In uniting successfully the twenty-two significations which emanate from these symbols, their ensemble is summed up in the term, The Synthesis of Magic.
>
> The human Will (1), enlightened by Science (2), and manifested by Action (3), creates the Realization (4), of a power which it uses or abuses according to good or bad Inspiration (5), in the circle which has been traced for it by the laws of universal order. After having surmounted the Trial (6), which has been imposed by Divine Wisdom, he will enter by his Victory (7), into possession of the work it has created, and establishing his Equilibrium (8), upon the axis of Prudence (9), he will rule the oscillations of Fortune (10).
>
> The Force (11), of man, sanctified by Sacrifice (12), which is the voluntary offer of himself upon the altar of devotion or expiation, triumphs over death. This divine Transformation (13), raises him beyond the tomb into the serene region of infinite progress and opposes the reality of Initiative (14), to the eternal falsehood of Fatality (15). The course of time is marked by Ruins (16), but beyond every ruin one sees reappear the dawn of Hope (17), or the twilight of Deception (18).
>
> Unceasingly, man aspires to that which ever flees from him, and the Sun of Happiness (19), will only rise for him beyond the Tomb (20), after the renewal of his being by death, which opens to him a higher sphere of Will, Intelligence and Action.
>
> Every will that lets itself be governed by the instincts of the flesh abdicates its liberty and is bound to the Expiation (22), of its errors. On the contrary, every will which unites itself to Deity in order to manifest truth and work justice, enters even in this life, into a participation of divine power over beings and things, Recompence (21), eternal of Freed Spirits (0).

I not only earnestly recommend to all students that they commit the above summary of the Major Arcana to memory and meditate upon it frequently, but that they use it as a mantram. It contains vastly more of truth and power than appears upon the surface, and used as a mantram has been singularly potent in establishing self-confidence and in building up positiveness and constructive power of will.

The Relation of Minor Arcana to Major Arcana

As previously indicated, the suit of Scepters, which in common playing cards is the suit of Clubs, symbolizes the element fire. This in human life becomes enthusiasm, ambition and enterprise. Consequently, this suit belongs to the department of life having to do with business, occupation, station, honor and profession. In astrology, it is represented by the M.C., where the sun appears at noon.

The suit of Cups, which in common playing cards becomes the suit of Hearts, represents the element water, symbol of the emotions and typical of domestic and affectional relations. It thus broadly corresponds to the western angle of a birth-chart, where the sun sinks below the horizon.

The suit of Swords, which in common playing cards becomes the suit of Spades, represents the element earth, symbol of struggle, allied to affliction and death. It thus corresponds to the Nadir, where the sun is in its grave, or lowest point in the diurnal cycle.

The suit of Coins, which in common playing cards becomes the suit of Diamonds, represents the element air, the breath of life. Air is merely one form of food, although the most essential of all. The other foods may be purchased with money, and thus money has become the symbol of life itself. It therefore corresponds to the Ascendant of a birth-chart, where the new-born sun each day rises above the eastern horizon.

The Aces

In astrology, Mercury is general significator of study, writing, correspondence and travel. As the Aces correspond numerically to Mercury, in their more common divinatory significance they relate to one of these things, according to the particular department of life signified by the suit. But in their application to higher planes, they reveal the influence of, and can be interpreted by, the first decanate of each zodiacal triplicity, starting, of course, with the movable signs.

The divinatory significance of the Ace of Scepters is news of a business opportunity; its inner interpretation is ACTIVITY.

The divinatory significance of the Ace of Cups is a letter from a loved one; its inner interpretation is MOODS.

The divinatory significance of the Ace of Coins is a short journey; its inner significance is POLICY.

The divinatory significance of the Ace of Swords is news of sickness or death; its inner interpretation is ORGANIZATION.

Veiled Isis—Arcanum II

Letter: Egyptian, Beinthin; Hebrew, Beth; English, B. Number 2. Astrologically, the zodiacal sign Virgo. Color, the darker shades of violet. Tone, low B. Occult science, the doctrine of signatures. Human function, clairvoyance. Natural remedy, such herbs as barley, oats, rye, wheat, privet, succory, skullcap, woodbine, valerian, millet and endive. Mineral, the talismanic gem Jasper, and among stones the flints.

B—2 expresses in the spiritual world, the consciousness of Absolute Being, which embraces the three terms of all manifestation; the past, the present, and the future.

In the intellectual world, the binary, reflection of unity; and the perception of things visible and invisible.

In the physical world, woman the mold of man, uniting herself with him in order to accomplish an equal destiny.

> *Remember, then, son of earth, that the mind is enlightened in seeking God with the eyes of the will. God has said, "Let there be Light," and light inundated space. Man should say, "Let truth show itself and good come to me." And if man possesses a healthy will, he will see the truth shine, and guided by it will attain all to which he aspires. If Veiled Isis should appear in the prophetic signs of thy horoscope, strike resolutely at the door of the future and it will open to you; but study for a long time the door you should enter. Turn your face toward the sun of justice, and the knowledge of the true will be given you. Keep silent in regard to your intentions, so as not to be influenced by the contradictions of men.*

In Divination, **Arcanum II** may briefly be read as **Science**.

Arcanum II is figured by a woman seated at the threshold of the Temple of Isis. She is seated between two columns, the one on her right being red to signify pure spirit and its luminous ascension over matter, and the one on her left being black to represent the bondage of matter over the impure.

The woman is crowned by a tiara of three stories surmounted by a lunar crescent. From the tiara a veil falls over her face. She wears upon her bosom the symbol of the planet Mercury, and carries upon her knees an open book which she half covers with her mantle. This symbolic ensemble personifies occult science, which awaits the initiate at the threshold of the sanctuary of Isis in order to tell him the secrets of universal nature. The symbol of Mercury (Hermes) upon the bosom of the Virgin, signifies that matter is fecundated by spirit in order to evolve mind, or soul. The cross below is matter, the circle is spirit. Together they figure the lingam of the Hindus, representing the union of the sexes; and the crescent above the union of spirit and matter represents the soul which is the evolved product of their union.

The seal on the breast of Nature also expresses the thought that knowledge comes from God and is as limitless as its source. The veil falling over the face announces that Nature reveals her truths only to the pure in heart, and hides them from the curious and profane. The book half hidden under the mantle signifies that but half of the truth can be discerned by the physical senses, the exoteric side. The esoteric, or other half, must be apprehended through the application of the psychic senses. Reason, divorced from intuition, can discern only in the realm of effects; but re-wed to intuition, can remove the obscuring mantle from Nature's most secret page and pursue her mysteries at leisure.

These mysteries are revealed only in solitude, to the sage who meditates in silence in the full and calm possession of himself. The tiara represents the power of the intellect to penetrate the three realms of existence—physical, astral and spiritual—which are signified by its stories. The lunar crescent, symbolizing the feminine attribute, is above the tiara to indicate that in occult science the intellect should be guided by the intuitional, or psychic powers. That is to say, in the occult sciences the feminine qualities of the mind are often of superior value to the masculine, or rational. The woman is seated to show that Will united to Science is Immovable.

Number

Numerically, 2 expresses polarity. It suggests night and day, inhalation and exhalation, heat and cold. In fact, the most evident thing in existence is duality, truth itself being dual, esoteric and exoteric, the truth of the real and the truth of appearances.

Astrology

Veiled Isis is none other than the immaculate Virgin who becomes a mother through union with the Holy Spirit. She sits in the doorway of the temple of Nature, veiling the knowledge that can only be gained through union, as depicted in Arcanum III. Arcanum II represents science. This is the harvest of experiences which have become assimilated as knowledge. Virgo is a scientific zodiacal sign, and it rules both the harvest and the processes of assimilation.

Human Function

Mind implies perception, and chief among the perceptive faculties is the sense of sight. Both the mind and sight are ruled by the planet Mercury, and Mercury also rules two zodiacal signs. When the sun is shining physical sight becomes available, but in the darkness of night the inner sight may be more effective. And as the night sign of Mercury is Virgo, it indicates that both this sign and Arcanum II correspond to the inner sense of sight, to clairvoyance.

Alchemy

Alchemically, Arcanum II is the universal solvent which, when properly used, can be made to reduce any metal to its first matter. Raymond Lully says in regard to this:

> Metals can not be transmuted...in the minerals, unless they be reduced into their first matter...Therefore I counsel you, O my friends, that you do not work but about Sol and Luna, reducing them into their first matter, our Sulphur and Argent Vive.

This means, in plain English, that in smelting ores the lowest melting point is obtained by mixing them so that the amount of acid is exactly equal to the amount of alkali; and that in fluxing experiences, when the polar opposites are exactly equal their vibratory rate is raised to a point in which transmutation is more readily accomplished.

Bible

The most notable mention of Arcanum II in the Bible is the story of the Virgin Mary.

Many nations of antiquity were familiar with the tradition of the immaculate conception; and the Christian account was borrowed

directly from Egypt, where the Jews at one time were held captive
and became familiar with traditional lore. For thousands of years in
Egypt it was taught that Isis, conceiving immaculately, gave birth to
Horus, the Sun God. The Egyptian Virgin is often depicted with a
New Moon in her arms, instead of the baby Jesus, which was
substituted when Isis became an object of Christian adoration.

The inner meaning of the immaculate conception is that matter,
or the feminine principle in nature, is impregnated by spirit, or the
positive principle. The gestation which follows is evolution, which
finally results in the birth of man, who possesses an immortal soul
and the potentiality of becoming a god.

Masonry

The F. C. degree of Masonry is founded upon Arcanum II. The two
Masonic pillars, Jachin and Boaz, are prominently pictured at the
entrance to Solomon's Temple.

Magic

In magic, Arcanum II depicts the principle of reception, which is the
polar opposite of the principle indicated in Arcanum I. It is the
feminine reaction of the magical agent, and teaches us the androgyne
nature of the astral light.

It is further exemplified in the production of physical phenomena
by mental means; for in order thus to move physical objects—a process
now recognized by university scientists as the PK (Psychokinetic)
Effect—there must be organic electromagnetism present of sufficient
volume to make the contact and do the work. Organic electromagnetism tends to take whatever form, and to do whatever work, it is
directed to do by the mental energy associated with it.

The ectoplasm of a materializing medium is an impressive example of this. The electromagnetism present is employed by the
directing intelligence to convert some of the material of the medium's
body temporarily into a plastic fluid outside the medium's form. This
plastic substance can then be molded into whatever image the directing
intelligence holds in mind. Electromagnetism is the magical agent
which forms the connecting link between mind and matter. And it must
always be present in sufficient volume whenever material conditions
are affected by the action of mind.

Initiation

In the pilgrimage of the soul Arcanum II represents a definite point in both the descending and the ascending arc of the cycle. In involution it represents the differentiation of the twin souls of one ego into opposite polarities. This takes place in the paradisiacal realm (highest spiritual state), just preceding their fall, as Adam and Eve, into material conditions.

In the upward cycle it signifies that point in initiation where it is realized that man or woman alone are not complete, but require another soul of opposite sex; and that reason alone is not sufficient with the aid of the physical senses to solve the problems of life, but that intuition and the psychic senses must be developed before adeptship is reached.

Occult Science

Astrological Signatures is the science of the correspondences between celestial influences and other things. The soul of each life-form had a point of differentiation from which it departed on its cyclic journey, and this point of departure is within the spiritual vortex of one of the seven planetary families. Thus the soul of any living thing responds more strongly to the vibrations of one particular planet, which is its ruler. And even things possessing no life, such as environments, also transmit the influence of one planet or zodiacal sign stronger than they transmit that of others, and thus the planet or zodiacal sign becomes their signature.

The Deuces

The sign Virgo is general significator of science and labor, therefore the Deuces, corresponding numerically to Virgo, in their more common divinatory significance must relate to these things as applied to the department of life indicated by the suit. But in their higher application they reveal the influence of, and can be interpreted by, the second decanate of each zodiacal triplicity, starting with the pioneer, or movable, signs.

The divinatory significance of the Deuce of Scepters is a business depending upon scientific methods; its inner interpretation is EXALTATION.

The divinatory significance of the Deuce of Cups is a work of love; its inner interpretation is REVELATION.

The divinatory significance of the Deuce of Coins is money acquired by hard labor; its inner interpretation is INDEPENDENCE.

The divinatory significance of the Deuce of Swords is sickness through over-work; its inner interpretation is MARTYRDOM.

The Pyramid Spread

In using the pyramid spread, the cards are first shuffled and cut, and this repeated three times, in the method employed for all the spreads.

Then they are dealt from the top of the deck, one by one, and laid face downward from right to left in pyramid form as illustrated on page 44, 21 cards in all being thus dealt.

The spread may be used to answer a question, to solve a problem, or merely to give the general run of events as they may be expected in some person's life. But before shuffling, what is desired from them should be clearly formulated, and held in the mind until the spread has been completed.

Starting at the lower right hand corner, and counting to the left, every fifth card is a Key, and this key is counted as the first card in the next five, as shown in the illustration. When a Major Arcanum falls upon one of the keys, it makes this key particularly important.

To read, first turn over, from top to bottom, key I, which shows the present. The four cards to the right indicate the past, the one farthest to the right as the more distant past, and the cards nearer the key as more closely approaching the present.

Then key II represents the next turn in the wheel of circumstances, and the cards between key I and key II represent the factors leading up to it.

Key III is read as the next circumstance of importance following this, and the cards between as the lesser factors; key IV is still further in the future; and key V, which crowns the pyramid, shows the ultimate of the thing, or the distant future.

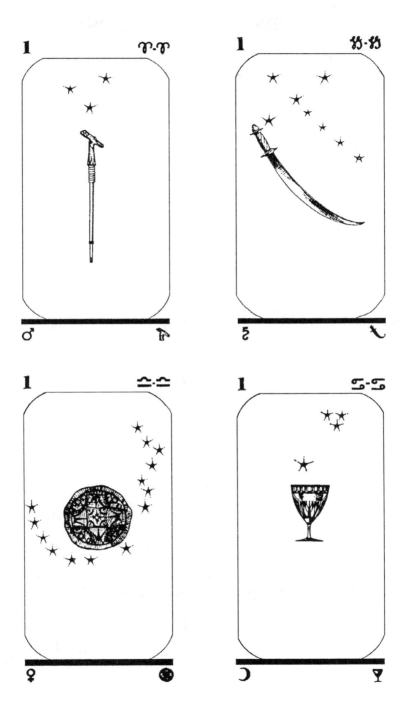

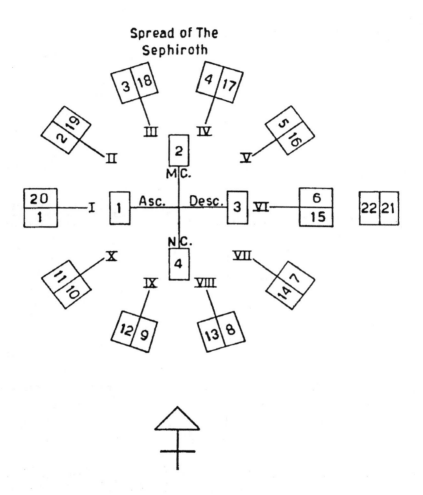

Spread of The
Sephiroth

Chapter 4

Involution and
Evolution of Numbers

A CCORDING to Hermetic Science there are 10 planets in the chain. But because it is a chain, the tenth planet (Pluto) not only closes the previous sphere of influence, but also commences a new gamut. That is, Pluto is a repetition, on a higher scale of existence, of the same influence as that exerted by the Moon; but in addition to being a higher expression of the influence of the Moon it serves an additional function as an influence of transition to an entirely new phase of existence. Neglecting this cycle-closing function represented by Pluto, there are 9 root planets.

These 9 root planets, however, express themselves also by virtue of overtone qualities, in keys that are denoted by the 12 zodiacal signs, in addition to the transition function of Pluto. Thus the principle expressed by Mars, expresses also in a distinctive manner through two other key influences, the sign Aries and the sign Scorpio; and the principle expressed by the Sun expresses in another key influence, through the sign Leo. But the number of such key influences is not unlimited, as shown by the fact that all things which we are able to discern can readily be correlated to one of 22 distinctive keys. That is, everything we contact corresponds to one of the ten planets or twelve Zodiacal signs. This we can prove by observing how a thing is influenced by astrological forces.

The system of numbers in common use is likewise based upon ten fundamental principles, the tenth influence closing the cycle, and starting a new gamut of existence. The 0 shows the completion of the cycle, or circle, and the 1 indicates that the first influence has been carried to a new plane, or phase of being. Thus either with planetary influences or with numbers, we work with 10 separate characters, but there are only 9 root influences.

Any number above 9 is merely one of the root numbers, to which 9 has been added a given number of times. This adding multiples of 9 to some number is called Theosophical Evolution, not because it derives from any particular group of people, but because Theosophy means Divine Wisdom, and because in its particular function, the number 9 is the key to Divine Wisdom in so far as numbers and cycles are concerned.

Due to this peculiar function of the number 9, when a number higher than 9 is given, instead of dividing it by 9 repeatedly until a remainder less than 10 results and thus obtaining its root, the same result may be obtained merely by repeatedly adding the digits of the number until there is but a single digit. That is, the adding of the digits is but a short-cut method of dividing the number by 9. Because this use of the key of Divine Wisdom, 9, to find the root of the number, is the reverse of Theosophical Evolution, it is called Theosophical Involution.

Dealing thus with numbers, we are considering mere abstractions. But when man thinks of a number, a name, or anything else, his thought is not an abstraction, but a definite astral vibration radiating outward. The astral counterparts of objects also radiate definite astral vibrations. And astral vibrations, as well as physical vibrations, and those electromagnetic vibrations known as light and radiant heat, have an influence upon the things they contact.

The tones of musical instruments are other vibrations with which we are even more familiar, and which have many parallels to the astral vibrations of thought. For even as a musical composition has a key, so every train of thought has its key, and influences its surroundings according to this key vibration. And each simple thought is a definite vibratory rate of astral substance, just as each musical tone is a definite vibratory rate of physical substance.

Now with physical tones, if the vibration is increased to a certain degree, the same sound repeats itself on a higher level. Raising the vibration still more causes the tone to be produced on each of many higher levels. We commonly call each of these higher levels an octave expression of the tone, because it was customary to use the diatonic scale in which the interval between one tone level and the next was divided into seven divisions, so that the eighth (octave meaning eight) repeated the tone on a higher level.

In the chromatic scale, however, the interval is divided into twelve tones, illustrated by the 7 white keys and the 5 black keys of a piano, the 13th expressing the octave. The Chinese have a reed instrument in which the interval is divided into 5 equal parts, certain Indians use a scale of 6 equal parts, the Siamese use a tone scale of 9, and certain Moravians use a scale of 24. Thus it will be seen that the interval between a tone on one level and the same tone (commonly referred to as an octave) on another level is variously divided by different people.

Now a thought has a vibratory quality very similar to a tone, except that it expresses in high-velocity substance, that is, in astral substance, and a thought can be sounded on different levels, just as a tone can thus be sounded. But it has been found convenient, and more in conformity to natural principles, to divide the interval between one thought-tone level and the next, not into 7, but into 9 divisions, so that the 10th shall express the same tone on the next higher level. Therefore, instead of calling the interval between a fundamental thought and its expressions on the next higher level an octave, we call it a decave (decave meaning ten). The word DECAVE has been coined, and will hereafter be used, to express the vibratory levels of thought and astral substance.

In the notation, analysis, and charting of thoughts as vibratory tones, therefore, we have 9 root tones. But even as in music overtones play an important part both in composition and in the effect produced, so with thought-tones, there are peculiar overtone effects that make it necessary to employ not merely 9 fundamental characters to express accurately all thought-effects; but to consider as distinct factors certain dominant overtone effects that observation shows to occur in the levels just above the 9 root tones. Thus to chart a train of thoughts it may be necessary to employ as many as 22 different characters.

When the string of a musical instrument is sounded the string not merely vibrates as a whole, giving rise to the tone, but it also divides itself into two equal segments, each of which tends to give forth a sound; into three equal segments, each of which tends to give forth another tone; into four equal segments, each of which tends to give forth still another tone, and so on. These tones produced by the smaller string divisions are called overtones, and are utilized in musical composition.

Certain musical instruments encourage certain overtones and discourage others, and thought-vibrations, likewise, produce specific overtone effects.

But because thought-tones are vibratory rates in high-velocity substance, we cannot follow the comparison with physical vibrations into too great detail. University scientists, through innumerable experiments conducted under strict test conditions, have demonstrated conclusively that on the inner plane, distance and gravitation each are of a different order than they are on the outer plane. And astrology indicates that inner-plane weather affects the individual, not merely according to his inner-plane constitution, but through certain time-space relationships. Astrological energies, in their various combinations, constitute the inner-plane weather.

There are inner-plane weather conditions that affect groups, cities, nations and world affairs, and through these influence each individual in the group, city, nation or world. But the chief weather conditions affecting an individual are restricted to him. In addition to the more general astrological weather conditions, each has his own individual inner-plane weather. Such personal weather is mapped by major progressions, minor progressions and transit progressions.

Also it has been found that with a thought-vibration the overtone quality is dominant from tone 1 up to tone 22, and not only any one of the 9 root-tones, but any one of the 22 types of thought-vibration, can express its individuality on a higher vibratory level or DECAVE.

Thus, in considering not merely thought-vibrations, but character-vibrations and astrological-vibrations, because these are all inner-plane vibrations, we can not confine ourselves merely to 9 root tones, but, due to the peculiar overtone properties of astral vibratory rates, we must give full tone value to 22 different qualities, which we shall, for convenience, call KEYS.

Every thought, every train of thought, every individual, every influence from the firmament and every force in nature, therefore, because its astral nature is thus tuned, vibrates to one of these 22 Keys.

And because each of the 22 key-tones may sound on various higher vibratory levels, or Decaves, in order to find the key to which the thought of a number, for instance, vibrates, it is necessary to reduce or involve it, by subtracting multiples of 9.

To thus apply the number of Divine Wisdom properly to obtain the Key of the number, the digits of the number are added together, and the digits of the number so obtained are added together again, and so on, until a number is obtained which is less than 23. This number is the Key of the number considered.

Thus to find the Key, or vibratory thought-rate, of the number

1932 we simply add 1 plus 9 plus 3 plus 2, which gives 15 as its thought-tone quality.

Now the Key itself is the first Decave of a number. The second decave is obtained by adding 9. In this case the second decave is 15 plus 9 which equals 24. The third decave of a number is obtained by adding two times 9, in this case giving 33. But due to the peculiar overtone properties of astral vibratory rates, the Key of 24 and 33 is not 15, but 6. Yet when we add six times 9 to 15 we get 69, the Key of which is 15, because in this number the overtone effect again becomes dominant.

From the above it will be seen that the way to find the decave in which the key is sounded is to subtract the key from the number and divide by 9; and then because the key itself is the first decave, to add 1 to the number thus found.

Thus 1932 minus 15 gives 1917. 1917 divided by 9 gives 213. That is, 9 has been added to 15 just 213 times to get 1932. But as 15 itself is the first decave, to get the number of the decave we must add 1 to 213, which gives us 214. This means that the thought-vibration is 15 sounded on the 214th vibratory level.

Now if we desire to get the Key of the Decave, which we use only for divinatory purposes, we merely add 2 plus 1 plus 4, which gives 7.

15 itself has a root, obtained through adding its digits—1 plus 5 gives 6 as the root. But from a vibratory-tone standpoint the Key is the important thing.

The ROOT is a number below 10.

The KEY may be any number below 23.

The DECAVE is the number of times 9 has been added to the Key plus 1, this 1 being the first Decave, which is occupied by the Key.

The Key of the Decave is found by using the Decave as a number and finding its key in the ordinary way.

When, therefore, we add the digits of a number together, let us not believe this is some arbitrary method of finding its significance; but understand that we are proceeding according to correct mathematical principles to find what number, as a Key number, has been raised to a higher level by adding to it multiples of 9.

And when we find the Decave of the number let us bear in mind that the number itself is on the first decave, and that to it has been added 9 a certain number of times. The number thus expresses a certain decave of a Key number, just as a musical tone sounded on a higher octave expresses itself as a tone which has been raised by multiples of 7.

Isis Unveiled—Arcanum III

Letter: Egyptian, Gomer; Hebrew, Gimel; English, G. Number, 3. Astrologically the zodiacal sign Libra. Color, the lighter shades of yellow. Tone, high E. Occult science, spiritual alchemy. Human function, the sense of feeling. Natural remedy, such herbs as white rose, strawberry, violet, water-cress, primrose, heartsease, balm, pansy and lemon-thyme. Mineral, the talismanic gem, diamond; and such stones as white quartz, white spar and white marble.

G—3, expresses in the spiritual world, supreme power balanced by eternally active intelligence and absolute wisdom.

In the intellectual world, the universal fecundity of being.

In the physical world, nature in labor, the germination of acts, which must hatch from the will.

> *Remember, then, son of earth, that to affirm what is true and will what is just, is already to create it; to affirm and will the contrary is to vow oneself to destruction. If Arcanum III should appear in the prophetic signs of thy horoscope, hope for success in thy enterprises provided thou knowest how to unite the activity which fecundates, to that rectitude of mind which will make thy works bear fruit.*

In Divination, **Arcanum III** may be read briefly as **Marriage** or **Action**.

Arcanum III is figured by a woman seated within a radiant sun. The rays from this sun number thirty, the number of degrees in one zodiacal sign. The woman is crowned with twelve stars, to represent the twelve signs through which the sun passes each year. Her feet rest upon the moon, symbol of the feminine in nature. And the cube upon which she sits represents the cross of matter, where rays of sun and moon meet, and so signifies the union of male and female forces.

From her brow the sacred serpent thrusts its head as a symbol of enlightenment. In her right hand she carries a scepter surmounted by a globe. This is essentially a phallus, and indicates the perpetual action of creative energy upon all things born or to be born. In her left hand she carries an eagle, the symbol of fruitfulness and of the heights to which the flights of the spirit can raise itself through the emotions engendered in union. The seat upon which she rests is covered with eyes, indicating that through union the eyes of the soul have been opened to a knowledge of good and evil.

This ensemble pictures, in terms of universal symbolism, generation, gestation, and universal fecundity.

Number

Numerically, 3 expresses the union of polar opposites, the relation between such forces as cause vibration and change. It thus represents the universal agent, action, or word, and is typical of fecundity. It is the union of forces of different polarity that is back of all action, all life and all intelligence.

As applied to human evolution it represents the ego joined to the body by the soul. The soul develops and makes progress because the ego is polarized to positive spirit and the body is polarized to negative matter. The interaction between these two generates the force that impells the soul forward in its journey.

On the physical plane, 3 represents man and woman in marriage. In science it stands for the dynamic laws; for the laws that govern the production and directing of energy. It is because of difference in polarity that nothing is free from change, that all nature is in constant motion.

Astrology

Having been tempted by the serpent of desire for material experience, the desire for offspring—astrologically the fifth house, presided over by the sign Leo—Eve falls into union. This union is astrologically the union of summer and winter, which, with the conception resulting, is represented by the natural ruler of all partnerships, the zodiacal sign Libra.

Arcanum III not merely pictures the union, but also the resulting enlightenment; for Adam and Eve after union discerned they needed clothing, and the serpent of desire, through desire's fulfillment, became the serpent of wisdom. This serpent, symbol of creative energy released by desire, is shown raised to the brow to indicate the power that union possesses to increase the range of mental activity.

Isis Unveiled should be distinguished from the second decave of 3, which is Arcanum XII and the sign Pisces; for this pictures negative union resulting in wasted vitality. Also from the third decave of 3, which is Arcanum XXI, ruled by the Sun, which reveals the use of union in making the highest spiritual attainment.

Human Function

Union is prompted by feeling. Also, the contact with objects which gives rise to feeling is a form of union. Thus the human function known as the sense of feeling quite naturally attaches itself to the arcanum which represents union.

Alchemy

Arcanum III represents the union of the various ingredients. Not only must all the proper ingredients be present before transmutation is possible, but they must enter into union. The reverberatory furnace imparts some energy to them, but not enough to complete the transmutation process. It is not, therefore, merely a matter of assembling suitable metals in proper proportions. But they must be joined in such a manner as mutually to increase their vibratory rates; adding the energy they thus mutually generate to the process. Physical proximity is not sufficient for this purpose. They must be intimately joined in their essential qualities.

Bible

The fall of Eve and the consequent expulsion of the human race from the Garden of Eden is pictured by Arcanum III.

The ark of Noah is another reference to the same arcanum. Its three stories correspond to the three realms of the arcanum which are represented by the Sun, typical of spirit, the Moon, typical of the astral, and the cube, typical of the physical world. The cube, or physical world, or square cabin of the ark, is where the soul undergoes its period of gestation.

Masonry

The Master Mason degree is based upon Arcanum III; and the meaning of the whole story of the assassination, the burial, the finding and the raising of Hiram Abiff is made plain by comparing it with the pictured symbols of this arcanum. It thus, in reality, is the key to the Master's Word which was lost at that time.

The G of Masonry, found traced upon the breast of the murdered Hiram, is the letter of this arcanum. High twelve, the time the master was attacked, is represented by the noon-day position of the Sun. Low twelve, the time he was buried, is indicated by the position of the moon at the nadir.

The grave, which is six feet due east and west, and six feet perpendicular, is represented by the six-sided cube upon which Isis sits. The sprig of cassia marking the grave is presented in the tarot as a phallic scepter. The twelve Masons sent out to hunt for Hiram Abiff are symbolized by the twelve stars above the head of Isis. The five points of fellowship upon which Hiram was raised by means of the Lion's paw grip are indicated by the five eyes traced upon the cube; and the final transcendent result of so being raised is pictured by the eagle on the left hand of Isis.

Magic

In Magic, Arcanum III reveals the principle of vitalization. This principle springs into existence as the result of that polarity represented in Arcanum II. That is, it is the vibratory effect of the interaction of polar opposites.

One of the first things we learn in the study of physics is that every action is accompanied by an opposite and equal reaction. Therefore, for every positive force in the universe there must be an exactly similar force of negative attributes.

It is impossible, for instance, to make a magnet possessing only a positive pole. For by the most fundamental law of nature, when a positive force of any kind is brought into existence it must be accompanied by an equal, but negative force. This is the principle upon which rests that great law of physics called the conservation of energy. For if one member of this duality were to be absent, and the energy spent in one direction were not always accounted for by an equivalent reaction, it would be possible not merely to transform energy, but to create new energies, or actually to lose energy already in existence. That such creation and such loss never take place constitutes the well known law of the conservation of energy.

The law of the conservation of energy does not apply merely to one plane of existence, but to all planes and states. Consequently, for every soul of positive, or male, polarity, which comes into existence through differentiation, there simultaneously springs into existence another soul of negative, or female, polarity. A soul is a definite force, and it has polarity, and it is as impossible to conceive of a male soul being launched upon the tide of involution and evolution without a similar female soul also being launched at the same time, as it is to conceive of a magnet with only one pole. Furthermore, because action and reaction are exactly equivalent, the female soul must be the exact replica of the male soul, except in the matter of sex, or polarity.

Other than sex, the only possible difference between souls which thus have been differentiated at the same time is due to the diversity of experiences which they have had since differentiation. Ultimately they are both born upon the earth, and sometimes they even meet in physical life as man and woman. But whether they meet upon earth, or in some higher state of existence, by virtue of their simultaneous differentiations and being originally exact counterparts, they are true soul-mates.

The ability of soul-mates spiritually to vitalize each other, although this may not be acquired until planes far above earth are reached, makes their joint immortality possible. But descending from such recondite considerations, in reality there is no action, no life and no consciousness that is not traceable to sex.

Chemical affinity, for instance, is due to the marriage of atoms. They are impelled to divorce less compatible partners and enter into union with those which have a greater attraction for them. And we use the power generated in such marriages to drive locomotives and to carry us about the country in automobiles.

Electricity and magnetism are due to positive energies endeavoring to unite with negative energies; and analysis could show that every force in the universe which has come under observation is the result of some similar sexual attraction.

Breathing, likewise, is dual, inhalation and exhalation, positive and negative. And in the process, in addition to the oxygenation of the blood, electromagnetic energies are picked up and lend their power to nerve, brain and electromagnetic body.

Initiation

In the soul's pilgrimage Arcanum III represents its descent into material conditions and then, having climbed the ascending arc of the cycle to the human state, finding a suitable companion to assist in developing the spiritual attributes. Spirituality implies an exalted emotional development.

Occult Science

Spiritual alchemy is the science which uses each and every event of life as a means of creating spiritual values. They are purified by separating the external appearance from their real significance, and fluxed in proper combination. Should some ingredients be lacking to perfect the transmutation, these events are sought out and added to life's collection.

The Treys

The sign Libra is the common significator of partnership, open enemies, lawsuits and dealing with the public; therefore the Treys, corresponding numerically to Libra, in their more common divinatory significance must relate to these things as applied to the department of life indicated by the suit. But in their higher application they reveal the influence of, and can be interpreted by, the third decanate of each zodiacal triplicity, starting with the active, or movable signs.

The divinatory significance of the Trey of Scepters is a business partnership; its inner interpretation is PROPAGANDA.

The divinatory significance of the Trey of Cups is a marriage for love; its inner interpretation is RESEARCH.

The divinatory significance of the Trey of Coins is a marriage for money; its inner interpretation is EXPIATION.

The divinatory significance of the Trey of Swords is a lawsuit or a divorce; its inner interpretation is IDEALISM.

The Sovereign—Arcanum IV

Letter: Egyptian, Denain; Hebrew, Daleth; English, D. Number, 4. Astrologically, the sign Scorpio. Color, the darker shades of red. Tone, low C. Occult science, imponderable forces. Human function, the absorption of electromagnetic essences. Natural remedy, such herbs as heather, horehound, bramble, bean, leek, wormwood, woad, charlock and blackthorn. Mineral, the talismanic gem, Spanish topaz, and among stones, bloodstone, vermilion and lodestone.

D—4 expresses in the spiritual world, the realization, perpetual and hierarchic, of the virtualities, the efficacies, contained in Absolute Being.

In the intellectual world, the realization of the ideas of contingent being by the four-fold labors of the mind; affirmation, negation, discussion, and solution.

In the physical world, the realization of acts, directed by the knowledge of the truth, the love of justice, the force of the will, and the works of the organs.

Remember, then, son of earth, that nothing can resist a firm will which has for a lever the knowledge of the true and just. To combat in order to secure its realization is more than right; it is a duty. The man who triumphs in that struggle only accomplishes his earthly mission; he who succumbs in devoting himself to it, gains immortality. If the Sovereign should appear in the prophetic signs of thy horoscope, it signifies that the realization of thy hopes depends upon a being more powerful than thyself. Seek to know him and thou shalt have his support.

In Divination, **Arcanum IV** may be read as **Realization.**

Arcanum IV is figured by a man; on his head a sovereign's helmet. He is seated upon a cubic stone; his right hand raises a scepter surmounted by a circle, and his right leg bent, rests upon the other, forming with it a cross.

The cubic stone, image of the perfect solid, signifies labor which has reached completion. The cat, pictured on the side of the stone, indicates that the vision of the soul penetrates the illusions of matter.

The sovereign's helmet is an emblem of force conquered by power. The ruler is in possession of the scepter of Isis, indicating that he has knowledge of the spiritual use of the creative energies; and he points downward with his left hand to indicate that he uses these energies in the subjugation of the physical.

The sacred serpent at his brow indicates enlightenment; and the hawk, sacred to the sun, indicates his ambition to attain spiritual supremacy.

The cross, formed by his legs, symbolizes the four elemental kingdoms he has mastered, and the expansion of human power through understanding.

The apron above the legs, together with them, figures a trine above a cross; the symbol of mind dominating matter, and of the conservation of energy.

Number

Numerically, 4 expresses the result of action, the fruit of the toil typified by 3. It is the realization from effort, and it is life springing into manifestation as the result of the union of polar opposites. It thus represents the practical, the concrete, and consequently that which has form.

It becomes, therefore, the type of the universal truth of reality, indicating that each realm is actual when viewed from its own plane.

It is also the practical as applied to everyday affairs.

In the macrocosm it signifies the result of motion; in man it is the knowledge which comes through experience. In science it relates to all those laws which govern the effective use of energy; to those which govern what is produced by motion.

Astrology

The Sovereign by his helmet and his attitude of dominating through force, expresses martial energy; and the prominence of the phallic symbol relates him to the sex sign of Mars rather than to the head sign, Aries. Furthermore, the fruitfulness and silent type of strength are attributes of Scorpio.

Scorpio is the zodiacal sign of sex, the magnetic forces of which conserved as indicated in Arcanum IV become a most potent power to dominate the elemental realms of life. The negative aspect of this principle is indicated by the second decave of 4, Arcanum XIII, which pictures the natural course of events when the force is undirected, life and death in different types of forms following each other in rhythmic cycles.

The inversive and degenerative use of the same principle is pictured in Arcanum XXII, representing the third decave of 4. Here the T is represented with its point down; but the other side of Pluto's influence is the T with its point skyward; which is the highest aspect of sex, the transcendent powers arising from a union of soul-mates.

Human Function

Magnetically, Scorpio is the most potent sign of the zodiac. Sex is back of all energy, and in man generates electromagnetic currents. Sexual vigor tunes the organism in on electromagnetic energies, which are all about us, and these give force to the personal magnetism, and vitalize the emotions and the procreative fluids. Scorpio, because of its rulership of sex, more readily than any other sign, is capable of receiving and transmitting these magnetic energies, and thus Arcanum IV, corresponding to Scorpio, is correlated to the faculty of electromagnetic absorption.

Alchemy

When the ingredients are brought together their union generates a force, or heat. The energy, thus liberated through the fluxing of polar opposites, when properly controlled, is an essential factor in proper transmutation. The control of it, however, is not accomplished by suppressing, or confining it, but by directing it into proper channels. In fact, the directing of this energy into those channels which prevent it from causing an explosion, or burning the various ingredients, is one of the most important secrets of the alchemical art. Diverting it to the end desired corresponds to Arcanum IV.

Bible

As Arcanum IV is the emblem of fruitfulness, there are numerous passages in the Bible which refer to it; for throughout, fruitfulness is considered a virtue and barrenness a crime. This applies more forcefully to the mental than to the physical plane; for when man is barren of thought his progress ceases and the body falls into decay.

Gen. 1:28. "And God blessed them, and God said unto them, Be fruitful and multiply, and replenish the earth, and subdue it; and have dominion over the fish of the sea, and the fowl of the air, and over every living thing that moveth upon the earth."

Rev. 12:5. "And she brought forth a man child, who was to rule all nations with a rod of iron; and her child was caught up unto God and His throne."

Thus is mentioned the fruitfulness of the sign Scorpio; its rulership, as belonging to Mars, of iron; the rod held in the hand of the Sovereign, its dominating character, and its possibilities of spiritual realization as symbolized by the hawk; for the child was caught up to the throne of God.

Masonry

The Mark Master's degree is founded upon Arcanum IV. As a whole the degree and the arcanum teach that, "To him that overcometh will I give to eat of the hidden manna, and I will give him a white stone, and in the stone a new name written, which no man knoweth, saving him that receiveth it."

The sovereign of Arcanum IV sits upon such a stone, and the symbol of a new name is engraved upon it, and he represents one who has overcome. The hawk pictured on his breast is reputed, in legend, to fly to the sun. It therefore carries the same purport as the eight Masonic letters which are interpreted either, "Hiram Tyrian, Widow's Son, Sent To King Solomon," or, "He That Was Slain Soars

To Kindred Spirit." Thus does Arcanum IV depict the key-stone which the builders rejected.

Magic

In Magic, Arcanum IV reveals the principle of realization. This implies the expectant attitude, and the preparation after the energy has been released to provide for that which is to be fulfilled. There must be confidence that the work is being properly performed, and that gestation will result in proper fruition. Worry, or anxiety as to results, is fatal to proper development of that which is desired.

Initiation

In the soul's pilgrimage, Arcanum IV indicates the result of marriage after the state of manhood has been reached.

Both Christian monks and Hindu ascetics were under the impression that to be holy one must be miserable. But modern psychology proves indisputably that happiness leads to efficiency, and that misery tends toward disintegration without necessarily adding anything to the spirituality.

Of all the avenues to spiritual development, the affections are the most potent. The union prompted by lust and selfishness is one of the most destructive forces. Through the emotions we raise or lower our vibratory rates, and thus tend to elevate ourselves to a higher condition or lower and degrade ourselves.

The creative energies, in union, customarily arouse intense emotional states. If these emotional states are such as inspire tenderness, kindness and the desire to be helpful to others, they tend vigorously to build up the spirituality; for they cultivate a higher basic vibratory rate. But if they engender brutal thoughts and encourage grossness, through cultivating a lower basic vibratory rate, they destroy the spirituality.

Furthermore, there is no power which can lift the soul to such exalted states of ecstasy as can love, and thus only through love can we of earth contact the higher spiritual states.

Occult Science

Imponderable forces is the science which deals with all the invisible energies not recognized by material science. In particular, it deals with the principles of ceremonial magic, in which there is a more or less definite ritual and often there is used specially prepared equipment such as wands, circles, seals, pentacles, inscriptions, etc.

The Fours

The sign Scorpio is the general significator of fruitfulness, legacies, spirit communion, the dead, and the partner's money. Consequently, each of the fours, in its more common divinatory significance must relate to one of these things according to its suit. But in their higher application these cards reveal the influence of, and can be interpreted by, the fourth decanate of each zodiacal triplicity, starting the count with the movable signs.

The divinatory significance of the Four of Scepters is a legacy; its inner interpretation is RULERSHIP.

The divinatory significance of the Four of Cups is an increase in the family; its inner interpretation is RESOURCEFULNESS.

The divinatory significance of the Four of Coins is money received through a partner; its inner significance is ORIGINALITY.

The divinatory significance of the Four of Swords is remorse for past action; its inner interpretation is DETERMINATION.

Reversed Cards

In all methods of reading the cards are dealt face downward; and they are turned over from top to bottom, one at a time, as read. This prevents the mind from wandering to other parts of the spread.

Any card right end up is considered slightly more fortunate than its common significance. It then becomes like a planet receiving a good aspect. Any card wrong end up is slightly more unfortunate than its common meaning. It then becomes like a planet receiving a bad aspect. But reversal never makes a good card bad, nor a bad card good. As Saturn and Mars are less evil when well aspected, and as Jupiter and Venus are more potent for good when well aspected, in the same manner any card is improved by being right end up.

Method of the Sephiroth

In this method only the 22 Major Arcana and the 4 Aces are used. The Aces are shuffled separately. They are the most potent of all; for they represent the four astral kingdoms symbolized by their suits.

They are called the Astral Keys, and outrank any of the other cards.

The 4 Aces after being shuffled and cut are then dealt as illustrated on page 66, the first on the kingdom marked Asc., the second on the M.C., the third on the Desc., and the fourth on the N.C.

Then the 22 Major Arcana are shuffled, cut, and dealt one at a time around the ten thrones, from I to X. This completed, the others are dealt back from throne X to throne I. This leaves two cards, which are placed face downward at the side. These are called the staff, and are only consulted when the figure proves contradictory. In such instances the staff indicates why there was failure to give a plain answer, and thus supports the devout student in his disappointment.

The first Astral Kingdom, marked Asc., is that of Life, and if the Ace of Coins falls there it shows strength, vigor and vitality; if the Ace of Scepters, it is favorable but denotes work and responsibility; if the Ace of Cups, that love of pleasure may deplete the vitality; and if the Ace of Swords, that there will be sickness or death.

The second Astral Kingdom, marked M.C., is that of Honor and Business. The Ace of Scepters falling there gives it great power; the Ace of Coins is favorable, but indicates much effort required; the honor is blemished through the pursuit of pleasure if the Ace of Cups falls there; and the Ace of Swords there presages failure.

The Astral Kingdom of Love is marked Desc. The Ace of Cups falling there indicates joy and happiness; the Ace of Swords there marks disputes; the Ace of Scepters there brings difficulties through difference in station; and the Ace of Coins signifies abundant strength.

The Astral Kingdom of Results is marked N.C. The Ace of Swords falling there indicates a favorable ending; the Ace of Cups there brings pleasant results; the Ace of Coins there is most unfortunate; and the Ace of Scepters there denotes a hard struggle which yields inadequate returns.

If the question relates to life begin with the Asc., if to love or war with the Desc., if to honor or business with the M.C., and if to secret things with the N.C.

First turn over, from top to bottom, the Ace, or astral key, of the question. Every question possible belongs to one of the four kingdoms, and the Ace indicating the general fortune of the matter is located as explained. After the significance of this Ace is noted, turn over the cards belonging to its thrones. You will note that the Asc. and Desc. have three thrones of two cards each, and that the M.C. and N.C. have but two thrones of two cards each. In considering the Asc. or Desc. the two cards on the center thrones, either I or VI, as the case may be, indicate the most important factors, and the other four cards signify modifying influences. The cards on the thrones of the question will indicate why the conditions signified by the Ace shown there exist and give some details.

Then turn over the opposite Ace, which indicates the opposition to the matter. The cards of its throne show the details of this opposition. Now if good cards occupy the kingdom and thrones of the question, and also the opposition to the question, it is most favorable. But if both the question and its opposition are held by evil cards, it is a bad omen. If the opposition holds more evil than the question holds good, the matter will fail after a struggle. If the question holds more evil than the opposition holds good, the matter lacks merit and will fail of its own accord. If the opposition is good enough, it will be carried to success in spite of its unworth. If the good in the question is stronger than the opposition it will succeed in spite of opposition.

The kingdom next in order always indicates the culmination of the matter, and the thrones opposite within their kingdom its end. Thus in a question of love, war, marriage, etc., the Desc. becomes the question and the Asc. its opposition. The N.C. then becomes its progress, and the M.C. its end. In a question of business, however, the M.C. becomes the question and the N.C. its opposition, with the Desc. its progress and the Asc. its end. If the question concerns psychic matters or hidden things the N.C. becomes the question and the M.C. its opposition; with the Asc. its culmination and the Desc. its end.

And in all cases the cards on the thrones will indicate the various factors, indicating how and why. The four cards on the thrones of the M.C. or N.C. are of equal importance.

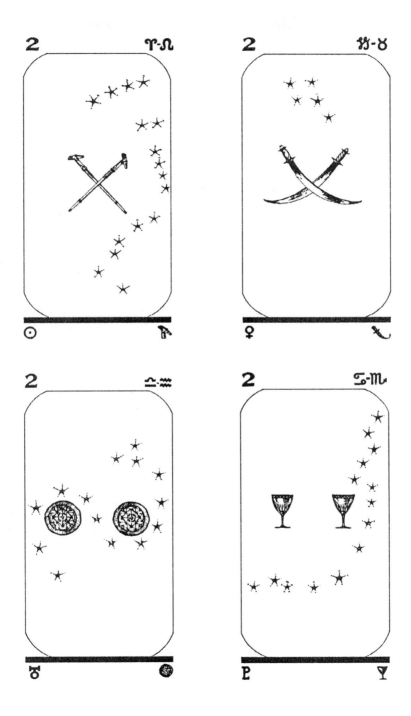

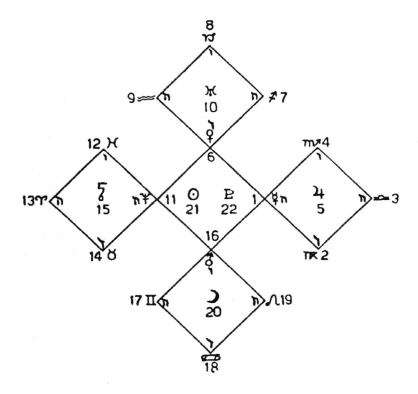

The Grand Pentagram

Chapter 5

Reading the
Meaning of Numbers

B Y MEANS of numbers we estimate the influence both of things and forces. The value of a material object, for instance, such as a house, is commonly expressed numerically in dollars and cents. The power of an engine is expressed numerically as so many horsepower. The speed of light is mentioned as so many thousand miles a second. And the pressure in an electric system as so many volts. In fact, the measure of quantity and quality would be very difficult to express except through the use of numbers.

When, therefore, we approach the study of the influence exerted by invisible energies, we quite naturally expect that they also should be expressed, in their power to cause changes, by means of numbers.

A vast amount of experimental and statistical evidence has been accumulated proving that man lives in, and is influenced by, two environments. And a vast amount of observation indicates that the inner-plane environment and its forces are as effective in determining his thoughts, emotions, behavior, health and the events which enter his life as are the outer-plane environment and its forces.

Man is influenced from the outer plane by what people say orally, over the radio, through the press and on the screen. And he is influenced from the inner plane by people's thoughts. He is influenced from the outer plane by objects. And he is influenced from the inner plane by the character vibrations of objects. He is influenced from the outer plane by the weather. And he is equally or more influenced from the inner plane by the astrological energies which constitute the inner-plane weather.

An individual ignorant of inner-plane energies is able to live up to only one-half his possibilities. Through knowledge of the inner-plane energies an individual who will apply such knowledge should be able to increase his spirituality, success, happiness and health 100 percent. Whatever his objectives may be, he stands a far greater chance of reaching them if he understands how the inner-plane environment influences his life, and how to take advantage of its energies.

As indicated, such energies may all be classified under these three categories:

1. Character-vibrations; which are the radiations of a thing or an intelligence due to its organization.
2. Thought-vibrations; which are the radiations of an intelligence due to thought processes.
3. Astrological-vibrations; which are the radiations from the heavenly bodies and the zodiacal signs.

The vibrations of physical substance within a certain range of frequencies give rise to tones or sounds. And electromagnetic vibrations within a certain range of frequencies give rise to colors. Likewise the range of frequencies of astral substance which has an influence upon human life gives rise to similar types of energy, producing effects comparable to physical tones or electromagnetic colors. Because we are more familiar with physical vibrations, it is convenient to refer to astral vibrations as tones.

There are thus astral tones arising from the signs and planets, astral tones arising from character radiations, and astral tones arising from thoughts. Tones may be isolated or in combination; and in either case there is often a dominant influence, or key. A character, for instance, is not just a single tone, but a combination of them. Yet there is usually a key note to the character. Likewise, a single thought radiates but a single astral tone. But a train of thoughts radiates a series of tones like a musical selection. Yet a musical composition commonly has a key tone. And a train of thoughts also has a key which can be determined from the nature of the thinking. In its influence the key tone is the most important vibratory rate.

We have all heard the story of how a building or a bridge can be demolished by a fiddler playing near it the tone to which it is keyed. And as already mentioned in chapter 2, the great Caruso, when he dined, would ask for a wine glass, tap it to find its tone, and have the waiter place it at the far side of the room. Then singing this tone in his powerful voice he would shatter the glass.

Now thoughts also have each a given tone quality. And just as Caruso's voice sounding a certain tone called forth that response in the tone of the wine glass, so a thought having the same tone as some particularly prominent vibratory center within ourselves, when it reaches us repeatedly, may set up a terrific vibratory intensity in that section of our astral body. That is, a specific thought reaching us from others, constantly being radiated to us by everyone who thinks about us, if it has the same tone as some section of our astral body, stimulates the thought-cells of that section of the astral body into unusual activity.

Of such thoughts sent to us regularly and with great frequency the name we use as signature may be the one from which we receive the greatest thought bombardment. However, the nickname by which our friends think of us, the given name by which relatives think of us, and the house number or telephone number which is used often by people while they visualize us, all have an influence. The amount of energy from each such name or number, of course, depends upon the frequency with which it is thought and the thought-power of those who thus think of us in such association.

Either a name or a number, as such, is merely an abstraction, and has no energy to do anything. But when a name or a number is thought, that thought is a definite energy radiated toward the one then thought about. As such it has also a specific vibratory key. Its influence, thus, is not to be measured by the sound produced in speaking; for the influence is quite as pronounced if it is only thought and not spoken. It is measured by the voltage, so to speak, of the thought; that is, by the energy supplied the thought by the thinker; and by the key to which it vibrates.

As to how much power to project their thoughts the various individuals who think our name have, and how often they think our name, we can only estimate in a very general manner. But as to the key to which any name or number vibrates we have a positive method of determination. Just as positive a method as we have of determining in which key a musical composition is written.

The Hebrew, Chaldean and Coptic square-formed letters served not merely as letters, but also as numbers. That is, there were no separate characters for numbers, each letter being a number. We thus have the numerical value of the letters of these ancient alphabets; that is, the vibratory quality ascribed to each by the early masters of occult science. And these values, as tested out today, prove correct.

And in tabulating the correspondence between the English alphabet and the ancient square-formed letters, the effort has been made, not merely to follow the precedent of translators of languages, but accurately to select the English equivalent in its thought-vibration quality of each of the ancient 22 letters. Thus we are able, by substituting the numerical vibratory equivalent of each English letter, to find the number which has the same astral vibratory rate as any name.

When the numerical equivalent of the name is thus found, the Key to which the name vibrates can be determined by finding the Key of the number. This Key is found by Theosophical Involution, as explained in chapter 4. That is, the digits of the number are added together, and this repeated, until a number results which is below 23. This gives the vibratory key of the number, and thus the vibratory key of the name.

By this method the vibratory rate of any name, whether it is associated with an individual or not, may be determined in a positive manner. And with this information at our disposal for determining the key of any name or any number, we have at hand a rather complete measure of all the astral forces that can have an influence over human life.

Character-vibrations are determined by finding the astrological signature. That is, the key to which a town, a person, a locality, an occupation, or what not, vibrates is made known when its astrological rulership is discovered. And astrologers have determined the rulership of most important things. In this connection, in subsequent lessons of this course, there will be some discussion of the influence of musical notes, of colors, of talismanic gems, and such things. The astrological vibrations, of course, are made known by astrological science. This leaves only the influence of thought-vibrations to be considered.

Thoughts are either abstract or concrete. Concrete thoughts are those that concern doing something, or which revolve about some definite object or action. We do not possess as yet any method of determining the tone of each separate thought in a thought-train. If we did we could chart any thought-train on a musical staff of 11 lines and 11 spaces. But we do possess a method of determining each separate tone in any name or any number; for each letter, or number, is one of 22 numbered thought-tones. Thus we can chart a number or name on such a staff as mentioned; the name C. C. Zain thus being charted on the frontispiece of Chapter 2 in Course 18, *Imponderable Forces.*

But the really important thing about a thought-train, or about a name or number, is the key to which it vibrates as a whole. This key to which a thought-train sounds can be determined by an analysis of it. Such analysis of a thought-train, or an emotion, reveals it to vibrate chiefly to the Domestic Urges (Key 20), to the Power Urges (Key 21), to the Safety Urges (Key 15), to the Intellectual Urges (Key 1), or to some of the other keys. From this the influence of the thought-train or emotion is made known. And in Course 9, *Mental Alchemy* the practical application of such knowledge is discussed in all its details.

Here, however, we are interested in abstract thoughts, such as names and numbers. The name FRED, for instance, when not associated in the mind with some particular person, is a mere abstraction. Yet when you, or anyone else, thinks the name FRED, there is radiated from the mind four thought-tones—17—20—5—4. No matter who thinks this name, the same thought-tones are radiated. And each of these four separate tones has a certain amount of influence.

But in thinking this name, or any other name, the various tones composing it are blended, just as the tones of a musical chord are blended, and the whole name as thought vibrates to a dominant key tone. And this key tone, the vibratory key of the name, has a far greater power than any tone embraced in it; in fact, it seems to have as much power as all the combined separate tones of the name.

Thus 17 plus 20 plus 5 plus 4 gives 46 as the number of the name FRED. Then as 46 is above 23, we add 4 plus 6 which gives us 10 as the astral vibratory Key of the name. No matter who thinks the word Fred, his thoughts send out a key-tone which vibrates to 10.

The meaning of this 10 tone, standing by itself, and unrelated to any individual, can be had by referring to the 10th Major Arcanum of the tarot. Its divinatory significance is there given as Change of Fortune. Its meaning is also there indicated in the spiritual world, in the intellectual world, and in the physical world. And still further information about it can be had from the detailed explanation of the number 10 tarot.

But as affecting human life things do not stand alone. Instead they exert an impact upon character. How the character is affected, depends not merely upon the vibration reaching it from without, but also upon the nature of the character thus reached. One individual is affected one way by a certain force and another individual is affected in quite a different way by this same force.

Therefore, if we are to have a positive science—as distinct from a divinatory method—of invisible vibrations as affecting human life and destiny, we must have a chart of the influencing vibrations, and also a chart of the character influenced. By a comparison of the two sets of vibratory rates we can determine, in the manner advocated by exact science, what response will be brought forth from the character by the vibratory tone reaching it.

And so far as human beings are concerned, I know of no method of accurately determining the various vibratory rates—their power, their harmony and discord, the department of life they affect, and the lines of energy exchange between them—that reside in the character, other than through the use of an astrological birth-chart.

The astrological birth-chart is a complete map of the astral body, revealing the strength and nature of all its dynamic thought structures, and how they are organized in relation to each other. It is a reliable map of the character.

Any invisible energy, whether character radiation, astrological radiation, or thought radiation, reaching the astral body of the individual stimulates into additional activity the same tone to which it vibrates as this tone exists already in the astral body. That is, it gives the thought cells of the astral body new energy. How this affects the individual then can be determined by the map of the astral body which is the astrological birth-chart.

The Heirophant—Arcanum V

Letter: Egyptian, Eni; Hebrew, He; English, E. Number, 5. Astrologically, the planet Jupiter. Color, indigo and purple. Tone, A. Occult science, Masonry. Human function, the electromagnetic form. Natural remedy, proper diet. Mineral, the metal tin.

E—5 expresses in the spiritual world, universal law, regulator of the infinite manifestations of being in the unity of substance.

In the intellectual world, religion, the relation of the Absolute Being to the relative being, of the infinite to the finite.

In the physical world, inspiration, communicated by the vibrations of astral substance, and the trial of man by liberty of action within the impassable circle of universal law.

> Remember, then, son of earth, that before saying of a man that he is fortunate or unfortunate, thou must know the use to which he has put his will; for every man creates his life in the image of his works. The genius of good is at thy right and the genius of evil at thy left. Their voice can be heard only by the conscience. If the hierophant should appear in the

prophetic signs of thy horoscope, retire into the sanctuary of thy heart, listen to the voice of the silence, and guided by it thou wilt reach the goal of thy aspirations.

In Divination, **Arcanum V** may briefly be read either as **Religion** or **Law**.

Arcanum V is pictured by a hierophant, master of the sacred mysteries. This prince of the occult doctrine is seated between two columns of the sanctuary; he leans upon a cross of three bars, and with his right hand makes the sign of the pentagram. From his brow the sacred serpent thrusts its head; and at his feet kneel two men, one dressed in red and the other dressed in black.

The hierophant, supreme organ of sacred science, represents the genius of good inspiration, of mind, and of conscience.

The column at the right symbolizes divine law, that on the left symbolizes the liberty to obey or to disobey.

The triple tau, or cross of three bars, is emblem of divine fire penetrating the three worlds, spiritual, astral, physical, in order that all manifestations of universal life may have their birth.

The left hand of the hierophant on the triple tau indicates his receptivity to the divine force; and the gesture of his right hand— making the pentagram—indicates his use of this divine energy to command the obedience of all sub-mundane atoms of life, and to hear the voice of heaven in the silence of the passions and the instincts of the flesh.

The sacred serpent at his brow signifies enlightenment; and the two kneeling men, the one red and the other black, denote the intelligences of light and shadow, both of whom obey the force of the pentagram.

Number

Numerically, 5 unites the first four digits into a harmonious unity, and thus explains all the apparent contradictions of nature. That is, the One Principle, the One Law, the One Agent and the One Truth are not independent factors, but imply and mutually sustain one another.

These four ideas, as represented by the four animals standing at the four gates of heaven, each quadrant of the sky having one, are brought together in the fourfold form of the sphinx. And the zodiac, so expressed, finds its counterpart in the constitution of one man.

Thus man or woman alone is symbolized by the number five. The hands, feet and head form five positive points from which the electromagnetic fluid is projected, health depending largely upon the equal distribution of the energies to these five points. Also, man, having passed through the four elemental realms of being, becomes their rightful sovereign by reason of his higher accomplishment.

In this sense, as 4 and 1, 5 signifies Realization which comes from the use of Intelligence and Will. For having attained true manhood, by virtue of wider experience, man directs the various entities, physical and astral, which have their orbits within his domain, and these become his willing and obedient servitors in proportion as they recognize his spiritual supremacy.

Astrology

Jupiter is the ruler both of law and religion. He has dominion over good inspiration, over the church and state, and over the authority of established institutions. He governs popes, hierophants and religious potentates of all kinds. The correspondence, therefore, between Arcanum 5 and the planet Jupiter is so obvious as to need no further comment.

Human Function

The carrying power of the will upon the physical plane depends upon the strength of the electromagnetic forces. These, in turn, depend upon the extent of vitalization—Arcanum II. In other words, the power of the electromagnetic body, and the carrying power of the will on the physical plane depend upon the ability to receive and transmit electromagnetic energies. These energies circulate through the body and build up the electromagnetic form even as the blood, ruled by Jupiter, carries nourishment to the physical body. Such receiving and transmitting are depicted by Arcanum V.

Alchemy

The various metals used in alchemy as they are collected are commonly found to contain other ingredients which would prevent them from properly combining in transmutation. Therefore, no matter upon what plane the hermetic art is carried out, there must be a thorough purification of the metals used. In this process of purification the dross is removed and cast aside and the true metal retained.

In spiritual alchemy, for instance, the dross is the apparent effect, while the real metal is the effect upon the soul. The spiritual metals, therefore, are purified by considering them not in the light of events influencing the material fortune, but as events which each can be made to yield spiritual values by taking the proper attitude toward them. In mental alchemy, the metals are purified, not by considering their effect upon the soul, but by casting aside the dross of discord and retaining the elements of harmony. Likewise, in other branches of the art, purification of the metals, which corresponds to Arcanum V, is always an essential step.

Bible

The most significant thing about the hierophant in Arcanum V is the sign of the pentagram, or five-pointed star, which he makes with his right hand. This is the symbol of man, the symbol of the intellectual power which dominates the four elemental kingdoms, and the symbol of the magical force of the human will. It gains its force by the gesture which bears token that the user is obedient to the laws of Deity, and thus participates in the divine power over all things.

Arcanum V, an ensemble expressing the idea of the pentagram in great detail, explains also the blazing star that led the wise men of the East to the place where the new sun-god was born that they might worship him. Their gifts of gold, frankincense and myrrh stand representative of the three worlds; spiritual, astral and physical; symbolized in Arcanum V by the triple tau.

These wise men, having been led by the star of religious devotion, into a knowledge of the three worlds and the laws governing them, departed into their own country by another way. That is, having gained illumination, their route to self-conscious-immortality—the return to the realm of spirit—was direct and certain, and not the devious path of the yet unenlightened neophyte.

This five-pointed star which they followed, has the same import as Arcanum V, signifying the Divine Law and Religion. Therefore, when it is inverted, the point of the star representing the head of man down, and the two points denoting his feet up, it signifies the opposite of the Divine Law, the opposite also of man governed by intelligence. Instead, it then denotes chaos, the devil, evil inspiration and the principle of destruction. Thus the Lamb of God is transformed into the Goat of Mendes; and to express this, in black magic the symbol is made by closing the hand so that two fingers are up—the horns of the goat, or feet of man—instead of three.

By such inversion Jupiter, or Jove, becomes Saturn, or Satan, and as such is represented by Arcanum XV. This is expressed in Rev. 8:10; "And the third angel sounded, and there fell a great star from heaven, burning as it were a lamp, and it fell upon a third part of the rivers, and upon the fountain of waters, and the name of the star is called wormwood."

The waters and fountains refer to the emotions and to love, which in magical practices of any kind are the chief sources of energy. They are turned bitter, like wormwood, when thus utilized for purposes of black magic and evil, for they are then converted into forces of destruction. In Arcanum XV, not only the lamp may be seen, but also the servants of evil in the art of making the inversive sign.

The tarot itself expounds a complete religious doctrine based upon a spiritual science. And not only do the Major Arcana set forth a system which is synthesized as a mantram, for strengthening the will, as explained in chapter 3, but they also synthesize the Religion of the Stars.

Eliphas Levi, the great French magus, expressed his conception of this religion in verse, setting at the head of each line the number of the Major Arcanum whose significance is revealed by it, each Arcanum thus representing one tenet of this ancient Wisdom Religion:

1. All things announce a conscious active cause,
2. Vivific Oneness, based on number's laws;
3. Who all containing is by naught confined,
4. And all preceding, hath no bound assigned.
5. This only Lord should man adore alone,
6. Who doth true doctrine to pure hearts make known;
7. But acts of faith require a single chief,
8. Hence we proclaim one altar, law, belief.
9. The changeless God will never change their base,
10. He rules our days and rules through every phase,
11. His mercy's wealth, which vice to naught will bring,
12. His people promises a future King.
13. The tomb's a path which to new worlds ascends, and life through all subsists, death only ends. Pure, sacred, steadfast truth we here repeat. The venerated numbers thus complete.
14. The angel blest doth calm and moderate.

15. The evil is the friend of pride and hate.
16. God doth the lightning and the fire subdue;
17. He rules the dewy eve' and the evening's dew.
18. The watchful moon he sets to guard our heights,
19. His sun's the source of life's renewed delights,
20. His breath revivifies the dust of graves
22. Where crowds descend who are of lust the slaves;
 0. Or, the mercy seat he covers with his crown,
21. And on the cherubs pours his glory down.

These impressive words are full of mystic significance, and when repeated in earnestness and with the soul lifted to the Author of All Being, they form a powerful inspirational mantram. The mantram of the will, given in chapter 3, is especially potent to increase the force, the power, and the accomplishment of the will. But this religious mantram serves another purpose; for it adds Faith, unites the human soul to its Maker, and thus lifts the will and its works to a higher plane where their force is expended in cooperation with the Divine Plan, and solely through constructive channels.

These two mantrams, therefore, stand as the masculine and the feminine of a complete system, the best results following the use of both. Although other methods may be used to advantage, one of the best systems of training commences the day, on rising, and while standing erect, with the mantram of the will; and closes the day, while reclining in bed, after retiring, with the mantram devoted to faith. Thus used together they form natural complements, and are important aids to soul growth.

Masonry

The Past Master's degree of Masonry is founded upon Arcanum V. It represents the Past Master who having passed the degree of this initiation is capable of presiding over a Master Mason's lodge. The lodge, of course, represents the human temple, over which the master must exercise constant dominion. Therefore, to indicate the rebellion of submundane atoms of life within the human domain, in this degree a riot is started.

Unless the one who would be master can use the force represented by the pentagram successfully to quell the elemental forces, as is done in Arcanum V, he is overpowered and made the slave of the very forces he sought to control, as indicated in the fifth degree of Masonry and illustrated by Arcanum XV.

Arcanum V also explains the Blazing Star of the Masonic Lodge. The compass joined to the square typifies both higher and lower union. Union is depicted by Arcanum III, and the Book of the Law, or polarity, is depicted in Arcanum II. Adding the 3 and the 2 we get Arcanum V, picturing obedience to that law, having thus the same symbolical import as the open Bible on which is laid the compass and square, as it is used in the fifth degree of Masonry.

Diamonds, the same suit in common playing cards as Coins in the tarot, are nothing more nor less than the united compass and square conventionalized, the G being removed from the center to show that the higher has superseded the lower.

Magic

In Magic, Arcanum V expresses the importance of using the proper symbols in all invocations and in ceremonial magic. It reveals the potency of rituals and such symbols as are used by secret societies and by the church.

The pentagram is the symbol of white magic, and thus constitutes the most powerful of all magical tokens; for it expresses the power of a mind which has devoted itself to assisting the progressive evolution of creation, and which knows, and is obedient to, the Divine Law. It is a symbol of constructive purpose.

The use of signs, rituals and symbols either in religion or in magic is a means of contacting invisible entities and other planes of being. The innocent use of an evil symbol in the course of a rite does not prevent the intelligence to which the symbol actually belongs being contacted. No more so than if one innocently calls the telephone number of a gangster, thinking it is the telephone number of a parson, one will fail to contact the gangster. Symbols and rituals tune the individual in on the intelligence corresponding to them just as a telephone number calls the individual to whom it belongs, regardless of his moral worth, or the intention of the one calling the number.

Initiation

Arcanum V represents the point in the ascending arc of the cycle of life where the voice of the conscience calls upon man to turn from the flesh-pots and devote himself to cosmic welfare. He decides henceforth to live, not for self alone, but to guide his every action in the direction of aiding cosmic progression. He determines that the good of cosmic society shall be his constant aim.

Occult Science

Masonry is that one of the seven branches of magic which treats in particular of the use of the emotions engendered by sex; and of the evolution of the human soul and its manifestations on the three planes of being, as set forth by means of signs, symbols and rituals.

In regard to such signs Eliphas Levi truly says:

> Four signs always express the absolute and are explained by the fifth. Thus the solution of all magical questions is that of the pentagram, and all contradictions are explained by harmonious unity.

As a single illustration of this method of solving occult problems, and because astrology and the tarot are the two keys to all mysteries, I will apply this formula to denoting the true correspondence between each tarot card and its astrological counterpart.

To begin with, the four suit cards of any numbered Minor Arcanum arrange themselves about the Major Arcanum bearing the same number in the form of a diamond; scepters being above, cups at the right, swords at the bottom and coins at the left. Thus arranged the four Minor Arcana express Jod-He-Vau-He, and the Major Arcanum in the center explains the pentagram as a whole as an expression of some planet or zodiacal sign.

The rulership of each Major Arcanum can be found in a similar manner by forming a Grand Pentagram of the whole 22 cards, as illustrated on page 88.

This diagram shows the grand pentagram as composed of five lesser pentagrams, each perfect in itself. And, of course, to be correct, the outer circle of tarots must represent the twelve signs of the zodiac in their natural position and sequence. The planets, in nature, may occur in any of the signs thus located; but their proper place here should bear some significance in relation to life.

Thus the first quadrant, the quadrant of life, is rightly explained by the selfish planet Saturn, showing that self-preservation, among lower forms of life, is nature's first law. But in the same quadrant, and more interior to it, is to be seen Neptune, the planet of universal brotherhood. And thus is also explained that when life has evolved to a spiritual conception, the law of self-preservation gives place to that of unselfish idealism.

The top quadrant, the quadrant of honor, is occupied by Uranus, indicating the struggle to make attainment through the overthrow of existing conditions and the downfall of opponents. But more interior to this is another principle which eventually supersedes. The planet Venus sets forth the idea that "Love lieth at the foundation," of any worthwhile attainment.

The third quadrant, that of companionship, is occupied by Jupiter, indicating that leniency and generosity are attractive to others. But more interior is to be seen Mercury, the planet of intelligence, indicating that a lavish purse does not compensate for lack of understanding, and that intelligence is necessary to make union spiritually advantageous.

The lower quadrant, the home and the end of life, is occupied by the Moon, indicating that physical life ends in the tomb. Yet there is an inner force, a lightning of the soul, typified by the planet Mars, which defies death, rends asunder the tomb, or pyramid, and liberates the soul to a new life in the beyond.

And as explaining all, the pentagram in the center holds the Sun, the source of all vitality, representing the ego which has sent its souls through the cycle of necessity. And the result of this pilgrimage, after the tomb has opened and liberated the souls, is explained by one of two symbols, that of the Earth, or that of Pluto. The soul, even after death, may be earth-bound, or held to the lower regions by its viciousness; or it may move rapidly above the astral into the spiritual realm to be reunited to its missing mate. This latter is the higher aspect—represented by the T with the point upward—of the planet Pluto.

The Fives

Jupiter, in astrology, is the general significator of good fortune; therefore the fives in their more common divinatory significance must relate to good luck in the particular department of life signified by the suit. But in their application to higher planes, they reveal the influence of, and can be interpreted by, the fifth decanate of each zodiacal triplicity, starting with the movable signs.

The divinatory significance of the Five of Scepters is good fortune in business; its inner interpretation is REFORMATION.

The divinatory significance of the Five of Cups is good fortune in love; its inner interpretation is RESPONSIBILITY.

The divinatory significance of the Five of Coins is abundant wealth; its inner interpretation is INSPIRATION.

The divinatory significance of the Five of Swords is escape from a danger; its inner interpretation is STRUGGLE.

The Two Paths—Arcanum VI

Letter: Egyptian, Ur; Hebrew, Vau; English V—U—W. Number 6. Astrologically, the planet Venus. Color, yellow. Tone, E. Occult science, kabalism. Human function, the astral body. Natural remedy, rest and recreation. Mineral, the metal copper.

U—6, expresses in the spiritual world, the knowledge of good and evil.

In the intellectual world, the balance between liberty and necessity.

In the physical world, the antagonism of natural forces, the linking of cause and effect.

Remember, then, son of earth, that for the common man, the allurement of vice has a greater fascination than the austere beauty of virtue. If The Two Paths should appear in the prophetic signs of thy horoscope, take care of thy resolutions. Obstacles bar before thee the path thou wouldst pursue, contrary chances hover over thee, and thy will wavers between two resolutions. Indecision is, above all else, worse than a bad choice. Advance or recede, but do not hesitate; and know that a chain of flowers is more difficult to break than a chain of iron.

In Divination, **Arcanum VI** may be briefly interpreted as **Temptation.**

Arcanum VI is figured by a man standing motionless at the angle formed by the conjunction of two roads. His looks are fixed upon the ground; his arms are crossed upon his chest. Two women, one at his right and the other at his left, each place a hand on his shoulder, showing him one of two roads. The woman at his right is modestly clothed, and has the sacred serpent, indicating enlightenment, at her brow. She thus personifies virtue. The one at the left wears less clothing, and is crowned with the leaves and vine of the grape. She represents vice, the temptress.

Above and back of this group the genie of justice, hovering in a flashing aureole of twelve rays, draws his bow and directs toward vice the arrow of punishment. The genie is crowned with a flame to show he is a spirit; and is represented in an aureole of twelve rays to indicate that justice will be meted out in due time to all as the sun passes through the zodiacal signs.

This ensemble typifies the struggle between conscience and the passions, between the divine soul and the animal soul, and that the result of this struggle commences a new epoch in the life.

Number

Six signifies two actions, or twice three. It does not represent forces in equilibrium, but a constant oscillation between action and reaction. It thus indicates a wavering, a vacillation, forces so uncontrolled and ill-directed that they tend to destroy one another.

Astrology

Venus governs the affections and the social relations. It gives love of ease, comfort, luxury and pleasure. It is not essentially evil, but in seeking the line of least resistance it may be led into vice. When it thus fails to resist the importunities of the wicked, it comes under the negativeness of Arcanum II, and is then under the dominion of Arcanum XV, or Saturn, which is the second decave of VI.

Human Function

Because the astral body is so responsive to every thought and emotion it is often called the desire body. The affections not only shape it, but give it nourishment; for it is organized by states of consciousness. Because it is so receptive and yielding, and the emotions play so important a part in its makeup, this astral body corresponds to Venus, and to Arcanum VI.

Alchemy

After the metals have been purified, before they are finally joined in transmutation they are first tested to be sure that no dross or impurities remain. This process of testing the purity of the metals, of applying the test of love, corresponds to Arcanum VI.

Bible

Of the sons of Isaac, Esau, who sold his birthright (spiritual heritage) for a mess of pottage (material things), listened to the voice of vice.

Jacob, however, who once successfully wrestled with the spirit of temptation, and though afflicted was not conquered, in this story listened to the voice of virtue.

Math. 4:8, "Again the devil taketh him up into an exceedingly high mountain, and sheweth him all the kingdoms of the world and the glory of them; And said unto him, All these things will I give thee if thou wilt fall down and worship me."

Masonry

The Most Excellent Master degree of Masonry is founded upon Arcanum VI. "When the Temple of Jerusalem was finished, those who had proved themselves worthy by their virtue, skill and fidelity, were installed as Most Excellent Masters."

Magic

Arcanum VI represents the temptations that always come to those who attain power. Especially is this temptation great among those who attain to the use of invisible energies. Should they yield to such insidious promptings, their lot is terrible; for they become the slaves of the very forces they imagined they had controlled. This Arcanum also represents the use of privation, hardships and obstacles to strengthen and test the will.

Initiation

The evolving soul, passing through the lower kingdoms, where strife and self-preservation are dominant factors, develops the animal propensities and instincts to a high degree. This is a necessary phase of its progression. But when self-consciousness has been reached, in order that the animal may partake of the Divine quality which makes self-conscious-immortality possible, these animal energies and instincts must be diverted into a higher than animal channel. They must be directed, or transmuted, into an organization of energy having for object the welfare of society as a whole. This higher-type organization, largely drawing its energies from the animal soul, or lower-type organization, yet containing many higher vibration rates, is called the divine soul.

Occult Science

Kabalism, corresponding to Arcanum VI, and therefore the feminine, embraces the written scriptures and the oral traditions of every land. It is really the science of traditional knowledge, the tarot being a condensation of the whole science.

The Sixes

Venus, in astrology, is natural significator of love, art, music and drama, as well as of social functions; therefore the sixes, corresponding numerically to Venus, in their more common divinatory significance must relate to these things as applied to the department of life indicated by the suit. But in their higher application they reveal the influence of, and can be interpreted by, the sixth decanate of each zodiacal triplicity, starting with the movable signs.

The divinatory significance of the Six of Scepters is music, art or the drama; its inner interpretation is AMBITION.

The divinatory significance of the Six of Cups is a love affair; its inner interpretation is ATTAINMENT.

The divinatory significance of the Six of Coins is a social event; its inner interpretation is REPRESSION.

The divinatory significance of the Six of Swords is dissipation; its inner interpretation is MASTERSHIP.

Method of Three Sevens

After shuffling and cutting, the cards are dealt from the top, one by one, from right to left, starting with the bottom row, in three rows of seven cards each.

The bottom row represents the past, the middle row the present, and the top row the future. In each row the central card, marked with an asterisk, is the most important, being the key to which the others merely contribute. In reading, the adjoining cards modify each other, and all should be blended as parts of a complete whole.

Future	21	20	19	18*	17	16	15
Present	14	13	12	11*	10	9	8
Past	7	6	5	4*	3	2	1

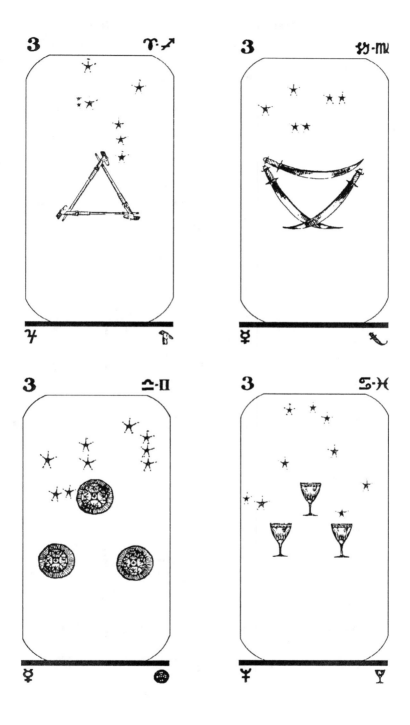

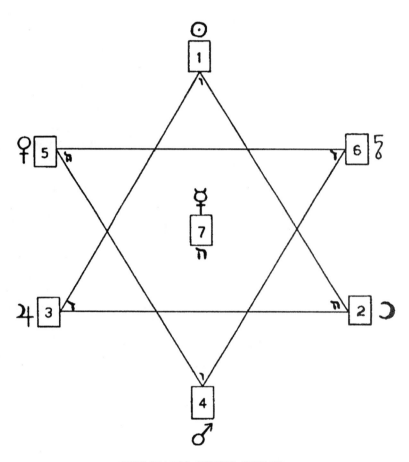

THE MAGIC SEVEN SPREAD

Chapter 6

Making an Astrological Chart of a Name

T HERE is just one way, in so far as I know, of determining in a positive, reliable and scientific manner how any invisible vibratory tone, or combination of such tones, will affect a certain person. That is by comparing the tone, or tones, with the astrological birth-chart of the person.

The planets and signs in a birth-chart each map thought-cells of specific tones, as revealed by their correspondences, which are set forth in these lessons. Any thought-vibration, character-vibration, or astrological-vibration reaching the individual adds its energy to the thought-cells having the same vibratory rate in the astral body of the person. The chief influence of a name, or number, as affecting a person is to give added energy to the thought-cells of that section of the astral body of the person which vibrates to the same rate as the Key-tone of the name or number.

That is, to determine how a name or number or other invisible influence will affect a person, first get the Key of the name or number, or other influence. This key is expressed by some number below 23. Thus the Mars dynamic structure vibrates to the tone 16, and the Virgo zone vibrates to tone 2.

Now if the Mars structure in a person's astral body is very discordant, as shown by inharmonious aspects to Mars in the birth-chart, any energy added to its thought-cells by objects, by thoughts, or other influences vibrating to tone 16 merely increases the power of these thoughts to attract such Catastrophe as is pictured by Arcanum 16. But if the Mars structure in a person's astral body is harmoniously organized, as shown by Mars having strong beneficial aspects in the birth-chart, this added energy will increase the power of its thought-cells to attract events which are constructive and beneficial.

The pictured arcanum corresponding to each of the signs and planets thus represents the more common influence of the tone apart from lines of force which, like aspects, conduce to harmony or discord. But in the astral body of man these dynamic structures and zones, which vibrate to the tones so depicted, are usually strongly modified and influenced by the manner in which they have been associated with other thought structures. Therefore, while tone 15 may in general be considered as Fatality; in a person's chart who has the planet Saturn exceedingly well aspected it might be the most fortunate influence in the life, and the one which, when given added energy, would bring the most benefit.

Therefore, in determining how a name, number, environment, or other invisible influence will affect an individual, the tone of the influence should first be determined, and then a study should be made of this tone as mapped in the astrological chart of birth. If the tone in the chart of birth is essentially beneficial, the same tone received from a name, number, other person, locality, birth-stone or anything else will be beneficial; because it will increase the power of beneficial thought-cells in the astral body. But if the tone as mapped in the birth-chart is detrimental, the same tone received from without, from any of the sources mentioned, will tend, through giving discordant thought-cells more energy, to attract misfortune.

Fortune or misfortune does not come equally through all departments of life. And a particular vibratory tone often stimulates one or two departments of life, and has little or no influence upon other departments. It thus may have an influence over finances and yet have no influence whatever over health or companionship.

The department of life influenced by a vibratory key is denoted by the compartment in the astral body ruled by the sign or planet in the birth-chart whose thought-structure is stimulated into activity by the key. Thus, disregarding whether the influence will attract or disperse it, if the key-tone is the same as a planet in the house of money (2nd house), or the same as the sign on the cusp of the house of money (2nd), its chief effect, for good or ill, will be upon money. But if the key-tone is the same as a planet in the house of partnership (7th), or the same as the sign on the cusp of the house of partnership (7th), the chief influence will be upon the relation with partners.

Now if on a pond of water there are several little sticks floating, and someone throws a rock into the pool, this disturbance of the water also disturbs the little sticks and they go bobbing about.

Likewise, if there is one or several planets in a zodiacal sign in the birth-chart, because these planets represent organized groups of thought-cells in that zone of the astral body indicated by the sign, if the sign is given increased activity, the groups of thought-cells in it are set in motion.

The precise power of a dynamic thought structure mapped by a planet or the common thought-cells mapped by an unoccupied sign to attract good fortune when thus given increased activity is directly proportional to its harmodynes, and the precise power of a dynamic thought structure mapped by a planet or of the common thought-cells mapped by an unoccupied sign to attract misfortune when thus given increased activity is directly proportional to its discordynes. How to calculate the astrodynes, harmodynes and discordynes of each birth-chart planet, sign and house is explained in Chapters 1 and 2 of Course 16, *Stellar Healing*.

An unoccupied sign occupying one house cusp has one-half the harmodynes or discordynes of its ruling planet. An unoccupied intercepted sign has one-fourth the harmodynes or discordynes of its ruling planet. An unoccupied sign occupying the cusp of two houses has the same number of harmodynes or discordynes as its ruling planet. Thus on an average the influence of a planet is twice as important as that of an unoccupied sign.

Thus it is that when we have before us that complete map of the astral body of any individual, which is a birth-chart, we can determine in a positive, scientific and detailed manner how any invisible vibratory rate of which we know the key will affect him. We can determine if the particular key will tend to attract to him fortune or misfortune. We can determine in what department of life that fortune or misfortune will be attracted. And we can determine, by calculating the astrodynes of the planet or sign mapping the thought-cells within his astral body responding to this key and the probable volume of energy added to them by the invisible influence, somewhat of the magnitude of the events that will thus be attracted into his life.

Now any name or any number can be converted into an astrological chart by the simple expedient of substituting the corresponding Major Arcanum for each of the letters or numbers. Each Major Arcanum also, of course, signifies a definite astrological influence.

These various letters of a name, or the astrological influences substituted for them, each represent one tone. Each letter of the name, therefore, as a tone, has some influence in stimulating into activity the corresponding tone in the astral body of the person wearing the name. Sometimes in a person's name certain letters are repeated several times. Sometimes there will be several A's, for instance, or the letter l may occur twice in each member of the name. In such cases, naturally, the influence of the particular tone so repeated is intensified, and may be taken into consideration in its relation to affecting the individual. But in all cases the Key of the name as a whole is by far the most important vibratory rate, and even letters that occur repeatedly in the name are of subsidiary influence.

To chart a name, therefore, we find the Key of the number of the name, and set it at the head of the chart as the dominant influence. In relation to the name itself, it represents the birth-chart. Then if we desire to do so we find the Key of the Decave and place it at the foot of the chart. It indicates the end of things, that which the fourth house in an astrological chart represents. Then the letters of the name may be placed between the Key of the name and the Key of the Decave as transitory influences.

Reading A Name Alone Does Not Give a Reading for the Individual Wearing It

By using such a chart we can give a reading of any name. But because people wearing the same name are different individuals, we must not assume that a reading of the name alone gives a reading applicable to the individual wearing it. On the contrary, to give a reading of the individual wearing a name, even by the process of divination by numbers, we must add an individual element. This individual element which is most suitable for such use is the Birth Path. And the method of using it and giving such a divinatory reading by means of numbers is set forth in chapter 8.

Apart from any individual, however, and not indicative of any person's fortune, we can make an astrological chart of any name or any number which will be scientifically correct; and to one delving in spiritual research such a chart often will yield information of value.

Let us take the name Jesus, for instance. J-10, E-5, S-21, U-6, S-21. 10 plus 5 plus 21 plus 6 plus 21 equals 63. 6 plus 3 gives 9 as the Key of the name. 63 minus 9 gives 54. 54 divided by 9 gives 6. 6 plus 1 gives 7 as the Key of the Decave. Then the astrological chart may be stated thus:

Aquarius (9), Uranus (10), Jupiter (5), Sun (21), Venus (6), Sun (21), Sagittarius (7).

As the birth date of Jesus is unknown we will attempt no reading of his life. But the motive actuating those who follow his doctrines is very apparent. The Key of the influence is Aquarius, or Major Arcanum IX, signifying Prudence and Circumspection. The prudence of the followers of Jesus causes them to accept Him in the expectation of finding heaven and escaping hell. And the end for which they hope, both here and hereafter, is Sagittarius, or Major Arcanum VII, signifying Victory. "Onward, Christian Soldiers," as sung in thousands of Sunday schools, might well be inspired by the pictured Arcanum VII with its conqueror riding forward to overcome opposition.

Aside from astrology let us consider the vibratory significance of some other holy names: The Jews called their stern and unyielding God, Jehovah, spelled in Hebrew, Jod-He-Vau-He (I-E-V-E): 10 plus 5 plus 6 plus 5 equals 26. 26 being more than 22 must be involved. 2 plus 6 gives 8 as the Key of the name. 26 minus 8 gives 18. 18 divided by 9, plus 1, gives 3 as the Decave. Thus the Key and the Decave, 8 and 3, indicate the moral code of Jehovah to have been inflexible Justice in Action.

To proceed with other deific names, the chief deity of Christianity is spelled G-O-D: 3 plus 16 plus 4 equals 23. 2 plus 3 gives 5 as the Key of the name. 23 minus 5 gives 18. 18 divided by 9, plus 1, gives 3 as the Decave. The Key and the Decave, 5 and 3, thus indicate that the idea behind the Christian God is beneficent (Jupiter) Law in Action.

Now turn to the deity of Egyptian initiates, Ra. R-A: 20 plus 1 gives 21, which needs no involving because it is already a Key, pictured by Arcanum XXI. Ra is thus, according to its Key and its astrological ruler, the spiritual Sun of our universe; the highest spiritual and intellectual entity; and those who worship Him strive to become the most spiritual and intelligent men on earth; they strive to be adepts. Astrologically, Ra is the Sun. The religion of His devotees is expressed still more in detail by the two arcana picturing the two letters of the word, 20 and 1, signifying Will and Intelligence (1), Resurrecting (20), the soul beyond the tomb.

What is the vibratory import of the Hindu deific word used so frequently as a mantram, and rendered into English as A-U-M? 1 plus 6 plus 13 equals 20. The Key (20) reveals that the object sought is to Awaken (20), the soul to its latent possibilities. The method employed to do this is indicated by the three letters: The Will (1), brought to bear upon Temptation (6), to induce a Transformation (13).

And this rendering of a foreign name brings up a point of some importance; that of the different ways of spelling a name.

Again I would call your attention to the principle that it is not the sound of a name, nor its phonetics, with which we are dealing, but its astral vibratory-rates. These astral vibratory-rates are set in motion by the person thinking the name, and they are set up irrespective of vocal action. Nor do people of different countries, who spell a name differently, have the same conception of its significance.

Because with most people, according to psychological experiments, sight registers its impressions more quickly and more strongly than sound, the spelling of a name commonly determines its thought-vibration when it is thought about. The English spelling, therefore, only indicates the vibratory significance of the name to those who use the English spelling. Any alteration of the spelling of a name, even though the phonetic value is unchanged, thus changes the vibratory-rate and the inner meaning of the name. The native spelling of a name gives its significance to such natives.

Buddha: 2 plus 6 plus 4 plus 4 plus 8 plus 1 gives 25. 2 plus 5 gives 7 as the Key. 25 minus 7 gives 18. 18 divided by 9, plus 1, gives 3 as the Decave. Thus our conception of the life and teachings of this great reformer is Victory (7), of mind in Action (3).

Brahma: 2 plus 20 plus 1 plus 8 plus 13 plus 1 gives 45. 4 plus 5 gives 9 as the Key. 45 minus 9 gives 36. 36 divided by 9, plus 1, gives 5 as the Decave. This deity, therefore, to us signifies Wisdom (9) acting through Law, (5).

Vishnu: 6 plus 10 plus 18 plus 14 plus 6 equals 54. 5 plus 4 gives 9 as the Key. 54 minus 9 gives 45. 45 divided by 9, plus 1 gives 6 as the Decave. This god of preservation therefore exemplifies the thought that Wisdom (9) overcomes Temptation (6).

Siva: 21 plus 10 plus 6 plus 1 equals 38. 3 plus 8 gives 11 as the Key. 38 minus 11 gives 27. 27 divided by 9, plus 1 gives 4 as the Decave. The Hindu trinity, Brahma, Vishnu and Siva are usually translated as Creator, Preserver and Destroyer. But while Siva does represent destruction, it is a destruction which implies a restoration, or reproduction, and thus the linga is used as his emblem. And this significance is conveyed by Force (11), undergoing Realization (4).

Devil: 4 plus 5 plus 6 plus 10 plus 12 equals 37. 3 plus 7 gives 10 as the Key. 37 minus 10 gives 27. 27 divided by 9, plus 1 gives 4 as the Decave. The Devil thus is the agent for a Change of Fortune (10), Realized (4).

Hell: 8 plus 5 plus 12 plus 12 equals 37. 3 plus 7 gives 10 as the Key. 37 minus 10 gives 27. 27 divided by 9, plus 1 gives 4 as the Decave. Hell, therefore, is a Change of Fortune (10), Realized (4).

The early Magi erected a tower to Bel: 2 plus 5 plus 12 gives 19 as the Key. As it is already below 23 no Decave influence need be considered. We chart this name in detail thus—19 (Key)—2-5-12, and read it as Happiness and Prosperity (19) devoted to Science (2), Religion (5), and Sacrifice (12).

Later generations forsook the worship of Bel for Baal: 2 plus 1 plus 1 plus 12 gives 16 as the Key. In detail it indicates that the desire for violence (16) prompted the energies to be turned to Science (2), Will (1), Intelligence (1), and Sacrifice (12).

Babylon: 2 plus 1 plus 2 plus 10 plus 12 plus 16 plus 14 equals 57. 5 plus 7 gives 12 as the Key. 57 minus 12 gives 45. 45 divided by 9, plus 1 gives 6 as the Decave. Babylon is mentioned in Revelations as the great prostitute; which is borne out by its vibratory significance which reads Sacrifice (12), to Temptation (6).

The above examples, I believe, are quite ample to denote how names may be handled as factors in themselves, apart from their influence upon any particular individual. But I must repeat, because it is so frequently overlooked by those who practice numerology, that when the influence upon an individual is to be revealed, or a reading is to be given an individual based on his name, that there is always an additional individual factor which must be included.

The Conqueror—Arcanum VII

Letter: Egyptian, Zain; Hebrew, Zayin; English, Z. Number, 7. Astrologically, the zodiacal sign Sagittarius. Color, the lighter shades of purple. Tone, high A. Occult science, spiritual astrology. Human function, the sense of smell. Natural remedy, such herbs as mallow, wood betony, featherfew, and agrimony. Mineral, the talismanic gem red garnet (often called carbuncle), and such stones as are mixed with red and green, including turquoise.

Z—7 expresses in the spiritual world, the septenary dominion of spirit over matter.

In the intellectual world, the sacerdocy and the empire.

In the physical world, submission of the elements and forces of matter to the intelligences and forces of man.

Remember, then, son of earth, that the empire of the world belongs to them who possess the sovereignty of spirit, that is to say, the light which makes clear the mysteries of life. If the Conqueror should appear in the prophetic signs of thy horoscope, it signifies that in breaking through obstacles thou wilt crush thy enemies; and all thy wishes will be realized if thou attack the future with audacity, armed in the consciousness of thy right.

In Divination, **Arcanum VII** may briefly be read as **Victory**.

Arcanum VII is figured by a war chariot of square form, surmounted by a starry canopy sustained by four columns. Upon this chariot advances a conqueror armed with a cuirass and carrying both sword and scepter. He wears a crown from which rises three pentagrams, or golden stars with five points.

The square car symbolizes the material world vanquished by the work of the will. The four columns supporting the canopy represent the four quadrants of heaven which surround the conqueror. They also represent the four elemental kingdoms that have submitted to the master of the scepter and the sword.

Upon the square front of the chariot is pictured a sphere sustained by two outspread wings; symbol of the immortal flight of the soul through the infinitude of space and time. The sacred serpent at the conqueror's brow signifies the possession of that intellectual light which makes clear all the arcana of fortune. The three golden stars rising from the crown symbolize the dominion of man in all three worlds; physical, astral and spiritual.

A T-square and two try-squares are traced upon the cuirass. The T-square, or Tau, symbolizes virile force, and the two try-squares indicate the rectitude of judgment that enables the conqueror to direct this force either to right or left, into mental or physical power as occasion demands.

The cuirass signifies resistance; the high held sword is the emblem of physical victory; and the scepter indicates mental conquest. This scepter is surmounted by a square, a circle, and a triangle. The square is the emblem of matter, the circle indicates the realm of spirit, and the triangle is the emblem of mind; together denoting the perpetual dominion of intelligence over all realms and forces of nature.

Two sphinxes, one white and the other black, are harnessed to the car. A sphinx, as composed of the four emblems of the zodiacal quadrants, indicates the passage of time. The white sphinx signifies fortunate periods, and the black one signifies periods of adversity;

both of which serve the soul victorious over the ordeals met in its pilgrimage of eternal progression.

Number

Numerically, 7, as composed of the numbers 3 and 4, expresses action and completion. It is the number of perfect form on the physical plane. It is thus the septenary, which is the complete and perfect three-dimensional gamut; even as 9 is the complete and perfect four-dimensional gamut. A scale of 7 is better, therefore, to indicate physical tones and electromagnetic vibrations; but a scale of 9 is more convenient to indicate astral tones and thought-vibrations. Thus in three-dimensional existence where perfection of form exists it will be found that the number 7 expresses it as 3 and 4. The 3 are active principles. The 4 are reactions, or forms.

In human life 7, as composed of 3 and 4, express the concrete 4 dominated by action, or 3; the realization of physical perfection through active effort. As composed of 5 and 2, it indicates man in full possession of the law of polarity, realizing the potency of sex force. As composed of twice 3 plus 1, it signifies body, soul and spirit united to body, soul and spirit, guided by intelligence and under control of will; thus representing the perfect nuptial union. It is dominion of intelligence over all actions, hence complete Victory over all Temptations.

Astrology

Astrologically, Sagittarius is pictured as the starry Centaur, with bow full drawn, indicating its combative qualities and its locomotion. Sagittarius is a dual sign, adapting itself to both scepter and sword. It is natural ruler of philosophy and travel; its chief mental characteristics being obedience to ruling authority, discipline, prompt decision, self-control and the power to command others. The conservative attributes are well represented by the cuirass; and the other qualities are all symbolized in detail by the various pictured emblems of Arcanum VII.

Human Function

It has been explained that the planet Jupiter corresponds to the electromagnetic body. This body is nourished by the electromagnetic energy liberated from protein molecules, as explained in Chapter 9 of Course 5, *Esoteric Psychology*. The electromagnetic energy of the nervous system enables it both to broadcast and receive short-wave radiations. As an aid to tuning in on the desired wave-length incense has been found helpful. Through stimulating the sense of smell in the proper way the mind is directed to a certain state of consciousness, which raises or lowers the individual's vibrations, tuning him in on the grade of energy it is desired to contact. Thus does the sense of smell correspond to Arcanum VII.

Alchemy

The various ores from which the metals to be used in the process of transmutation are obtained are not of equal richness, and are not of equal suitability as furnishing the required metals. And when the metals are extracted from these ores, or are otherwise obtained, they are not of equal purity, or of equal value. Thus it is that every ingredient used in the process should be assayed to determine its refinement, to determine its value, and to determine how best it may be treated to purify it to the extent required if it is to be used in the alchemical work.

In spiritual alchemy, for instance, each experience needs to be appraised as to its possibilities of providing spiritual values, and to determine exactly what attitude will recover the highest percentage of these spiritual values. In mental alchemy, a still different appraisal is made to determine the value in terms of harmony, and the treatment necessary to gain these values in highest measure. Such determinations are secured through assaying, which corresponds to Arcanum VII.

Bible

Joseph, sold into Egypt, representing the soul born into matter and fettered by carnal desires, represents Arcanum VII.

But Joseph overcame all obstacles and rose to great power, as indicated by the sword. And in addition to having at his command the material forces thus indicated, he also became an interpreter of the Divine will, as symbolized by the scepter.

He was tempted by Potiphar's wife, Arcanum VI, but he Triumphed (Arcanum VII) over the temptation, even though it meant certain affliction. The dream of Pharoah which he interpreted, of the 7 fat kine and the 7 lean kine, and the 7 good ears and the 7 bad ears, related to periods of good and evil, such as the white sphinx and the black sphinx of Arcanum VII signify. The result of his triumph through periods of good and periods of evil, and of his not yielding to temptation, is set forth in Gen. 41:41, and is symbolical of what may be expected by others who triumph over temptation; for they also shall be made rulers over the physical plane, which is the land of Egypt.

"And Pharaoh said unto Joseph: See, I have set thee over all the land of Egypt. And Pharaoh took off his ring from his hand, and put it upon Joseph's hand, and arrayed him in vestures of fine linen, and put a gold chain about his neck: and made him to ride in the second CHARIOT which he had: and they cried before him: Bow the knee: and he made him ruler over all the land of Egypt."

Masonry

The Royal Arch degree of Masonry is based upon Arcanum VII. The chariot, like the tabernacle, is an oblong square; but instead of being divided into four veils the canopy is supported by four columns.

The captivity in Babylon is denoted by the square-formed chariot; and the release from bondage by the scepter. The return journey to Jerusalem is denoted by the two sphinxes hitched to the wheeled car. The arcanum also symbolizes the vault into which the candidate is lowered; where he finds the Ark of the Covenant containing the four emblems which are the suits of the tarot cards. Of these the scepter represents the rod of Aaron; the sword is the symbol of the tablets of the law, the gomer is represented by the cuirass, and the sacred serpent indicates the manna, or intellectual food.

The three jewels, or trying squares of the three ancient Masters, are to be seen on the cuirass, and the wonderful scroll, which is the key to the ineffable characters of the degree, is present as the starry canopy overhead. The long lost Master Mason's Word, which is recovered in the Royal Arch, is fully exemplified by the four symbols mentioned, and is written in three languages as indicated by the golden stars. All of which, plainly stated, signifies harmonious union of positive and negative forces, such as the Masonic trowel suggests, on all three planes of existence.

Magic

In magic, Arcanum VII represents the power of projection, of sending the astral form to a distance; and the power of attraction, of compelling the astral of another to appear and obey whatever commands may be given. And it is also of the same symbolical import as the Seal of Solomon, the two interlaced equilateral trines.

Next to the pentagram, Solomon's Seal is the most important magical diagram; for it represents the macrocosm and its laws, thus indicating its user to be familiar with nature, and to be endowed with intelligence.

Initiation

In the soul's pilgrimage, Arcanum VII indicates physical initiation completed. It shows proficiency in both science and magic. The temptations of the material world have been surmounted and the neophyte has gained complete mastery of self. The body is under the control of a disciplined will, and whatever knowledge concerning spiritual things is obtainable in the external world has been gained.

The scepter and the sword balance each other, positive and negative, indicating that the neophyte has a partner whose physical temperament, mental polarity, and spiritual aspirations are in complete harmony with his own. And as shown by the Tau and squares on the cuirass, they both implicitly obey the divine laws governing physical union, having mastered which they become candidates for regenerate union as signified by Arcanum XIV, and later for true soul-union represented by Arcanum XXI.

Neither 7 nor 14 are decaves of 3, the number of union; but 7, composed of 3 and 4, expresses union and its issue, which is perfection of form. And the multiples of 7, though not decaves of 7, relate to some octave of the perfect form.

Occult Science

Spiritual astrology reveals the facts which the wisest men of all time have learned regarding the nature of the soul, its destiny, and how it may best make progress. Such facts have been recorded still more specifically in the pictured constellations. These pictured constellations thus form a positive key to the sacred books of the world, and give detailed instructions on how the soul may best proceed to scale the spiritual heights.

The Sevens

The sign Sagittarius is general significator of philosophy, long journeys, publishing, teaching and out-of-doors sports; therefore the

Sevens, corresponding numerically to Sagittarius, in their more common divinatory significance must relate to these things as applied to the department of life indicated by the suit. But in their higher application they reveal the influence of, and can be interpreted by, the seventh decanate of each zodiacal triplicity, starting with the movable signs.

The divinatory significance of the Seven of Scepters is success in teaching or publishing; its inner interpretation is DEVOTION.

The divinatory significance of the Seven of Cups is a successful change of home; its inner interpretation is VERITY.

The divinatory significance of the Seven of Coins is money earned through a journey; its inner interpretation is INTUITION.

The divinatory significance of the Seven of Swords is danger through travel or sport; its inner interpretation is ACHIEVEMENT.

The Balance—Arcanum VIII

Letter: Egyptian, Helitha; Hebrew, Cheth; English, H-CH; Number, 8. Astrologically, the zodiacal sign Capricorn. Color, the darker shades of blue. Tone, low G. Occult science, horary astrology. Human function, the sense of hearing. Natural remedy, such herbs as henbane, nightshade and black poppy. Mineral, the talismanic gem sardonyx, and ash-colored or black minerals such as coal.

H—8 expresses in the spiritual world, absolute justice.

In the intellectual world, attraction and repulsion.

In the physical world, relative justice, fallible and limited, which comes from man.

> *Remember, then, son of earth, that to be victorious over thyself and dominate obstacles is but a part of the human task. To accomplish it entirely thou must establish equilibrium between the forces that thou hast brought into play. All action produces reaction. The will should foresee the shock of opposite forces in order to temper or annul them. If the Balance should appear in the prophetic signs of thy horoscope, it signifies that the future is balanced between good and evil, and warns that an unbalanced mind is like an abortive sun.*

In Divination, Arcanum **VIII** may be read as **Justice** or **Equilibrium**.

Arcanum VIII is figured by a woman, blindfolded and seated upon a throne. She wears a crown of lance-heads, holds in her right hand a raised sword, in her left hand a balance, and from her brow the sacred serpent thrusts its head.

This is the ancient symbol of justice, which weighs all acts and opposes to evil as a counterweight the sword of expiation. Justice, emanating from God, as symbolized by the overshadowing protection, is the equilibrium between right and duty.

Justice is crowned with lances to indicate inflexibility, adorned with the sacred serpent to signify she acts with enlightenment, and her throne is placed on a platform of three steps to represent her action in all three worlds. At her side is a lion, symbol of the force over which she rules; and a sphinx, symbol of the passage of time which enables her to manifest. Above is a winged turtle, symbol of the repentance which may bring forgiveness. At the back is a divine messenger, signifying that the justice of God will be the final judge of the justice of men. The sword is here a sign of protection to the good and a menace to the wicked.

The eyes of Justice are covered with a bandage to show that she weighs and strikes without taking into account the conventional differences that men establish for themselves.

Number

Numerically, 8 expresses complete balance and equilibrium, hence stagnation and death. As composed of two fours it indicates two realizations of an opposite nature, and is thus the antithesis of progress. In nature it signifies the polarization of the forces that bind together, or that produce motion; hence dissolution of matter and inactivity of energy. It is the number of annihilation, unconsciousness and mortality.

Astrology

Perfect equilibrium of forces produces crystallization. A solid is the result of an equilibrium established between at least eight forces. First, two forces converge. And about this point of equilibrium two forces meet from above and below, two from right and left, and two from behind and in front; eight forces in all, well represented by a cube with its six faces and a center. Verily, matter is nothing but spirit in a state of equilibrium. The most earthy sign of the zodiac, the sign which the sun enters when life's forces are lowest and the waters and vapors of earth crystallize into ice and snow, is Capricorn. Capricorn well expresses that equilibrium which results in crystallization, and thus corresponds to Arcanum VIII.

Human Function

Capricorn is receptive, and is also a reflective zodiacal sign which pertains to earthly endeavor. These qualities which express as receiving and not giving, of utilizing all to its own advantage, are well typified by the sense of hearing. It is often quoted that where speech is silver silence is gold; and Arcanum VIII pictures this stable attitude of listening.

Alchemy

In all branches of alchemy different ingredients are brought together. And it is of utmost importance that they shall be present in just the right amounts. In order that they shall form the proper fluxes for each other, and in order that some essentials shall not be too small in quantity, the ingredients are weighed. If there is not sufficient of some substance, as indicated by such weighing, it must be sought out and added to the mixture. Both the weighing and the seeking of ingredients thus found lacking, correspond to Arcanum VIII.

Bible

The descent of the spirit into matter, and the result of the equilibrium so established is set forth in Gen. 3:19: "In the sweat of thy face shalt thou eat bread, till thou return unto the ground: for out of it wast thou taken, and unto dust shalt thou return."

Surely the wages of sin is death; but the only real death is the polarization of the spiritual forces by the animal propensities as indicated in Rev. 3:16: "So, then, because thou art lukewarm, and neither cold nor hot, I will spue thee out of my mouth." Still more explicit, as indicating the reaction upon those who once see the truth and later turn to evil ways, turning back from a higher vibratory level to selfish motives, is the account of Lot's wife, Gen. 19:26: "But his wife looked back from behind him, and she became a pillar of salt."

Masonry

The Royal Master degree is founded upon Arcanum VIII. As a Just reward for the most skillful and faithful Masons in building the

Temple, it was decided to impart to them the Omnific Word as soon as the Temple was completed. "And behold I come quickly: and my reward is with me, to give every man according as his work shall be," etc. It also represents the judgment which ultimately was passed upon the assassins of Hiram Abiff, and the state of disintegration in which the body of Hiram was found.

Magic

Nothing is more sure than that in magic any thought or desire projected to another will in time return to influence the sender. The magical forces of the soul traverse the spaces almost instantly and fasten upon the object of its ceremony, and may act with terrible force. But if such a force launched toward another has not the power to penetrate his aura it at once reacts upon the sender and affects the other not at all.

In repelling any evil influence there should be no thought either of vengeance or of mercy, but instead an attitude of unbending justice. Efforts at retaliation attract fearful dangers. To launch a destructive thought is to attract denizens who are destructive by nature, and who may linger long afterwards.

Initiation

In the soul's pilgrimage a time comes when the individual accepts some definite work to perform for the benefit of humanity. In carrying out this spiritual work, his body must have sustenance. Thus he can not entirely ignore the physical, nor can he devote his energies exclusively to financial ends. He also has certain obligations to his family which he should not ignore. Too much energy spent in gaining wealth and caring for the physical body prevents the accomplishment of the spiritual work; and upon his faithfulness to it depends his further progress. Thus he must learn to "Render, therefore, unto Caesar the things that are Caesar's, and unto God the things that are God's."

Occult Science

Horary astrology depends upon the relation between the mental factors and the positions of the heavenly bodies. A question receives additional stimulation when the factors corresponding to it in the sky reach such a situation as to represent the facts concerning it. This equilibrium between the mind of man and the astrological influences at the time he is stimulated to ask a question, permits the astrologer to give a correct answer to the question.

The Eights

The sign Capricorn is general significator of station, honor, business, and government affairs; therefore the Eights, corresponding numerically to Capricorn, in their more common divinatory significance must relate to these things as applied to the department of life indicated by the suit. But in their higher application they reveal the influence of, and can be interpreted by, the eighth decanate of each zodiacal triplicity, starting with the movable signs.

The divinatory significance of the Eight of Scepters is a political appointment; its inner interpretation is EXPLORATION.

The divinatory significance of the Eight of Cups is extravagance; its inner interpretation is SELF-SACRIFICE.

The divinatory significance of the Eight of Coins is a costly law suit; its inner interpretation is FIDELITY.

The divinatory significance of the Eight of Swords is loss of honor, or business failure; its inner interpretation is EXPERIENCE.

The Magic Seven Spread

Ten completes a cycle, but seven completes a form. Common divination is concerned with external life, hence with form, the problems of which are readily solved by the application of the Seal of Seven, or Solomon's Seal, as it is commonly called.

This Seal is an astrological chart in abstract; for the sum of the angles of the two triangles equals 360 degrees, measuring exactly, but in a more concrete form, the number of degrees in a circle. The six external points of the star, together with the point in the center, express the planetary septenary in terms of Jod-He-Vau-He, both above and below, the final He, or product, being common to both and occupying the center of the star.

To use this magical figure as a tarot spread, first, as usual, clearly formulate the information sought and keep it constantly in mind while shuffling and cutting the cards. Then deal them face downward, one by one, on the points of an imaginary six-point star, in the order shown in the diagram on page 110, the seventh card taking the center.

Turn the cards over one at a time, and read as turned.

The first card dealt, the upper Jod, signifies the past of the matter inquired about. It is the Cause of the present condition.

The second card dealt, the upper He, represents the present of the thing inquired about. It is the effect of past causes already indicated.

The third card dealt, the upper Vau, signifies the past and present united. It represents the immediate future of the matter.

The fourth card dealt, the lower Jod, represents the power of the individual to control the matter. It is also the influence of those favorable to it to control the matter through initiative and effort.

The fifth card dealt, the lower He, designates the part that fate and environment will play in the matter.

The sixth card dealt, the lower Vau, shows the combination of fate and individuals in the future taking the form of opposition to the venture.

The seventh card dealt, the final He, corresponding to the seventh seal of the Apocalypse, reveals all the factors of past and future after they have undergone gestation and given birth to the final issue. It, therefore, represents the result of the thing asked about.

At the front of this booklet both Hebrew characters and planetary symbols are added to the figure to assist those studiously inclined to discern the astral and kabalistical meaning of the seal, and the method used in divination. These additional characters need not be considered by those interested in divination only. The question asked may embrace any phase or activity of life, and thus the application of this method in divination is universal.

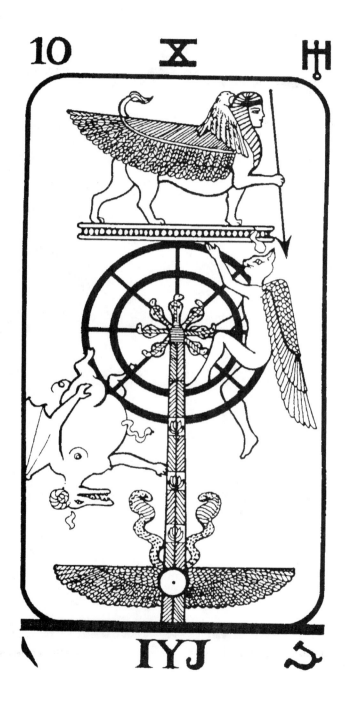

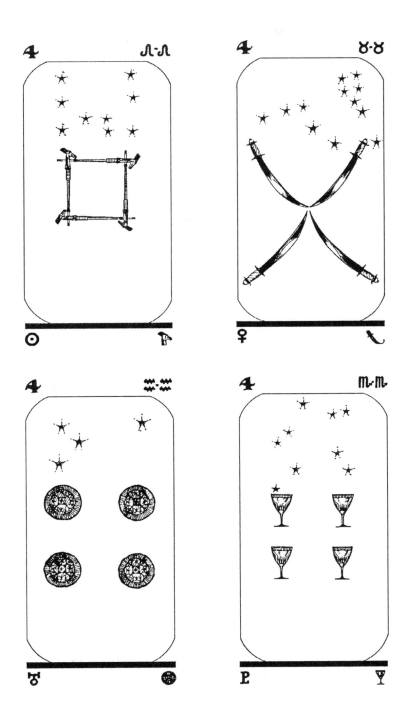

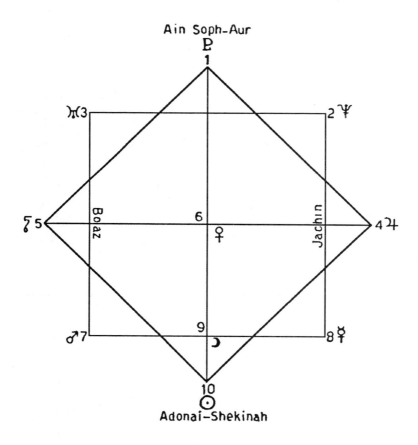

The Kabala Spread

Chapter 7 _____

Influence of Changing the Name

_____

T HE USE of the name as a divinatory instrument is the use to which it is put in the various systems of numerology. And because divination may be approached from so many angles and yet give good results it does not follow that any of the different systems of numerology in use are valueless. The method we have found to give the best results is set forth in the next chapter.

But the use of the name as a vibratory influence that affects the individual wearing it in a particular way is not related to divination. Nor can there be more than one interpretation which is correct, of the vibratory force exerted by a particular name as affecting a given individual. The vibration of a name, or of a number, is a positive thought-force of a definite quality; as much so as that light-vibrations of a certain frequency give rise to the color blue. You can not correctly call blue red, yellow, green or some other color. Such is the difference between the system I am now explaining and numerology.

A name has a definite thought-vibration quality which is radiated to the individual by everyone who thinks of him by that name. If different people think of him by different names, they thus bombard him with different types of thought-vibration. But because an individual usually thinks of himself by the name he customarily uses as his signature, and because the thought-vibrations of the person wearing the name probably have more influence upon him than the combined thought-vibration of all others who think about him, the way an individual signs his name becomes very important as a vibratory influence in his life.

If such a signature were something unalterable this would be an interesting but not very useful fact. But as a matter of observation, it is quite common for people in all walks of life to use a different signature at different periods in the life: using an initial instead of a given name, dropping the use of a middle name or initial, or even changing the spelling of the name. A woman when she marries, and therefore coincident with a marked change in her fortune, commonly changes her name. Others, also, who change the spelling of their name, or alter the signature, are discerned to change in fortune coincidentally. A change in name is nearly always accompanied by a change in the life.

Writers quite commonly use a pen name, and actors, more frequently than not, use a stage or screen name. And these names by which they are known to the public not only influences them according to the key of the name, but also from a divinatory standpoint often markedly differentiates their public life from the private life in which they are known by another name.

The practical application of the knowledge of thought-vibrations, character-vibrations and astrological-vibrations is in selecting those invisible influences which assist to bring into the life the things which are desired, and which prevent attracting events and conditions which are undesirable.

The Positive, Scientific Method

Yet one can not know, by a positive method, what types of astral vibrations will prove beneficial and what types detrimental, and in what way this benefit or detriment will manifest, without a map of the astral body, such as is furnished by the astrological birth-chart. But with the astrological birth-chart at hand, it can at once be seen just what the effect will be upon the life of stimulating into unusual activity any particular section of the astral body, or any particular center of energy in the astral body. Even the connecting aerials, or aspects, between such centers of energy are there clearly shown, so that the effect upon other departments of life through secondary influences can also be determined in advance.

A scrutiny of an astrological birth-chart will reveal to anyone who has even a slight acquaintance with astrology just what zone of the astral body, or what thought structure, it is advisable to give added force. If the individual wishes to attract favorable conditions in some special line, a glance at the birthchart will reveal what influence there shown most pronouncedly is beneficial to it. Then by stimulating this influence, by using a name having the same keytone, and by having things in the environment which radiate the same key-tone, the activities of this favorable influence can be built up in a manner that will markedly attract the condition desired into the life.

The changing of the name, it will thus be seen, if the change causes the name to vibrate to a different key, adds the thought-energy of all those who think of this name in connection with the individual, to some different section or center in the astral body, and this causes a change in the fortune commensurate to the transfer of energy thus effected.

Unless the individual wishes especially to stimulate some one thing in his life in a favorable manner, the best plan in selecting a name or the objects and people of the environment, is first to find what influences in the birth-chart are more fortunate. This can be determined in a general way by inspecting the house positions and aspects of the planets. But by calculating the harmodynes and dis-cordynes of the chart the relative harmony and discord of each planet and sign can be precisely determined.

It may be desirable to give the added intensity to a section of the astral body not occupied by a planet because the department of life it rules may be deemed more important. When this is the case, the favor or disfavor that may be expected from such stimulation is determined by the harmony of the planet ruling the sign governing the zone thus selected. The common thought-cells of the astral body are mapped by the signs, and the dynamic thought-cells by the planets. The power and harmony or discord of an unoccupied sign is one-half that of the planet ruling the sign.

In seeking the influence that will conduce most to the general good fortune the best planet and the best sign in the chart should be located. Then, if possible, the name should be spelled, abbreviated, or otherwise altered, so as to have the same key as the best planet or best zodiacal sign. If a sign is occupied by a planet, or planets, accentuating the sign also accentuates the planet, or planets, in the sign. As a planet has twice as much influence as the unoccupied sign it rules, the harmony or discord of a planet, or planets, in a sign may be more important than the harmony or discord of the planet ruling the sign elsewhere located. Thus in selecting the best zodiacal sign, the harmony or discord of any planet, or planets, in it must be given due consideration.

Usually without much alteration a name may be given such spelling or abbreviation as to cause it to vibrate to the key which has been selected as most desirable. A long name, however, can not vibrate to Key 1, and thus accentuate the influence of Mercury in the astral body; for to get this key the number of the name must be either 1 or 100. A name vibrating either to the number 99 or the number 198 gives key 18; but to get key 19 the number of the name must be either 19, which is low, or not less than 199, which is quite high for the ordinary run of names.

Yet when it is desired to get a special type of vibratory key in the name—for there is no number above 21 which gives key 21 until 399 is reached, and thus it is impractical to accentuate the Sun thought-cells in the astral body through using key 21—often almost the same result may be had by accentuating the sign the Sun occupies in the birth-chart. Thus if the Sun were the only planet in Virgo, the number 101—1 plus 0 plus 1 gives 2 (Virgo)—would accentuate key 2, and because the Sun thought-cells are in Virgo, it would be the influence chiefly accentuated. Of course, Mercury, as the ruler of Virgo, would be somewhat stimulated, wherever located; but the most pronounced influence would be the energy thus added to the Sun structure.

To illustrate by a personal example: When the author was selected to write the various lessons and other publications issued by The Brotherhood of Light, he felt it advisable to use a distinct name for these publications that would indicate that whatever appeared under this name had the sanction of The Brotherhood of Light, and was, therefore, in this respect authoritative.

In addition to his occult interests he is also a naturalist, writing and lecturing on natural history subjects. He also has, as does everyone, a private life. And while it is unlikely that any of his private opinions would differ from those of The Brotherhood of Light, he did not wish to carry the responsibility of having any chance utterance he might make in an unguarded moment quoted as a Brotherhood of Light doctrine. So he decided he would select a pen name, that whatever appeared under that name should have the weight and careful thought of a Brotherhood of Light teaching; and that he would retain the name Elbert Benjamine for business purposes and for such writings as he did on other than occult subjects.

Now as he had entered into an agreement with The Brotherhood of Light to write a series of courses of lessons, each of the 21 occult sciences to be treated in a separate course, and ultimately to be published as a separate book, he felt that the chief requisite of the name should be to stimulate the tendency and ability to study and write about occult subjects. The announcement of the titles of these 21 courses to be written was made in the Declaration of Principles published early in May, 1915.

In his birth-chart the author has the sign Aquarius on the cusp of the third house, the house of writing. Its ruler, Uranus, is the most elevated planet in the chart. The aspects it receives are not all beneficial; but some of them are strongly harmonious, and those that are not, tend to attract just such discords as any person must attract who ventures to write and publish ideas that are as yet unaccepted by the vast majority of the race. So to give an impetus both to writing and to the acquisition of occult knowledge (for Uranus as ruler of Aquarius governs occultism) he decided that the chief thing to add energy to was the zone of his astral body ruled by Aquarius. The name, therefore, must vibrate to key 9.

Because the ability to gain information from the inner planes is chiefly ruled by the planet Neptune, and because it is the best planet in his birth-chart, it was thought advisable also to accentuate key 11. This could be done, although only in a minor degree, by using the initial C.

There were other considerations also of a symbolic nature. Zain (or Z) is the seventh letter of the Egyptian alphabet, and not only means victory, but corresponds to the sign Sagittarius, which is the natural ruler of the house of religion. And the writing and work to be accomplished was of a religious character; the re-establishment of The Religion of The Stars. Z also is a very peculiar letter, representing two 7's, one above and one below. Also 7 is an open trine, indicating giving out rather than receiving; and it was the author's purpose in issuing The Brotherhood of Light lessons to give as wide dissemination, both to material facts and to spiritual doctrines, as possible.

Furthermore, the author is a double Sagittarian; that is, he has Sagittarius both for a rising sign and for a Sun sign. So that not only were the vibratory ends sought gained by the use of C. C. Zain as a pen name—C-11, C-11, Z-7, A-1, I-10, N-14: 11 plus 11 plus 7 plus 1 plus 10 plus 14 gives 54; 5 plus 4 gives key 9 adding energy to the section of the astral body ruled by Aquarius—but it is an accurate translation of the strongest influences in his birth-chart into letters combined in a name. Whoever, therefore can read this name aright, can know the source from which these writings come, the motives prompting their expression, the method by which the information they contain was gained, and much about the inner life of the author.

The name in full, given as a tarot chart is—IX—XI—XI—VII—I—X—XIV—VI. This may be read as Wisdom (9), and early Spiritual Power (11), followed by Psychic Strength (11), leading to Victory (7) over obstacles. Will and Intelligence (1), after a time dictate a Change of Fortune (10) and this brings Regeneration (14) and still other Trials (6).

Changing a Name

At first thought it may seem that using a name in business other than that conferred at birth is exceptional other than in a few professions. But a little reflection will indicate that most people in business abbreviate, or otherwise alter the name, in using it as a signature.

And because people become familiar with this signature, it becomes more strongly associated in their minds with the person using it than any other name. The person signing himself in a given way, because he writes his name thus, and both makes and sees the signature, comes to think of himself according to the signature as written. And the name by which an individual thinks of himself, because his own thoughts are more powerful to influence his life than the thoughts of others, is commonly the most important name of all.

Therefore, because the business signature determines the thought-vibrations sent him by those who see this signature, and the thought-vibrations which he generates when he thinks of himself by name, it should be selected with an end in view of stimulating some department of life as desired, in a favorable manner. This is done by selecting for a business signature a name the vibratory key of which corresponds to the sign or planet in the birth-chart most favorable to the department of life it is wished to strengthen.

The Sage—Arcanum IX

Letter: Egyptian, Thela; Hebrew, Teth; English, Th. Number, 9. Astrologically, the zodiacal sign Aquarius. Color, the lighter shades of blue. Tone, high G. Occult science, mental alchemy. Human function, clairaudience. Natural remedy, such herbs as myrrh, frankincense and spikenard. Mineral, the talismanic gem, sky-blue sapphire, and such stones as obsidian and black pearl.

Th—9, expresses in the spiritual world, absolute wisdom.
In the intellectual world, prudence, director of the will.
In the physical world, circumspection, guide of actions.

Remember, then, son of earth, prudence is the armor of the wise. Circumspection enables one to avoid snares and abysses and to foresee treason. Take it for thy guide in all thy actions, even in the least. Nothing is indifferent here below. A pebble can overturn the chariot of the master of the world. If Arcanum IX should appear in the prophetic signs of thy horoscope, keep in mind that speech is silver and silence is gold.

In Divination, **Arcanum IX** may briefly be read as **Wisdom** or **Prudence**.

Arcanum IX is figured by an old wanderer leaning on a staff and carrying before him a lighted lamp which he half conceals behind his mantle. This sage personifies experience gained in the journey of life. The cloak is of square form, symbolizing the physical world in which man may acquire knowledge of good and evil. That this knowledge has been gained is signified by the man having partially removed the cloak of material limitations, and by the lamp, emblem of intelligence, shedding its rays over the past, present and future. The lamp being concealed by the mantle symbolizes discretion, and also expresses the truth that if we are ever to know the real nature of anything we must delve deep beneath the cloak of external appearances.

The staff, which in form is the sixth letter of the Egyptian and Hebrew alphabets, indicates that man progresses through struggle, alternately overcoming obstacles and being vanquished by them, and that when finally he realizes he only develops his abilities through recurrent efforts to triumph over difficulties, this knowledge becomes his staff of prudence supporting him in all his endeavors.

Number

Nine is the Deific number, the highest digit, which possesses the unique property that it may be multiplied by any number and the digits so obtained when added together always resolve into 9. On the inner-plane, where thought-vibrations and astral-vibrations of all kinds become effective, 9 is the perfect scale, even as 7 is the perfect scale of physical form. Such vibratory rates, consequently, are measured by decaves instead of by octaves.

As the multiples of 9 resolve, when their digits are added, into 9, it is the symbol of manifested Deity whose different manifestations may all be reduced to the one primal source. It is the figure unlocking the cycles of the ancients, and as composed of 3 times 3 indicates action on all three planes. As composed of 4 plus 5 it represents man realizing all earth can teach, and thus is the number of wisdom. As consisting of 7 and 2 it adds polarity, intuition and wisdom, to the union of man and woman, giving knowledge of good and evil, or wisdom gained through union. As 8 and 1 it is death, mortality and stagnation overcome by will and intelligence; hence new action, life, immortality.

Astrology

The zodiacal sign of the Sun, Leo, is represented by the symbol of a serpent. This serpent, natural ruler of the fifth house of a birth-chart, and thus of pleasures and love-affairs, is the symbol of desire.

And while the Man of the zodiac, Aquarius, is represented commonly by the two wavy lines representing water from the urn, these wavy lines were also depicted in ancient times as two serpents, or two desires, one traveling in either direction. Desires thus kept in equilibrium through knowledge gained in experience with good and evil are true wisdom. Hence the serpent is sometimes referred to as the tempter and sometimes as the essence of wisdom. Math. 10:16; "Be ye therefore wise as serpents and harmless as doves."

This is a clear statement of the import of Arcanum IX. The love nature is signified by doves, which are sacred to Venus; and the power of Aquarius to properly direct the love nature is indicated by the reference to wisdom. Aquarius astrologically represents the highest form of intelligence, expressing progressively in scientific and occult interests, such as are depicted in the arcanum of the Sage.

Human Function

The highest wisdom, such as symbolized by the Sage, comes both from within and from without. Experience with good and evil is garnered in the external world and stored together with the experiences garnered in the interior realms. The two sources of knowledge are thus symbolized by the two wavy lines, anciently also depicted as two serpents. The Sage thus not only has listened to the teachers in the external world, but he has also been guided by those speaking from the inner plane; and to hear them he has developed the faculty of clairaudience, which thus corresponds to Arcanum IX.

Alchemy

In alchemical processes of any kind, danger is sure to be present if the conditions are forced. Transmutations, for instance, can not be made to take place instantly. They require time. To try to alter a condition too quickly is apt to result in an explosion. Whatever energies are present must be taken care of through gradually diverting them into those channels which will promote the object sought. More failure in alchemical work results from undue haste and impatience for results than from any other cause. The prudence which alone enables the alchemist to be successful in his endeavors is depicted by Arcanum IX.

Bible

In the Bible we find that the tempting serpent of desire denied the word of God that man would die when he should eat of the forbidden fruit.

"For God doth know that in the day ye eat thereof, then your eyes shall be opened; and ye shall be as gods, knowing good and evil." (Gen. 3:4).

But it is true that when spirit descended into matter it died to its celestial nature and was no longer pure and innocent. Yet through yielding to Temptation (Arcanum VI) and entering into material incarnation, the words of the serpent also were verified: Gen. 3:7; "And the eyes of them both were opened, and they knew that they were naked, and they sewed fig leaves together, and made themselves aprons."

That is, after partaking of the Tree of Good and Evil they gained knowledge and immediately put forth an effort to overcome matter and Triumph over circumstances, as indicated by Arcanum VII.

After the Judgment (Arcanum VIII) of the transgression—8 expressing crystallization—we learn: "Unto Adam, also, and to his wife, did the Lord God make coats of skins and clothed them." In other words, they had spiritual bodies while living in the realm of spirit, but upon descending to the material plane they were clothed with physical bodies. The result of incarnation through the various lower life-forms is symbolized by coats of skins, verifying the wisdom of the serpent, and in the final result being depicted by Arcanum IX. Gen. 3:22; "And the Lord God said, behold, the man is become as one of us, to know good and evil."

Still another reference to Arcanum IX is Solomon's choice of Wisdom instead of worldly goods.

Masonry

The Select Master degree of Masonry is founded upon Arcanum IX. It signifies the ninth arch of the secret vault of Solomon's Temple, where are stored exact copies of all that is contained in the sanctum sanctorum above. It is what might be called the lowest degree of adeptship on the physical plane, being the Intellectual degree in which man has recognized the correspondence between the heaven above and his soul. Arcanum IX corresponds also to the three triangular tables arranged in a row with a triangular plate of gold in the center of each and a lighted candle at each corner. It corresponds likewise to the three times three of the ritual.

Magic

In Magic, Arcanum IX corresponds to the various magical methods of obtaining information about occult subjects.

In such endeavors there are two chief methods which are followed. One is to leave the physical body and travel in the astral form. Through this process it is possible to visit the homes of the dead, to sit at the feet of the wise in the Halls of Learning on the astral plane, and to gather information through personal contact and observation, while the physical body slumbers on earth.

The other method, which is beset with far fewer dangers, is to tune in on the plane from which it is thus desired to gain information. In this tuning in process the proper astrological conditions are usually observed, and often it is assisted by an appropriate ceremony.

Initiation

In the soul's pilgrimage, Arcanum IX indicates the attainment of cosmic consciousness.

Upon arriving at this state of his upward ascent the neophyte is able to discern the proper relations of the various entities in the universe, both to himself, and to each other. This is not merely an intellectual conception, but is borne home to him also through tuning in on the universal organism. He recognizes that each soul is being trained to perform a work which the expansion of the cosmic organization makes needful.

As a result of this higher state of consciousness he comes to recognize quite clearly the nature of his own function in universal work, and thus sets about his task with the knowledge that he is a valuable factor in the scheme of things, with a certain and definite mission to perform. And upon his faithfulness in performing what he comes to recognize as his present task in contributing to cosmic welfare, depends his future opportunities for progression.

Quite important in arriving at this higher state of consciousness, wherein he perceives his cosmic work, is the development of his affectional relations. That is, the power to tune in on either higher or lower states is chiefly regulated by the emotions. Passion and gross expression, therefore, must be supplanted by more exalted expressions of love. That which is gross and degrading tends to tune the mind in on lower states. But acts which engender strong emotions of tenderness, and kindly feelings that are so expansive as to embrace all, and which uplift the energies in intense desire for noble work, are the most effective agents known to tune the individual in on higher realms and to develop cosmic consciousness.

Cosmic elementals—sylphs, salamanders, undines and gnomes—as well as magnetic elementals such as fauns, elves, nymphs and fairies, have relation to man; but they are not dependent upon him for intellectual and spiritual force, as are the so-called degrees of life. Yet his thoughts and desires do arouse them into activity, and may enlist them in the performance of such work as is within their special province. His proper relation to all such life-forms, and the work he should do aiding cosmic progression, are revealed to him when he attains cosmic consciousness.

Occult Science

Mental alchemy treats of the mental factors and how they may be made most effective to attract into the life just the conditions required. The process consists largely in transmuting discord into harmony and in providing the proper flux to annul undesirable conditions.

Under Arcanum V we found that four signs express the absolute and are in turn explained by a fifth. And now, rather paradoxically, we find that 9 symbolizes the absolute in expression. But if we use the lamp of the Sage to look beneath the surface of this apparent contradiction, we find that 5, or intelligent man must have a medium through which to express; a place in which to move and work, as signified by the square mantle of the Sage. This universal medium, of course, is symbolized by the number 4. Thus Arcanum IX sheds much light upon how mantrams, suggestions and the processes of mental-alchemy bring about their results.

For those with a penchant for symbolism to add further light upon their researches, this whole subject will be given clarity through a study of the diagram, page 19 of chapter 1. The square marked 1 should be colored yellow; 3 should be colored green; 5 should be colored purple; 7 should be colored red, and 9 should be colored violet. These are the five odd, or active, numbers. The colors yellow and red signify power (love) and motion (life).

However, activity must take place in a medium, which is represented by the four squares marked with even numbers, which should be colored the other primary, blue. Then the squares 5 and 3 represent the reaction of yellow and red on blue, and as stated are purple and green. And the central square, representing the highest vibration, the evolution of all below, should be colored violet.

Finally, the border around the whole figure, the solar combination of power and activity, should be colored orange.

The Nines

The sign Aquarius is general significator of friends, associates, hopes and wishes; therefore the nines in their more common divinatory significance must relate to one of these things, according to the particular department of life signified by the suit. But in their higher application they reveal the influence of, and can be interpreted by, the ninth decanate of each zodiacal triplicity, starting the count from the movable signs.

The divinatory significance of the Nine of Scepters is a wise and profitable friendship; its inner interpretation is ILLUMINATION.

The divinatory significance of the Nine of Cups is that the hopes will be realized; it is the WISH-CARD; its inner interpretation is VICISSITUDES.

The divinatory significance of the Nine of Coins is money spent on associates; its inner interpretation is REASON.

The divinatory significance of the Nine of Swords is a quarrel resulting in enmity; its inner interpretation is RENUNCIATION.

The Wheel—Arcanum X

Letter: Egyptian, Ioothi; Hebrew, Jod; English, I—J—Y. Number, 10. Astrologically, the planet Uranus. Color, dazzling white, like snow in the sunshine. Tone, the astral chimes. Occult science, natal astrology. Human function, intuition. Natural remedy, electricity and mesmerism. Mineral, uranium.

I—10, expresses in the spiritual world, the active principle which vivifies all being.

In the intellectual world, the governing authority.
In the physical world, good and evil fortune.

Remember, then, son of earth, that for power thou must will, that is, will strongly; thou must dare, and to dare with success thou shouldst know how to be silent until the moment of action. If the Wheel should appear in the prophetic signs of thy horoscope, know that to possess the Key of Power you must learn to will persistently only for what is good and true. And in order to maintain thyself upon the heights of life, shouldst thou reach them, thou must have learned how to sound with a look, and without dizziness, the vastest depths.

In Divination, **Arcanum X** may be read as **Change of Fortune**.

Arcanum X is figured by a wheel of eight spokes suspended by its axis upon a dual column. At the right Hernanubis, genius of good, strives to mount to the summit of the circumference. At the left, Typhon, genius of evil, is precipitated. On a circular platform in equilibrium on the Wheel, is poised a sphinx, holding in its claws a javelin. At the foot of the dual column two serpents raise their heads.

This is the wheel of destiny. The circular platform upon which the sphinx stands represents the zodiac; and the sphinx, as a composite of the four constellations marking the zodiacal quadrants—Eagle, Lion, Man and Bull—signifies the passage of time.

It holds a javelin in its claws to indicate that time is always fructifying events and ever ready to strike to right or left as the wheel turns under its impulsion, raising the humble and lowering the proud.

The eight spokes of the wheel, eight being the number of justice, symbolize that time and opportunity, in the course of divine providence, are justly meted out to all. The dual column supporting the wheel indicates that all nature is polarized into positive and negative. The serpents signify that the law of all action is that of sex.

Number

The number 10 represents the completed cycle, and therefore the starting point of another. It thus indicates transition to a new phase, or plane, of existence.

The absolute having expressed itself through all the various manifestations up to and including 9, which signifies perfection of consciousness in addition to perfection of form, commences a new gamut. 1 is the absolute unmanifest, and 9 is the perfection of its manifestation.

In humanity, as composed of two 5s, 10 indicates the whole man to consist of both man and woman, and that their union commences a new and higher phase of existence; that is, that it enables them to contact a higher plane of endeavor. 1 symbolizes will and intelligence, and 10 shows that they are now used by both in a new and higher field of endeavor.

Astrology

Uranus is the octave expression of Mercury, even as Arcanum X is the second decave of Arcanum I, ruled by Mercury. The unsexed quality of Uranus is depicted in Arcanum X by the two serpents in equilibrium.

Uranus transits one sign of the zodiac in about 7 years, and the whole zodiac, completing the circle through the 12 houses of a horoscope, in about 84 years. That is, it corresponds to perfection of form in each department of life, its complete cycle coinciding with the present natural life of man. More than any other planet it gives sudden changes of fortune, either for good or for evil, and sudden change of the mental viewpoint.

Human Function

In natal astrology it is found that those individuals who have Uranus prominent in their birth-charts have the ability to short-cut their reasoning. Instead of the ordinary slow mental process of the objective mind, the processes are carried out by the unconscious mind which has more complete data at its disposal, and which acts almost instantly in drawing conclusions from them. These conclusions thus arrived at then rise into the objective consciousness as intuition.

Alchemy

No matter what the plane of alchemical procedure, it is a decided aid to observe the astrological conditions which are operative at the time. The energies of the planets have an influence upon all processes, and it is easier to perform a given type of work when the astrological influences favor it. Of course, alchemical work of many kinds can not await favorable conditions. But the knowledge that astrological influences are hindering at certain times, both incites to more careful and energetic effort and prevents discouragement when it is observed that small progress is being made.

Bible

Arcanum X depicts the Wheel of Ezekiel. Ezek. 1:15; "Now, as I beheld the living creatures, behold, one wheel upon the earth by the living creatures, with his four faces." These faces were the composite symbols embraced in the sphinx; the Lion, the Eagle, the Man and the Bull.

The geni on the wheel of Arcanum X are mentioned thus: Ezek. 1:13; "As for the likeness of the living creatures, their appearance was like burning coals of fire, and like the appearance of lamps: it went up and down amid the living creatures: and the fire was bright and out of the fire went lightning."

The change in the fortune of Solomon also has to do with Arcanum X. I Kings, 2:3; "And he had seven hundred wives, princesses, and three hundred concubines; and his wives turned away his heart."

Masonry

The Super Excellent Master degree of Masonry is based upon Arcanum X. Its ritual depicts the fate of Zedekiah, who did evil in the sight of the Lord, and underwent a sudden and extreme change of fortune.

Magic

In magic, Arcanum X represents the orbit of action of the blessing and cursing energy of the human soul. This orbit is elliptical, with a periodic action of its own, sure to react upon the individual; for to cause a condition in another one must create within himself the matrix of that condition.

It is quite useless to fight a discordant emotion or a discordant thought sent to one by another. To fight it merely draws the attention to it and thus tunes in on its vibrations and enables them to gain a still greater potency. Thinking about either a harmony or a discord adds energy to it and gives it more force.

Whether it be events, the thoughts and emanations of people who think discordantly but without malice, or the actual malicious attempt to injure one by black magic; in all cases anxious attention feeds the undesirable condition. And except to recognize that it has an existence and should be thwarted, the discord and its source should be ignored. And in addition to this judicious indifference, the attention should be given as enthusiastically as possible to something harmonious. A discordant vibration can not live in the same place as a harmonious vibration.

Initiation

As the soul progresses up the spiral ascending way of attainment, it gradually refines its organism to the end of living a richer life. On both planes, however, there is always the impact of environment; and some of the conditions contacted are sure to be discordant.

If, therefore, the life-form occupied by the soul becomes sensitive without at the same time developing the power of control there may be actual danger. No matter how sensitive it becomes, so long as the soul has the power to direct the thoughts and attention, no other entity can gain control of the organism or do it injury from the inner plane. But if sensitiveness becomes greater than the power of control, other entities or discordant conditions are able to hold the attention and can cause the individual to suffer.

Yet as abilities are developed only through the effort to overcome such obstacles as are shown by progressed afflictions in the birth-chart, at the state of progress here considered, astrological afflictions are viewed as opportunities to develop ability, and astrological harmonies are viewed as opportunities to use the abilities thus developed in assisting universal progression.

Occult Science

Natal astrology is the science of discerning the character from a map of the mental factors within the astral body as pictured by the birth-chart; and of determining when certain events will have a tendency to be attracted due to the stimulation of these mental factors by energies from the planets.

Here also should be mentioned the doctrine of the Ten Emanations of the Sephiroth. The kabalistical scheme of three pillars is given in most works on the kabala, but someone a hundred or more years ago inserted a blind by placing Hod on the left and Netzach on the right, knowing that real intimates would discern that Netzach is the victory of woman. Yet this error has been copied by kabalistical writers ever since.

The correct astrological correspondences of each emanation has not been placed in writing before, but the chart on page 132 of chapter 6 gives the emanations in proper sequence and relations.

Above all is the Limitless Light, Ain-Soph-Aur (1). Pluto, is Kether, or Crown, the point of differentiation, where soul-mates separate and where ultimately they must again rejoin. (2) Neptune is Chocmah, or Wisdom. (3) Uranus is Binah, or Intelligence. (4) Jupiter is Chesed, or Mercy. (5) Saturn is Geburah, or Justice. (6) Venus is Tippereth, or Beauty. (7) Mars is Netzach, or Victory. (8) Mercury is Hod, or Splendor. (9) Moon is Yesod, or Foundation. (10) Sun is Malkuth, or Kingdom. And below all is the region of Adonai—Shekinah.

Benefic planets, of course, are on the tree of good, and malefic planets on the tree of evil, while Pluto, Venus, Moon and Sun form the Shekinah, or Tree of Life.

The upper story of the diagram is Atziluth, or Emanation; the next lower is Briah, or Creation; below this is Yetzirah, or Formation; and the lowest of all is Assiah, the realm of Action.

Of course, the river that waters the garden of Eden and parts into four heads is the planet Venus in the diagram and the four lines radiating from it. Each of the 10 emanations manifests in all four kingdoms, and the 12 triangles of the circumference are the 12 houses of a birth-chart; the 32 lines in the circumference representing the paths of wisdom.

The ten emanations operating through the four kingdoms, or suit cards of the tarot, are expressed in verse by Mr. A. E. Waite admirably, thus:

> Four signs present the Name of every name. Four brilliant beams adorn his Crown of flame. Four rivers from his Wisdom flow. Four proofs from his Intelligence we know. Four benefactions from his Mercy come. Four times four sins avenged his Justice sum. Four rays unclouded make his Beauty known. Four times his Conquest shall in song be shown. Four times he Triumphs on the timeless plane. Foundations four his great white throne maintain. One fourfold Kingdom owns his endless sway. As from his crown there streams a fourfold ray.

The Tens

The planet Uranus is general significator of uncommon pursuits, of sudden changes of fortune, of inventions, discoveries, and of unconventional relations and actions; therefore the tens in their more common divinatory significance must relate, according to their suit, to one of these things. But in their higher application they reveal the influence of, and can be interpreted by, the zodiacal triplicities.

The divinatory significance of the Ten of Scepters is an invention or discovery; its inner interpretation is ENTHUSIASM.

The divinatory significance of the Ten of Cups is a decidedly unconventional affectional interest; its inner interpretation is EMOTION.

The divinatory significance of the Ten of Coins is alternate financial loss and gain; its inner interpretation is ASPIRATION.

The divinatory significance of the Ten of Swords is sudden loss of employment; its inner interpretation is PRACTICALITY.

Spread of the Kabala

When the influence and outcome of anything is sought, the cards may be dealt on a diagram similar to the one on page 132, one after the other, until 10 cards are laid out according to the sequence there indicated.

The cards of the Tree of Good are on the right, and indicate favorable events. The cards of the Tree of Evil are on the left, and indicate unfavorable events. The four cards in the middle are on the Tree of Life, and represent the outcome.

Card 1 signifies the spiritual result, and card 10 the material result. 6 is the result concerning life and love, and 9 the result as affecting the home. The cause of the influence exerted by each card is signified by its kabalistical name. Thus if on 2, Wisdom is the cause; if on 3, Intelligence is behind it; if on 4, Mercy has an influence; if on 5, there is a desire for Justice. 6 indicates love of Beauty, 7 desire for Victory, 8 Splendor and show, 9 home conditions, and 10 physical power as distinct from spiritual aspirations signified by 1.

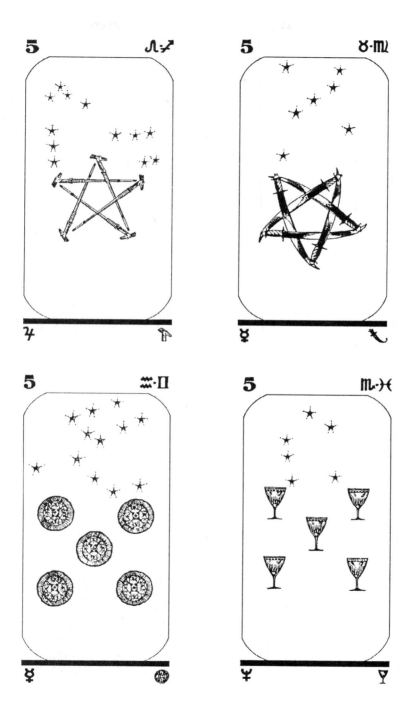

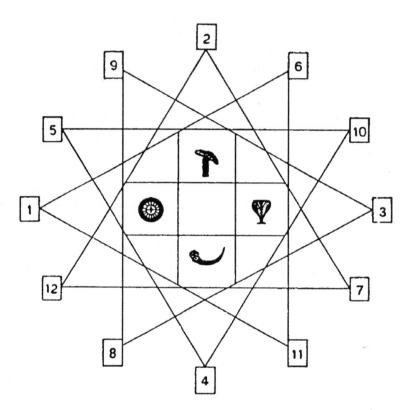

THE HOROSCOPE SPREAD

Chapter 8

Reading Names in Detail

ECAUSE the name John Brown when present in any person's mind always radiates the same component thought vibrations, and always reverberates to the same vibratory key, it is easy to map the influences of this name in a positive and scientific manner. And by substituting the divinatory significance of each numerical factor, it is possible to give a divinatory reading of the name, as such, without reference to any particular person.

But such a divinatory reading is a delineation of the name only, and should not be expected to reveal much concerning the life of any particular John Brown. Quite certain it is that of the thousands and thousands of John Browns throughout the world, their fortunes are markedly varied, and have no such uniformity as would be necessary if all their lives were to be represented by a single set of divinatory symbols.

When we have the astrological birth-chart of an individual we possess a positive map of his various important vibratory rates and how they are related to each other. When we have a name and find its key we possess a map of the vibratory qualities of that name. By comparing the two maps we can determine with all the exactitude of positive science how the name will influence the individual.

From the astrological birth-chart and the progressed aspects we can plot the invisible influences operative in the life of the individual at any given time, and thus have a positive way of mapping the probable events and the time they will happen, in the individual's life.

But when we do not have the birth-chart of the individual by which to determine his various vibratory rates, we have no positive method of determining how a name will affect him, and we possess no positive method of determining either the events of his life or the time they will happen.

But man is not dependent exclusively upon positive methods in the acquisition of knowledge. Reason is positive, but often intuition, which is not positive, yields information even more valuable. The physical senses are positive, but the psychic senses, under certain circumstances, are even more reliable. And while the positive method of gaining information by means of numbers is very valuable, it is not the only method of using numbers to acquire knowledge. Numbers may also be used as divinatory instruments. All systems of numerology are purely methods of divination; and the one now to be presented is no exception. But it is the best system we have been able to find.

In order to have a constantly varying factor which provides a proper basis for the exercise of divination, it is customary to use the name of the individual, but to this name add another distinctive factor which is unique to the individual. This distinctive factor, which has come to be known as the number of the Birth Path, is merely the number which is obtained by adding crosswise the factors of the birth date as commonly expressed numerically.

Thus the number of the Birth Path of Jan. 13, 1872, is 1 (January is 1st month) plus 1 plus 3 plus 1 plus 8 plus 7 plus 2, which gives 23.

The number of the Birth Path of May 8, 1932, is 5 (May is the 5th month) plus 8 plus 1 plus 9 plus 3 plus 2, which gives 28.

The number of the Birth Path of July 4, 1776, is 7 (July is 7th month) plus 4 plus 1 plus 7 plus 7 plus 6, which gives 32.

The number of the Birth Path of December 7, 1941, is 1 plus 2 (December is 12th month) plus 7 plus 1 plus 9 plus 4 plus 1, which gives 25.

The number of the Birth Path of November 2, 1948, is 1 plus 1 (November is 11th month) plus 2 plus 1 plus 9 plus 4 plus 8, which gives 26.

The Birth Path is really the birth date, and therefore it is true that the number of the Birth Path does belong specifically to the individual; for it is a number obtained from the record of his birth; yet it must not be lost sight of that using it thus is not a method depending upon the vibratory influence of thought, but is merely a divinatory method of using the Birth Path, or date of birth, in a particular way.

Then having found the number of the Birth Path, this number is added to the number of the name, the sum giving a Divinatory Number, which affords a chart which should reveal to one whose intuitions are active, the character, the chief events of the life and the conditions surrounding the individual when life ends.

To obtain this chart the Key of the Divinatory Number is found and placed at the beginning of the chart as signifying the chief influence in the character. The Major Arcanum corresponding to this Key of the Divinatory Number is considered in the nature of symbolically representing the birth-chart of the person.

Then in the chart this is followed by a Major Arcanum substituted for each letter of the name. That is, each letter of the name, commencing with the first, is considered as a separate influence in the life. It is considered in the nature of an astrological major progression. And the nature of the event which it brings into the life is symbolized by the Major Arcanum corresponding to the letter. The first letter of the name thus represents the influence in the life immediately following birth, the next letter an influence somewhat later, the third letter a period following this, and so on up to the end of the name.

Then the Key of the Decave of the Divinatory Number is found and placed at the end of the chart, after the Major Arcanum representing the last letter of the name. The Major Arcanum corresponding to the Key of the Decave does not so much represent a specific event, as the conditions which surround the person at the close of life. That is, it represents in a divinatory way, that which is signified by the fourth house of a birth-chart.

Abraham Lincoln was born Feb. 12, 1809.

A	I	L	12	(Feb.)	2
B	2	I	10		1
R	20	N	14		2
A	1	C	11		1
H	8	O	16		8
A	1	L	12		0
M	13	N	14		9
	46		89		23 Birth Path

46 plus 89 plus 23 gives 158 as the Divinatory Number. 1 plus 5 plus 8 gives 14 as the Key of the Divinatory Number.

158 minus 14 gives 144. 144 divided by 9, plus 1, gives 17 as the

Key of the Decave.

14 (Key, or Character)—1—2—20—1—8—1—13—12—10—14—11—16—12—14—17 (Condition at end of life).

The numerical chart as given in the line above shows that Abraham Lincoln's character was based upon 14, or Temperance. A much more detailed description of it can be had by substituting the astrological correspondence, Taurus, which shows clearly the deep sympathy and the intense practicality of his nature.

Very early in life he began to develop himself through the application of Will in the expansion of his Intelligence (1).

Science (2) next comes under his scrutiny as a child, and exerted its full influence in his life as he ciphered on the back of a wooden shovel by the firelight.

But there was an Awakening (20) also in his early years, by which his thoughts were turned into higher channels.

And some travel (Mercury influence) which gave full material for his developing Intelligence (1).

This was followed by gaining for himself a reputation for Justice (8); for he came to be known as honest Abe.

Then further application to study and the development of his Intelligence (1); for he began to prepare himself to practice law.

And a Transformation in his affairs due to taking part in a military expedition (Aries) (13).

Then came the first great Sacrifice and sorrow (12) of his life through the loss of his beloved Ann Rutledge.

Followed by a Change of Fortune (10) as he was thrust forward into the political arena.

In which capacity his fairness and Temperance (14) in handling the issues of the day;

Lent to him a Spiritual Force (11) which swept him into the highest office in the land.

And brought to him the responsibility of that great Catastrophe (16), the Civil War.

This was an Expiation (12) of the sin of human slavery; and enabled him to set free these slaves at the Sacrifice of his own and other lives.

Then the war was ended, and he embarked upon a full program of Regeneration (14) for the country, when his own end came.

And while this end came suddenly, and violently, nevertheless, he had accomplished his work. The surroundings of his life at its end (Key of the Decave of the Divinatory Number) is well shown by 17.

Truth had prevailed, Faith had been vindicated, and he left behind him a message of Hope that has continued unabated to this day.

George Washington was born Feb. 22, 1732.

		W	6			
		A	1			
		SH	8	(Feb.)	2	
G	3	I	10		2	
E	5	N	14		2	
O	16	G	3		1	
R	20	T	22		7	
G	3	O	16		3	
E	5	N	14		2	
	52		104		19	Birth Path

52 plus 104 plus 19 gives 175 as the Divinatory Number. 1 plus 7 plus 5 gives 13 as the Key of the Divinatory Number.

175 minus 13 gives 162. 162 divided by 9, plus 1, gives 19 as the Key to the Decave.

13 (Key, or Character)—3—5—16—20—3—5—6—1—18—10—14—3—22—16—14—19 (Condition at end of life).

13 (Aries) indicates that Washington was typically a pioneer destined to bring about a Transformation by the use of the sword. A more detailed reading of the character may be had from the sign Aries.

His early life was spent in Action (3) rather than in study.

Then the influence of Law and Religion (5) played their part.

At an early age a commission as midshipman was offered to him, but his mother blocked this, which was a Catastrophe (16) to his ambitions.

The death of his brother brought him an inheritance and an Awakening (20) to new responsibilities.

Then he married (3) Mrs. Curtis, and settled at Mt. Vernon.

His life as a planter brought him into contact with the Law (5) in that he was elected repeatedly to the legislature of Virginia.

Then came a time of Trial and Temptation (6) in regard to Governor Dunmore, in which his position was always that of a radical.

His appointment to Congress in 1774 gave him opportunity for the exercise of his Will, Intelligence and Dexterity (1) for which later he became famous.

In this period, just prior to the Revolutionary War, Deception (18), subterfuge, and secret enemies were encountered on every hand.

And then, with the war, came a decided Change of Fortune (10).

When named commander-in-chief of the armed forces of the United Colonies his Temperance (14) caused him to refuse a salary, and to announce that he felt himself unfit for the command.

Then came the Action (3) of War.

But the stupidity, Foolishness (22) and impatience of his supporters during 1775 almost wrecked the enterprise.

It was a Catastrophe (16) when Benedict Arnold and his sympathizers turned against him.

But his persistence and Temperance (14) brought him through, established his fame, and placed him uncontested in the presidential chair.

From this position he later retired to his home at Mt. Vernon, to find the rural life he enjoyed so much, surrounded by his family and friends. Away from the conflicts of political quarrels, with the highest honors his country could bestow, with wealth and the affection of many, his closing years are well represented by the Key of the Decave of the Divinatory Number (19), the number of Happiness.

I believe these two illustrations will quite suffice to indicate the manner in which divination by numbers can be used to give a detailed reading of a name. The number representing the Key of the Divinatory Number should always be taken to represent the character. Then each letter of the name, in its proper sequence, should be taken to represent a period of the life, and the influence of this period can be expanded by using the astrological correspondence of the number.

There is no way, by this system, to know just how long any period lasts. The duration of time is the most difficult thing to determine by any method of divination. The general rule here, however, is to divide the total life—whether short or long—into as many periods as there are letters in the name. Each letter represents one of these periods. If the life is long, it represents a longer period than if the life is short.

Then the Key of the Decave of the Divinatory Number is taken to represent the condition at the end of life, whether this end comes early or late.

And it must not be forgotten that in such divination rigid interpretations are to be avoided. The numbers in such a chart are to be used merely as guides to the intuition; not to limit it. All impressions and intuitions, therefore, should be expressed freely, even when they somewhat contradict the rigid interpretation of the numerical chart.

The Enchantress—Arcanum XI

Letter: Egyptian, Caitha; Hebrew, Caph; English, C—K. Number 11. Astrologically, the planet Neptune. Color, changing iridescence. Tone, the music of the spheres. Occult science, divination. Human function, thought-transference. Natural remedy, spiritual healing. Element, neptunium.

C-11, expresses in the spiritual world, the principle of all force, spiritual and material.

In the intellectual world, moral force.

In the physical world, organic force.

Remember, then, son of earth, that for power one must believe in one's ability. Advance with faith. To become strong, impose silence upon the weakness of the heart. If Arcanum XI should appear in the prophetic signs of thy horoscope thou shouldst study duty, which is the rule of right, and practice justice as if you loved it.

In Divination, **Arcanum XI** is **Force, Spiritual Power,** or **Fortitude**.

Arcanum XI is figured by the image of a young girl who opens and closes without effort, with her hands, the jaws of an angry lion. The maiden wears a crown surmounted by a vase and crowned eagles, and at her brow the sacred serpent.

The vase is symbol of the affections, and the crowned eagles represent force spiritualized. The sacred serpent signifies that she acts in full knowledge of her power, and not blindly. The lion symbolizes force, also the animal desires in man which are subdued by the spiritual nature.

The whole ensemble symbolizes the power over violent forces of nature that faith in oneself and an innocent life will give; also the spiritual power that is the natural result of unsullied affections which dominate and rule the animal instincts. It signifies that purity is the touchstone, and that goodness alone is power.

Number

Numerically, 11 indicates the extreme magnetic and feminine forces of nature. It exemplifies the doctrine that evil should not be resisted, but be overcome with good. The finer forces of woman, while not giving the physical strength of man, enable her to govern him by appealing to him interiorly, and thus she molds his efforts through his affectional nature. She enters occultly into his life; and liberating the powers which lie latent in the structure of his genius, enables him to realize the ideals she in her love has formed of him.

As composed of 7 and 4, the number 11 symbolizes the power that is realized as a result of the perfect union denoted by 7. As 9 and 2, it represents Wisdom carried into the realms of Occult Science, giving control of the magnetic currents of the astral world. As 6 and 5, it signifies Temptation banished through devotion to Religion. As 10 and 1, it denotes Fortune dominated by Will.

Astrology

Neptune is the octave expression of the planet Venus, signifying spiritual love as distinct from the material love ruled by Venus. Neptune is the planet of psychic manifestation, its prominence in a birth-chart being an indication of psychic ability. It exerts little power upon the physical world directly, but by its action upon the imagination of people it becomes singularly potent. Its influence is to spiritualize, and it usually is a prominent planet in the birth-chart of all types of genius, denoting that peculiar power so well expressed by Arcanum XI.

Human Function

The peculiarly high-strung and sensitive organism given by the planet Neptune enables its natives to receive mental messages from others. It is capable of great negativeness, giving it capacity for reception, and is sensitive enough to perceive the import of thought vibration. At the same time it has an inward power by which it can send potent thought-forms to do its will, or through the faculty of imagination impress its messages upon the minds of others. It is like the strings of a cello, sensitive to impinging sounds and readily set vibrating by them, and at the same time powerful to cause vibrations in other instruments. These qualities requisite for thought-transference are indicated by Arcanum XI.

Alchemy

Arcanum XI represents the energy liberated during the process of transmutation. When the metals join, and the heat of the reverberatory furnace is applied, they flux and reduce to the first matter before the alchemical transformation takes place. And in this process heat, electricity, magnetism, and still finer forces are set free. These forces, so generated, are not violent, and are so subtle that they would go entirely unnoticed by the careless. Nevertheless, they are of great importance in the alchemical process, and especially essential in the completion of the Great Work.

Bible

The most notable reference to the principle pictured by Arcanum XI which occurs in the Bible is the story of Samson. His strength lay in his purity and his virility; for his mother was commanded while carrying him; Ju. 13: 14; "She may not eat anything that cometh of the vine, neither let her drink wine nor strong drink, nor eat any unclean thing."

Samson slew the lion of Arcanum XI with his hands, and later took honey from its carcass; honey being symbolically the nourishment the spiritual body receives from that creative purity represented by the highest work of the bee. In other words, Samson overcame his animal nature; and the bees, or creative attributes, utilized his virile powers to build up spiritual strength.

So long as Samson was pure his strength was boundless, but when he fell into sin his strength departed. Ju. 16:5; "And the lords of the Philistines came up unto her, and said unto her, Entice him, and see wherein his great strength lieth, and by what means we may prevail against him, that we may bind him to afflict him, and we will give thee, every one of us, ELEVEN hundred pieces of silver."

The three times Samson was bound and easily broke his bondage signifies that the power of purity prevails in physical, astral and spiritual realms. Hair is coincident with the age when sexual virility is attained, and Samson having been unshaved since his birth, indicates his natural ability, due to purity of life, to use his virile forces in a constructive manner. But Delilah was a harlot, and robbed him of his purity, shaved him of his constructive powers, and delivered him into the hands of his enemies, who put out his eyes, or spiritual sight, and the spirit of the Law departed from him.

Masonry

The Masonic degree known as the Heroine of Jericho is founded upon Arcanum XI. The scarlet line let down by the heroine, and the red handkerchief used in making the sign of the degree, denote feminine power.

The story is that by means of this cord two spies from Israel made their escape from their enemies in Jericho. It is symbolic of woman's creative periods, and signifies the spiritual escape from physical limitations that the higher use of their creative powers will bring to man and woman. They are here alluded to as spies in a foreign land because the physical plane which they occupy is a domain foreign to their spiritual estate.

Magic

In magic, Arcanum XI corresponds to thought-diffusion. This process, sometimes used maliciously, and sometimes used unconsciously, is a dominant factor in our political life, and is the means by which the so many occult absurdities and religious imbecilities are kept alive and gain a following.

Some strong, self-willed individual elects himself leader, and formulates some doctrine—political, occult, religious, or what not. This doctrine may, or may not, contain much of truth; and it may be an earnest conviction, or merely the means by which the leader hopes to further his own unscrupulous ambitions.

But in any case he attracts to himself other mentalities less dominant than his own, who unite with him in promulgating this doctrine. The combined thought-force radiates the thought-form of the doctrine outward with much force, and it reaches and dominates a number of receptive minds. These, in turn, convinced the doctrine is true, even though they have never subjected it to keen analysis, add their thoughts to the thought-form group. And in this manner, the dominant power of the thought-form overpowering reason through emotional energy, a chain is formed extending from the leader as the positive pole, through various links, to the masses as the negative pole.

Every additional person who accepts the doctrine and becomes its proponent makes its power stronger. As a snowball gains in size as it rolls down hill; so the thought-power of such a group of thoughts gains strength with each new adherent.

The viciousness of this thought-diffusion process is that it works so subtly. It attacks the unconscious minds of people quite unknown to themselves. The vast thought-power gives an emotional trend to the unconscious minds of the people it reaches, and this emotional element is often sufficiently strong to override any tendency to use reason or to bring to bear the critical faculties.

Thought-diffusion, minus the chain effect, is the kind of power used by a high-pressure salesman to sell a customer something for which the customer has no earthly use. But as employed by statecraft or by priestcraft, with the chain effect, it is used to sell the populace whatever ideas those in authority wish people to accept. And these ideas, all too often, are those that support decaying theological dogmas, those that keep people subservient to their exploiting rulers, or which cause Occidental students to accept, in spite of their logical absurdities, certain mystical follies from the Orient as a part of the real Secret Doctrine.

The real adept never utilizes such methods; and the only image he radiates systematically is his own ideal of himself in greater perfection than he has yet attained; and this ideal he receives through reflection, from his mate.

Initiation

In the soul's initiation Arcanum XI represents the spiritual and psychic powers that are the outcome of the neophyte's occult training.

His training, as well as the general trend of his life, has been to give greater refinement to his body, his thoughts, and his feelings. And as this change, denoted by Arcanum XI takes place, he becomes increasingly more potent to use his spiritual and astral powers; for the power of a force depends upon the plane from which it emanates, and the finer the organism the finer the force which it is capable of receiving and transmitting.

This refinement and training also increase the sensitivity of the psychic senses, enabling him to register and interpret vibrations quite outside the range of perception of the less developed man.

As shown by Arcanum XI, the animal nature must be entirely subdued; but it certainly must not be killed. Man is dependent for energy upon the attributes developed while in the lower kingdoms; but these energies, to be spiritual, must be diverted from animal expression into purely constructive channels. Not the suppression of the animal nature is real purity, but the use of all energy, sexual energy included, in channels which are constructive and aid others instead of merely benefiting self.

This Arcanum does not represent the repression, or destruction of sex; for every energy in existence is dependent for its potency upon polarity, or sex. The power of an electric current depends upon the difference in potential; that is, the difference between the positive pole and the negative pole. And a man or woman to be able to exert any real power must be strongly sexed. The more feminine a woman is, and the more masculine a man is, the more power they possess. The mistake here must not be made, however, of concluding that intellect and will are strictly masculine qualities. Mercury is convertible, and not the exclusive property of either sex. A woman may be an intellectual genius and still be strongly feminine, and a man may have strong tender emotions and still be masculine. But to have great power, as amply demonstrated by the outstanding people of the world's history, the individual must be strongly sexed.

Things have been accomplished by hermaphrodites; that is, by those of dual sex; but an investigation of such accomplishment discloses that these hermaphrodites were merely the mediumistic and negative instruments through which some other strongly sexed intelligence was able to manifest. The lack of individuality, the lack of character, and the lack of sex, alike give easy access to some dominant force, and encourage the expression of a multiple personality. But it hinders the development of individuality, makes for the disintegrative phases of mediumship, and precludes real soul development. Real power depends upon an energy controlled by the individual, and this energy has great dependence upon sex; but if it is a real power it must be projected from a high plane and only into constructive channels.

Occult Science

By divination the attention of the unconscious mind is directed to obtaining information which is not readily accessible to the objective consciousness through external channels. The psychic senses, thus directed, perceive the information sought. This information then resides in the astral brain like a memory. Then, through the divinatory process, whatever it may be, this memory residing now in the unconscious mind, is brought up into objective consciousness to be utilized in everyday affairs.

King Court Cards

Strictly speaking the king, queen and youth of each suit have a numerical value of 10 each; for they represent all of humanity, both men and women, as born under the twelve zodiacal signs.

Man alone, or woman alone, is represented by the number 5; but each king not merely signifies a man of given temperament, but also, when reversed, a woman of that temperament, thus giving two 5s, or 10 for the whole card. Either the king, the queen, or the youth, is numerically 10.

The kings represent the first degree of emanation of each zodiacal triplicity; the queens represent the reaction, or second degree of emanation of each triplicity; and the youths or product of action and reaction, represent the third degree of emanation of each triplicity.

The horsemen, however, do not represent people, but the thoughts of people. Thoughts are ruled by Arcanum I; therefore, each horseman has a numerical value of 1.

The King of Scepters signifies a person ruled by the sign Aries: fiery, headstrong, ambitious, courageous and energetic. Right way up it denotes an Aries man; reversed it indicates an Aries woman. The dominant idea is I AM.

The King of Swords signifies a person ruled by the sign Taurus: reserved, sullen and practical. Right way up it denotes a Taurus man; reversed it indicates a Taurus woman. The dominant idea is I HAVE.

The King of Coins signifies a person ruled by the sign Gemini: intelligent, restless, volatile and fickle. Right way up it denotes a Gemini man; reversed it indicates a Gemini woman. The dominant idea is I THINK.

The King of Cups signifies a person ruled by the sign Cancer: mild, reserved, home-loving and pleasant. Right way up it denotes a Cancer man; reversed it indicates a Cancer woman. The dominant idea is I FEEL.

The Martyr—Arcanum XII

Letter: Egyptian, Luzain; Hebrew, Lamed; English, L. Number, 12. Astrologically, the zodiacal sign Pisces. Color, the darker shades of purple. Tone, low A. Occult science, natural alchemy. Human function, sensing the spiritual aromas. Natural remedy, such herbs as mosses which grow in the water, ferns and seaweed. Mineral, the talismanic gem peridot; and such stones as sand, gravel, pumice and coral.

L—12 expresses in the spiritual world the revealed law.

In the intellectual world, the precept of duty.

In the physical world, sacrifice.

Remember, then, son of earth, that sacrifice is a divine law from which none is exempt; but expect any ingratitude from men. Always hold thy soul in readiness to render its account to the eternal. If Arcanum XII should appear in the prophetic signs of thy horoscope, a violent death will spread its snares upon the way. But if the world attempts thy earthly life do not die without accepting with resignation this decree of God, and pardon thy cruelest enemies; for whosoever does not forgive here below will be condemned in the next life to eternal solitude.

In Divination, **Arcanum XII** may be read as **Sacrifice** or **Expiation**.

Arcanum XII is figured by a man suspended by one foot from a gallows which is supported by two trees, each having six cut branches. His hands are tied together, forming a down-pointing triangle, above which one leg crosses the other in the form of a cross. From the hands gold pieces drop to the earth.

It is the sign of a violent death, coming unexpectedly by accident, or in the expiation of a crime, or accepted voluntarily through heroic devotion to truth and justice.

The twelve cut branches indicate the destruction of the twelve houses of the horoscope, signifying the extinction of life.

The cross above the triangle, a symbol the reverse of that on Arcanum IV, indicates that material forces have gained the ascendency and subdued the mind.

The coins dropping upon the earth signify wasted effort and the ebbing of the life forces. They also indicate that the efforts of the martyr who loses his life in furthering truth and justice are never lost, but remain on earth after he has passed. Ideals as yet unrealized persist in the astral about the earth until they contact some other person through whom they find suitable and more complete expression.

Number

Numerically, 12 being the second decave of 3, may be represented by Arcanum III expressing on the vibratory level indicated by Arcanum II. That is, union expressing on the negative plane, the result of which is depicted by Arcanum XII.

But it also has another aspect; for union may also be on the plane of science, as denoted by Arcanum II. And thus considered, Arcanum XII indicates that the science of union rests upon sacrifice and devotion; for selfishness is the antithesis of higher union. This thought, however, is perhaps better expressed by adding 3 and 9 to indicate union guided by wisdom; while the adverse significance is more completely denoted by 6 plus 6, indicating trials upon trials. The 8 plus 4 aspect is better; for it reads, justice realized.

Astrology

As the sign Pisces is the last sign of the zodiac, and rules the house of self-undoing, of expiation and crime, as well as sacrifice and disappointment, the astrological correspondence with Arcanum XII is obvious.

Human Function

As a symbol of religious devotion, or for the expiation of sin, it was anciently the custom to offer a sacrifice unto the Lord, or universal law. This taking of life and offering it upon the altar of expiation was to be a sweet savor unto the Lord. But its higher import was the implication of the sacrifice of the animal part of one's nature upon the altar of devotion to cosmic welfare, and that such sacrifice, through the aspirations which prompt it, nourishes the spiritual nature. Such exalted emotions, in addition to building a spiritual body, cause radiations to emanate from a man similar to those spiritual aromas which can alone be apprehended by the psychic senses.

Alchemy

Because life is short and the processes of the alchemical art take time, the variety of the ingredients which enter into transmutation becomes limited. Some such ingredients, therefore, which, had we more time, might be used successfully must be Sacrificed to the need of other ingredients. Thus are we compelled to exercise choice in their selection. This choice should be made only after careful analysis has revealed the quality of each, the effort at all times being made to retain that which already is far advanced and truly useful. When such a choosing becomes imperative the grosser metal must be

Sacrificed that we may retain the more refined.

Bible

Arcanum XII pictures Judas after he repented. Math. 27:5; "And he cast down the pieces of silver in the temple, and he went and hanged himself."

It also symbolizes the fig tree that was cursed for not being fruitful. Mark 11:20; "And in the morning, as they passed by, they saw the fig tree dried up from the roots."

The other aspect of this symbol is that of voluntary sacrifice instead of expiation. This is exemplified in the persecution and violent death of the apostles, and also in the conversion of the rich publican, Zacchaeus. In mythology it is Prometheus undergoing perpetual torment for his immortal theft of the divine fire from heaven with which to benefit humanity.

Masonry

Arcanum XII is represented by the ritual in the Christian Mark degree where the Grand Ministers execute the Judgment of the Lord and the candidate bewails his fate because his lips are unclean. Before conferring the mark, in some obediences, a live coal is taken from the altar and pressed to the candidate's lips to signify expiation.

Magic

Arcanum XII symbolizes the certain fate that ever follows those who use magical powers without discrimination. The cross above the triangle signifies that the magician has become the servant of the very elemental forces he sought to master. The practice of magic, unless with wisdom and unselfishness, inevitably leads to tragedy. And those who attempt to use sex in magic to attain selfish power merely fasten upon themselves evil elementaries that often force them to follow the example of Judas Iscariot and commit suicide in their attempt to get free from them.

The benefic side of the arcanum is this exposition of magical law: "Give all thou hast of breath, of power, or life, in just duty and lawful motive; expire honestly the corrupted or contaminated matter; and you shall instantly be filled with the celestial fire and become refined."

Initiation

Arcanum XII indicates the neophyte's absolute devotion to the cause of truth and progress. It exemplifies the summons of the Nazarene: "Go thy way, sell whatsoever thou hast, and give to the poor, and thou shalt have treasures in heaven; and come, take up thy cross, and follow me." Henceforth the struggling soul takes no thought what it shall gain personally by its efforts, but devotes its energy to assisting in the progressive evolution of creation; sacrificing life itself if necessary in the cause of truth and justice.

Occult Science

Natural alchemy embraces those processes which take place slowly in nature, but which man can hasten and utilize for himself if he possesses sufficient knowledge. To this end, therefore, he studies all the transformations that have taken place in the world; physical, biological, mental and religious, that he may perceive just what nature has thus accomplished. Having arrived at a comprehensive knowledge thus of relations of things to each other and to himself, he utilizes this information to bring those transmutations to pass which, in this new wisdom, he now most desires.

The Horoscope Spread

The diagram on page 88 of chapter 4 illustrates the principle that four signs always express the absolute and are explained by the fifth. The diagram on page 19 of chapter 1 shows how the five must move in a medium expressed by four signs, thus completing the number of deific manifestation, 9. But when we consider man, we find him the medium through which stellar forces act. So considered, the signs reverse and he is represented by cells 2, 4, 6, 8, and 9 in the diagram of chapter 1.

Furthermore, we know that everything possessing life is a trinity of positive, negative, and union, so that each of the active cells, 7, 1, 3, 5, shown in chapter 1 expands into a trine as indicated by the diagram on page 154. These are the twelve houses of life constituting a horoscope.

To use the diagram as a tarot spread the cards are dealt one by one upon the houses of the horoscope in the order indicated by the numbers in the diagram. The reading is used to foretell the near future of every department of life of the one making the consultation. The card falling upon any house of the chart will reveal the fortune of those things ruled by that house astrologically. The cards should be turned over only as read.

Trine 1—6—11 is the trine of life. 1 relates to personal things and health. 6 is the life of the mind, governing philosophy, publishing, and travel. 11 is the life of posterity, ruling children, love affairs, pleasures, and speculation.

Trine 2—7—12 is the trine of power. 2 is the power to attract honor and authority, ruling business, credit, and reputation. 7 is the power given by environment, governing sickness, servants, and labor. 12 is the power of wealth, ruling cash and personal property.

Trine 3—8—9 is the social trine. 3 is the society of partners, and rules the husband or wife, open enemies, and law suits. 8 is the society of kindred and thoughts, governing brethren, studies, writing, and short journeys. 9 is the society of associates, ruling friends and hopes.

Trine 4—10—5 is the trine of concealed things. 4 is the environment more or less concealed, ruling the home, real estate, and the end of life. 10 is the concealed things of death and fatality, ruling legacies and the partner's money. 5 is the concealed afflictions, governing disappointments, restrictions, and secret enemies.

A good card falling on any house signifies good luck in that department of life, and an evil card on a house signifies evil luck will come from the things it rules, the nature being shown by the card.

"Everything that has been, is, or will be, has its foundation and is built up, in four trines."

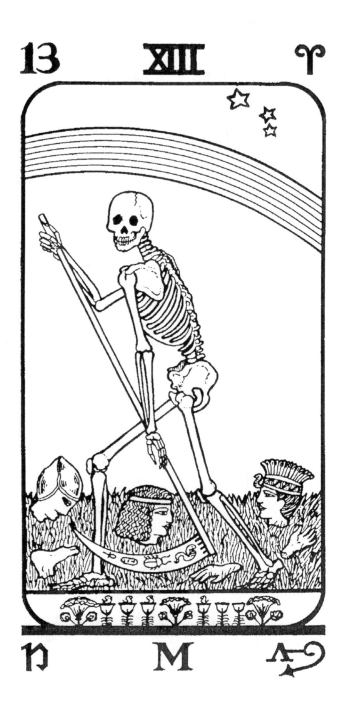

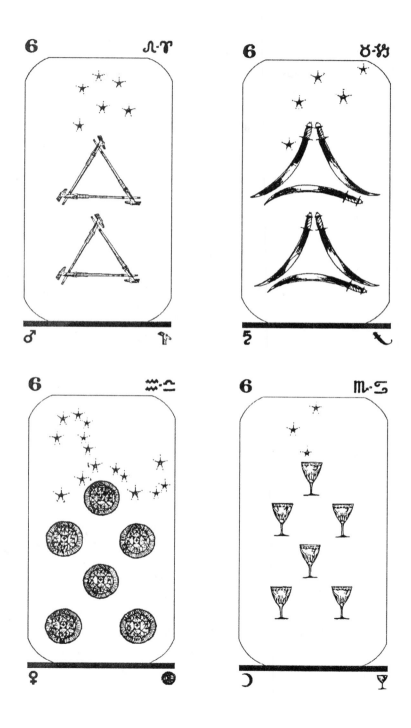

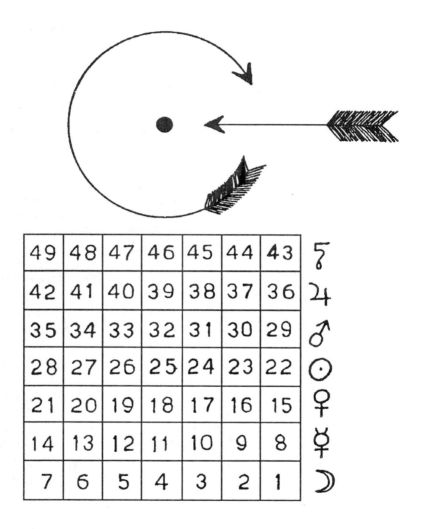

The Solar Spread

Chapter 9

The Color of a Name

PARACELSUS, one of the greatest physicians, and one of the most learned of occult students, several hundred years ago set forth the principle upon which depends the influence of a name, a number, a color, a musical tone, a locality, or other invisible vibratory rate.

He said: "If I have manna in my constitution I can attract manna from heaven. Saturn is not only in the sky, but also deep in the ocean and earth. What is Venus but the artemisia that grows in your garden, and what is iron but the planet Mars? That is to say, Venus and artemisia are both products of the same essence, while Mars and iron are manifestations of the same cause."

What you have in your constitution is mapped by your birth-chart. If you have the dynamic stellar structure in your astral body mapped by the position of the planet Mars powerful, you will, of necessity, attract events into your life of the nature of Mars; events of violence, either constructive or destructive in character. If you do not have much iron, or Mars, in your constitution, as shown by Mars occupying a weak house and having almost no aspects, you will not have aggressiveness nor much courage, and you will not attract violent events.

And what has been said of the Mars structure is also true of the other nine thought-structures mapped by the various planets, and of the twelve zones of the astral body mapped by the zodiacal signs. If the section of your astral form mapped by a particular zodiacal sign is shown to have much activity, as indicated by planets in the sign having many astrodynes, or by the ruler of the sign having many astrodynes, the department of life indicated by the house position of that zodiacal sign will come into unusual prominence all through your life. And thus it is that the type of events attracted to the individual depends exclusively upon the activity of the thought-cells within himself that have the same vibratory rates as these events. If the money structures and money zone of the astral body have considerable activity, money will enter the life as of considerable importance; but if the money structures and zone are weak, there will be neither large gains nor large losses, and money will not be as important a factor as some other of life's activities. If the structures and zone ruling marriage are unusually active, this phase of the life may dominate in importance all the other matters entering the life; but if they are passive, this department of life may prove of negligible importance.

Now any of these structures or zones mapped in the birth-chart can be given additional energy, and thus made more active than it normally is, through associating with things or thoughts of a similar vibration. Whether we will or no, some of them are thus given additional activity through the progressed positions of the planets.

There are three sources of invisible energies that have the power to stimulate the thought structures and thought-cells of our astral body into exceptional activity: astrological influences, the influence of thoughts, and the influence of objects. And when a planet by progression reaches a zone of the astral body, it gives its thought-cells new activity, and this attracts events corresponding to the department of life ruled by the zone into the life. In particular, when a planet by progression also forms an aspect to a dynamic thought structure in the astral body mapped by a planet in the birth-chart, the additional energy thus gained by the thought-cells enables them to attract some pronounced event into the life. And thus, from such progressed positions of the planets, and the dates when they make aspects with structures in the astral form, the astrologer is able to predict what events will transpire and when they will come to pass.

But progressed planets are not the only source of such additional energy that may be made available to thought structures and zones within the astral form. Both thoughts and objects have a similar power, though varying in the amount of energy contributed. In Course 9, *Mental Alchemy,* I have considered the deliberate use of certain types of thought, and in this course considerable attention has been paid to the use of abstract thoughts, such as names and numbers. And right here I wish to indicate how the character vibrations of colors may be employed in a similar manner.

Sound is caused by vibrations ranging from the 4th to the 12th octave of vibration, or from 16 to 32,768 vibrations per second.

Vibrations either slower or faster than these must be apprehended by other means than the ear. Electricity, for instance, which is not perceptible to either eye or ear, includes the 25th to the 35th octave, or from 33,354,432 to 34,359,738,368 vibrations per second.

Radiant heat, such as that coming to us from the sun, ranges from the 46th to the 48th octave, or from 70,368,744,644 to 281,474,976,710,656 vibrations per second.

The effect of these vibratory rates, as producing physical changes in our organism, is readily apparent. But there are other vibrations which have quite as pronounced an effect in producing physical results that are less easily discerned in their action. Thus, the chemical ray, used in photography and producing sunburn when we stroll the beach in scanty attire, belongs to the 50th octave of vibrations; and the X-ray, which without sensation burns tissue within the human body, belongs to the vibratory rates within the 59th to 61st octave.

Within the range of the 49th octave of vibration, around 562,949,853,421,312 vibrations per second, the rates of motion are perceived by the eye as light. This white light when refracted divides itself into vibratory rates slightly faster and slightly slower than the average, and these different rates give rise to the seven colors of the solar spectrum.

These seven colors, as ascertained by the effects they produce when associated with, each tend to stimulate, or add energy to, the structure within the astral form mapped by one of the planets of the septenary. And the various shades of these colors, produced by slightly higher or lower vibrations than the type color, are found to add activity to the zone of the astral body ruled by a zodiacal sign. Thus any color, or combination of colors, has an effect upon the astral body which can be determined from the correspondence of the color, or combination, to the zones and structures mapped in the birth-chart. These color correspondences, from which the structure or zone of the astral body stimulated can be ascertained, are given in the treatment of each major arcanum, and also in the table at the front of chapter 1.

Now as each letter, and each number below 23, has the same astral vibratory rate as the astral vibratory rate of some color, or its shade (the astral vibratory rate of a color must not be confused with the electromagnetic vibratory rate which affects the sense of sight), it is easy to find the color correspondence of any number or any name by first finding the vibratory key of the number or name, and then discerning to which color this key corresponds. In applying such correspondences it will be noted that the night signs of a planet correspond to the darker shades of the color ruled by the planet, and the day signs of a planet correspond to the light shades of the same type color.

Thus to find the color of the name, "Teddy": T-22, E-5, D-4, D-4, Y-10 added gives the number 45. 4 plus 5 gives 9 as the Key of the number, and by referring to Arcanum IX we find the color of this key to be light blue.

To find the color number 1918 we add 1 plus 9 plus 1 plus 8, which gives 19 as the Key to which it vibrates, and referring to Arcanum XIX we find the color to be light orange.

Thus by associating with the name Teddy there is the same kind of influence, but probably of different intensity, as that obtained by associating with the color light blue, such as wearing a light blue dress, or even a light blue necktie.

But the most important factor is yet to be mentioned. For while the type of event attracted is determined by the structure or zone of the astral form to which energy is thus added; whether the event will be favorable or unfavorable must be determined by how that structure is organized as shown in the birth-chart.

If the structure or zone as mapped in the birth-chart is shown to be decidedly discordant, adding energy to it (except as a mental antidote as explained in Course 9) gives it additional power to attract misfortune. Therefore, by names, by numbers, by colors, or by other means, pains should be taken not to associate with those astral vibrations that have the same rate as discordant conditions mapped in the birth-chart. Instead, those should be associated with which will add energy in large volume and intensity to such structures and zones of the astral body as the birth-map shows to be especially harmonious. Thus will more favorable conditions be attracted from without.

The Reaper—Arcanum XIII

Letter: Egyptian, Mataloth; Hebrew, Mem; English, M. Number, 13. Astrologically, the zodiacal sign Aries. Color, the lighter shades of red. Tone, high C. Occult science, mundane astrology. Human function, the sense of taste. Natural remedy, such herbs as hemp, mustard, broom, holly, dock, thistle, fern, garlic, onions, nettles, radishes, poppies, peppers and rhubarb. Mineral, the talismanic gem, amethyst, and such stones as ochre, brimstone and red stones of various kinds.

M—13 expresses in the spiritual world, the perpetual movement of creation; destruction and renewal.

In the intellectual world, the ascension of the spirit into divine spheres.

In the physical world, natural death; that is to say, the transition through which the soul leaves its physical form henceforth to function in an astral form in the astral world.

> *Remember, then, son of earth, that terrestrial things are of short duration and that the highest powers are reaped as the grass of the field. If Arcanum XIII should appear in the prophetic signs of thy horoscope, the dissolution of thy organs will come sooner than thou expectest. But do not dread it; for death is but the parturition of another life. The universe reabsorbs without ceasing all which springs from her bosom that has not spiritualized itself. But the releasing of ourselves from material instincts by a free and voluntary adhesion of our souls to the laws of universal movement constitutes in us the creation of a second man, a celestial man, and begins our immortality.*

In Divination, **Arcanum XIII** may be read as **Death** or **Transformation**.

Arcanum XIII is figured by a skeleton reaping human heads, hands and feet. On the blade of the scythe wielded by Time is a serpent and a scarabeus, and back of all is seen a rainbow.

The progression of the scythe in its work is the emblem of the perpetual destruction and rebirth of all forms of being in the domain of time.

The serpent on the scythe represents the virile energy that has carried the soul, symbolized by the scarab, in its pilgrimage of births and deaths through the mineral kingdom, the vegetable kingdom and the animal kingdom up to the estate of man.

The skeleton mowing human heads, hands and feet signifies that the thoughts, works and understanding of man eventually pass from the earth. But the rainbow promises a new life of thought, effort and knowledge in a superior realm.

Number

Numerically, 13 is the 2nd decave of 4, indicating Arcanum IV, or realization, operating on the negative plane of frequency of Arcanum II. It is what is Realized from the efforts of life when Polarizing forces disintegrate the physical body.

What this new plane of realization, to which the efforts have now been transferred, will offer, depends entirely upon how the energies have been used on the plane left behind. If this use can be represented by 9 and 4, the Realization of Wisdom, self-conscious progression gains momentum. But if the transition is only 10 and 3, Change of Action, 5 and 8, the operation of the Law of Justice, or even of 6 and 7, Victory over Temptation, the activities of life are merely transferred, without much gain or loss, to the inner plane.

Such transition is possible, however, as 1 and 12, Will directed to the Sacrifice of all selfishness, or as 2 and 11, under the Science of Spiritual Power. And when such is the case, the new life witnesses a great gain in freedom, in consciousness, in ability, and in enjoyment.

Astrology

Aries is the beginning of the zodiac, where the circle is completed and the cycle of one life ends in the start of another. When the Sun crosses the first point of Aries the astronomical year commences, and when it again crosses into Aries, that year is ended, cut off, destroyed. And thus is Aries, as indicated by Arcanum XIII, Brahma as well as Siva, both creator and destroyer.

Human Function

Life subsists upon life. The energy and substance of each physical organism is largely gained through the Death of others. To sustain the life of man there is a constant sacrifice of the lives either of plants or of animals. This life of the lower kingdoms, when taken into the body of man undergoes a Transformation by which it is made available for his use.

The cosmos depends upon the innumerable conscious entities embraced in it for expression and progression. And likewise man depends upon the innumerable cells of his body for expression upon the physical plane. Each of these cells is as independent of man as man is independent of the earth on which he lives. That is, each cell has its own individual consciousness, nor do the sum total of the cells comprise the man; for the man has a consciousness independent of these cells. Yet while these cells are a portion of man's anatomy they should each obey the dictates of man, just as man should obey the mandates of the Supreme Intelligence.

Even as man is undergoing a progressive cycle on the earth, so each cell in his body is undergoing its progressive cycle in association with him. Therefore, while the Death of the organism that serves as food liberates the soul that has polarized the protoplasm and energy contained in the form, this transition to the body of man is not without compensation to the life of the individual cells. For their substance and energy is now Transformed into cells occupying the body of man, and thus in association with an intelligence which affords them greater opportunity by far for evolutionary progress.

To the cell-life, at least, the serving as food for a higher form of life than that previously occupied is not without its advantages. And the human function by which man selects what shall thus be Transformed to his own use is the sense of taste, which corresponds to Arcanum XIII.

Alchemy

Arcanum XIII represents that Transformation which occurs in the substance and form due to transmutation. The fluxing of polar opposites or natural antidotes produces not merely a blend of the substances, but the Death of the old properties in the production of a new and more highly refined substance with entirely different properties. There is thus a Transformation of both the substance and the form.

Bible

As related in the 49th chapter of Genesis, Jacob, being about to die, called together his sons, who are the fathers of the 12 tribes of Israel. To each he gives his blessing, together with a prophecy; and this deathbed pronouncement reveals without error to any competent astrologer just which tribe is ruled by each zodiacal sign.

It should be evident, for instance, that when he speaks of Reuben being as unstable as water, that he refers to the Waterbearer, Aquarius, and the abrupt changes made by those in whose chart Uranus, its ruler, is prominent. Likewise, when he speaks of Simon and Levi as being brethren, he can be referring to no other sign than the Twins, Gemini.

That Judah is a lion's whelp must mean Leo, the Lion; and when he says that Zebulon shall dwell at the haven of the sea, he certainly refers to the home of the Crab, Cancer. Isaachar mentioned as a strong ass, is the sign Taurus; because Taurus rules donkeys as well as the Bull. And because justice is weighed in the scales of Libra, Dan, who shall judge his people, must belong to this sign.

Speaking of Gad, he says that a troup shall overcome him, but he will overcome at the last; because Scorpio has a multitude of desires, but has the power to divert them to a high purpose as symbolized by the Eagle, which also is a token of this sign.

That Asher shall yield royal dainties and his bread shall be fat, of course, indicates the food sign, Virgo; and Naphtali being a hind, or deer, or Goat, signifies Capricorn. So, too, when we read that in Joseph's bow abode his strength, we look for a bow among the signs, and find the Archer, Sagittarius.

Now Aries has a constructive and a destructive, or warlike, aspect; the latter being signified by the wolf, as when there is a wolf in sheep's clothing. So when we learn that Benjamin shall rave as a wolf, we know he belongs to Aries. And then when we come to Ephram and Manassah, we find that Ephram, who was the younger, was blessed first, contrary to customary usage, and that Manassah, who was older, was blessed later, thus indicating that at the end, or last sign, the dual sign Pisces, that the last shall be first and the first shall be last. This not merely signifies the sign of disappointments, but also indicates that the priesthood, who belong to this sign of Universal Brotherhood, should be willing, when necessary, to renounce worldly advantages for the good of mankind.

At the death of Jacob the twelve signs were thus represented, and Jacob himself, after delivering his blessings, was straitway gathered to his fathers, a Transformation such as is represented by Arcanum XIII.

The twelve disciples who were called by Jesus also represent the 12 zodiacal signs; Jesus making the 13th member, the lamb of God, or transitional influence of Aries.

He said on that occasion, Math. 26:23; "He that dippeth his hand with me in the dish, the same shall betray me."

Now of the four zodiacal quadrants the Scorpio, or Eagle, is represented by the suit of cups. Jesus is crucified on the autumnal cross of Libra, and was betrayed for 30 pieces of silver. And from the point where the sun is slain on the cross of Libra, the nights, or powers of darkness prevailing over the days, to the sign Scorpio, is just 30 degrees. Judas, therefore, is the sign of death, Scorpio, the realization of material forces, indicated by Arcanum IV, who betrays the sun into the winter signs; delivers the spiritual influence into the power of matter.

Judas later repents and hangs himself, as shown by Arcanum XII. This, however, but depicts the expiation of the sin; for Judas himself belongs essentially to Scorpio and not to Pisces.

The bread of the Lord's supper is the symbol of the physical nourishment that sustains the material body. The wine is token of the emotional nourishment which alone builds up the spiritual body and makes immortality possible. Man requires both forms of sustenance.

Because thirteen were gathered at the Lord's supper, and one passed on, even today some persons will not sit at a table where thirteen are present. To some it is an omen that one of them shortly will die.

But 13 is not merely the symbol of death and dissolution. It is the number of the vernal cross, of spring-time, of the sign Aries in which the sun commences a new cycle of life. It is thus also the promise of immortality; for the Sun God then arises from the tomb of winter. So while 13 means physical death to the vulgar, to the initiate it signifies more frequently the Death of Selfishness and Crystallization through the Sacrifice and Devotion signified by Arcanum XII; and the commencement of a new life through the Transformation of material desires into spiritual aspirations.

Masonry

In modern Masonry there are something like six degrees of the Cross, all dealing with some aspect of Arcanum XIII. But because in the zodiac there are two crosses, the vernal cross of Aries and the autumnal cross of Libra, these degrees of the cross have reference to both of them.

The Christian cross of crucifixion is Arcanum III, astrologically Libra. But there is also a militant cross of resurrection, Arcanum XIII, or Aries, symbolized by a sword, which in form is but an inverted cross, even as Libra and Aries are polar opposites in the zodiac.

The meaning of these degrees of the cross is that man is born upon the earth through generation, or Arcanum III, and is born into the next life through physical death; yet his real birth into a spiritual life is brought about through the Transformation of his animal tendencies into those that have for their chief object the welfare of the whole of cosmic society.

Magic

In magic, Arcanum XIII represents the ability to separate the astral body from the physical at will and use it as a vehicle to visit other parts of the earth, to visit the homes of the dead, or to explore the tremendous regions of space. It is that process which is referred to in Masonry as "travelling in foreign countries."

Various methods are employed to bring about this separation of the astral body from the physical without a break in consciousness. One of the safest ways is to go out during sleep, passing out through the pineal gland, retaining the consciousness by a realization all the while that one is dreaming, and holding to the recognition of things seen as a true astral experience. Full details of this method are set forth in the 11th Award MS.

Others quite successfully bring about this condition by gradually incapacitating the physical body and voluntarily slowing down the heart action. While lying in a relaxed state, and after thus slowing down the heart action, they induce a tremendous desire to move to some particular spot; and this, under such training, takes them out of the physical and permits them to maintain consciousness while moving about in the astral form.

Orientals commonly use mantrams, rhythmic breathing and a spiral swaying motion of the body to loosen the astral from the physical. The astral body by means of this method passes upward out the top of the head.

Mediums also leave the physical body during trance, and may bring back accounts of what has been seen on such journeys. But this method, because it is done under the influence of some controlling entity, is disintegrative and highly dangerous.

Such experiments are not to be undertaken lightly; and considerable precaution should be taken to protect the physical body from shock; as the too sudden awakening, or bringing back to the physical, is a great jolt to the nervous system, and might be so great as to sever the astral cord binding the finer to the grosser body, and thus result in death. Also some precaution should be taken that in case there is difficulty getting back into the physical that relatives do not conclude hastily that death has ensued and cause an untimely burial.

Initiation

The soul has its birth into the next life, just as it has its birth into this one. This new birth does not always coincide with the moment of physical death, for there is commonly a short or longer period of unconsciousness in transition.

If one is too strongly attached to the things of earth, and unable to relinquish the strong desires for them, he may be bound, for a time, close to the earth, and not awaken into the consciousness of the new life. Or one may have become so dominated by some idea that one lives in the image of this idea and for a time shuts out the reality by which he is surrounded. That is, until something or someone awakens him to a realization of his true condition, he may live in an imaginary world of his own thought-creation.

But whether one passes through the doorway to astral existence quickly or slowly, ultimately the time arrives when he awakens into full consciousness of his surroundings. This is the moment of his birth into the next life, and it coincides with his new astrological birth-chart.

Then comes the period of judgment, in which he is both judge and the one on trial. He perceives the actions of his life and the motives which prompted them. He finds, perhaps, that his progress now depends first upon rectifying certain mistakes made while on earth. And this he does either through contact again with those he injured, or at least through rendering some constructive service to others.

After a period of adjustment to next-life conditions he gravitates, or levitates, to the particular plane which corresponds to his own dominant vibratory rate. And on the plane where he now finds himself, whether high or low, depending upon his spirituality, he moves into the environment which corresponds to the harmonies and discords within his finer form.

But whether high or low, there is always opportunity for progress. There are works to be performed, joys to be experienced, and an even greater variety of interesting events than is possible on earth. But in this new realm money has no value. There is but one currency which is legal tender, and his progress and any assistance rendered him by others depends upon it. This currency of the next life is constructive service such as in some manner brings benefit to others.

Occult Science

The events which happen to nations, to cities, to communities, and to the world in general are chiefly shown astrologically in Cycle charts. These charts, by which the events that thus affect groups of people are predicted and explained, are chiefly those erected for the moment some planet has circled the zodiac and crossed from south to north declination.

The point of the zodiac where the sun thus crosses from south to north declination is always the first point of Aries, and thus the first point of Aries becomes the accepted symbol for the commencement of a new cycle. And as Mundane Astrology largely depends upon such cycles, it corresponds to Arcanum XIII, which pictures the sign Aries.

Queen Court Cards

The Queen of Scepters signifies a person ruled by the sign Leo: haughty, high spirited, ambitious and resolute. Right way up it denotes a Leo woman; reversed it indicates a Leo man. The dominant idea is I WILL.

The Queen of Swords signifies a person ruled by the sign Virgo: studious, rather even tempered, ingenious and witty. Right way up it denotes a Virgo woman; reversed it indicates a Virgo man. The dominant idea is I ANALYZE.

The Queen of Coins signifies a person ruled by the sign Libra; good, high minded, noble and amiable. Right way up it denotes a Libra woman; reversed it indicates a Libra man. The dominant idea is I BALANCE.

The Queen of Cups signifies a person ruled by the sign Scorpio: active, selfish, proud, resentful, reserved and thoughtful. Right way up it denotes a Scorpio woman; reversed it indicates a Scorpio man. The dominant idea is I DESIRE.

The Alchemist—Arcanum XIV

Letter: Egyptian, Nain; Hebrew, Nun; English, N. Number, 14. Astrologically, the zodiacal sign Taurus. Color, the darker shades of yellow. Tone, low E. Occult Science, Practical Occultism Applied to Daily Life. Human function, psychometry. Natural remedy, such herbs as daisies, dandelion, myrtle, gourds, flax, lilies, larkspur, spinach and moss. Mineral, the talismanic gem, moss agate; such stones as alabaster, white opaque stones and white coral.

N—14 expresses in the spiritual world, the perpetual movement of life.

In the intellectual world, the combination of ideas which create the moral life.

In the physical world, the combination of the forces of nature.

Remember, then, son of earth, to conserve thy forces, not to recoil at thy works, but in order to wear out obstacles, as water, falling drop by drop, wears away the hardest stone. If Arcanum XIV should appear in the prophetic signs of thy horoscope, a well formulated plan of action followed perseveringly will raise thee by degrees to the heights thou wouldst attain.

In Divination, **Arcanum XIV** is **Regeneration** or **Temperance**.

Arcanum XIV is figured by the genie of the sun holding a golden urn and a silver urn, and pouring from one to the other the conducting fluid of life. The genie is crowned with flame to indicate that it is a spirit; and its feet are winged to signify its rapid movements. The fluid transferred from one urn to another is the symbol of transmutation; and the eight rays of the sun which show behind the genie's head signify that the positive, or masculine, forces of the universe are exactly equilibriated by the negative, or feminine, forces. The cloak over the shoulder of the spirit indicates the perpetual fecundation of matter, as symbolized by the cloak, by spirit.

This ensemble pictures the combination and interchange of masculine and feminine forces throughout nature, working ceaselessly in all kingdoms, as the instigators and cause of all movements and life.

Number

Numerically, 14 is the second decave of 5, and thus represents the Law, Arcanum V, operating upon the next interior plane as signified by Arcanum II. As 5 is the dominion of man's intelligence over the physical plane, so 14 must be the dominion of man's intelligence over the astral plane.

Now 7 signifies the perfect nuptial union on the physical plane, the union of body, soul and spirit with body, soul and spirit. Therefore, the double 7, or 14, must signify the perfect union on the inner plane, the perfect regenerate union, in which the finer forces, as shown in Arcanum XIV, completely blend and fuse. And herein lies the secret of rejuvenation; for, in the exchange of these finer energies, controlled and directed by love, there is a power to restore and maintain youth and vigor.

Astrology

When, in the spring of the year, the sun crosses the vernal equinox and enters Aries, represented by Arcanum XIII, the forces of nature commence to move and new processes are set in motion within the laboratories of Isis.

But the solar force in Aries is not alone capable of regenerating the world; for such regeneration, or any other regeneration, requires also that the feminine forces shall be mixed with the masculine. This transmutation, therefore, is not celebrated at the vernal equinox, but on Easter, which can not occur until after the full moon has brought a partnership and exchange with the sun, from the natural sign of marriage.

This process, started at Easter, is carried forward as the Sun enters Taurus, the exchange of the finer forces fecundating the earth (Taurus) to bring forth the grass and flowers. For while Aries is the exaltation of the Sun, Taurus is the exaltation of the Moon, and the Sun moving thus into the exaltation of the Moon after the partnership has been formed carries forward the process of fructification. This process by which fecundity is assured is pictured in Arcanum XIV; and is thus associated with the sign Taurus; for the bull also is a symbol of fecundity.

Human Function

Already it has been shown that Libra, and Arcanum III, correspond to feeling in its external aspect. Libra is the sign of generation. The other Venus sign, Taurus, is the sign of regeneration, and rules the inner sense of feeling known as psychometry. Psychometery, therefore, is the human function corresponding to Arcanum XIV, which esoterically depicts the sign Taurus.

Alchemy

Arcanum XIV represents the fluxing of polar opposites, or mental antidotes. When the minerals are predominantly acid, or positive, just enough of the alkaline, or negative, minerals should be added to balance the mixture; and when the minerals are predominantly alkaline, just enough acid minerals should be added to balance the mixture. When positive and negative, acid and alkaline, male and female, energies are of like volume and intensity the ingredients readily fuse and undergo transmutation into a different and far more valuable product. But when either positive or negative elements are not thus balanced by their polar opposite, it takes more energy than can be generated to affect the transmutation.

Bible

The mystery of union as a spiritual force is set forth symbolically in the story of Jacob. First he wrestled with Temptation, as shown by Arcanum VI, and was Victorious, Arcanum VII. Then falling in love with Rachel, as symbolical of proper physical union he served for her 7 years. Gen. 29:30; "And Jacob served seven years for Rachel; and they seemed unto him but a few days, for the love he had of her."

But this perfect physical union signified by 7 did not suffice; for it relates that he was deceived into marrying Leah of the tender eyes. That is, his spiritual sight was not thus opened. Therefore, he served another 7 years for Rachel, the 14, as shown by Arcanum XIV, indicating regenerate union.

And so much more satisfactory was this higher fusion that in his great love for her he served voluntarily another 7 years. This 21, as shown by Arcanum XXI, designates the true spiritual fusion, the union of twin souls, the attainment of the Great Work.

In Math. 28:2, we have mention of the Transformation to a new life indicated by Arcanum XIII; "And, behold, there was a great earthquake; for the angel of the Lord descended from heaven, and came and rolled back the stone from the door and sat upon it." And following this, in Math. 28:18; this new life entered into, or Regeneration accomplished, Arcanum XIV, is indicated thus: "And Jesus came and spake unto them, saying, All power is given unto me in heaven and in earth."

Masonry

The Rosy Cross is but another method of expressing the process portrayed by Arcanum XIV. And the same principle is more briefly indicated by the compass. 14 is the second decave of 5; and when wine, symbolical of spirit, is added to the 5, as in the fifth libation of pure wine which is drunk from a skull—the skull represents Arcanum XIII—we again have the principle of regenerate fusion expounded, this time in ritualistic form. And as of universal application, instead of merely personal, Arcanum XIV is well rendered by the mystical letters, INRI, which more correctly stand as the initials of Igne Natura Renovature Integra, meaning, All Nature is Renewed by Fire.

Magic

Love manifests on all planes and in various degrees of grossness and refinements; for it is convertible as passion, enthusiasm, heat, affection, fire, deific solicitude. In truth, in some form of expression, it lies at the foundation of all activity, all intelligence, and all feeling.

As to man, there are three planes upon which his love-life can express while he is still embodied. And when we consider that the power of an energy to benefit or to destroy depends upon the volume liberated and the intensity of feeling which accompanies it, it should be apparent that grossness, lust and viciousness in sexual matters is one of the most destructive forces upon earth.

Yet as life depends upon harmony, and death follows in the footsteps of discord, when sex is actuated by mutual esteem, and mutual harmony results, it has even as great a building power. The harmonious exchange of energies between husband and wife tends to build health, to prolong youth, and to increase the vitality.

Then as to the offspring, the intensity of the father furnishes the vital force, and the intensity of the mother the magnetic constitution.

The general health is thus usually more dependent upon the mother than the father, but the length of life more dependent upon those vital energies furnished by the father. And upon a balance between these two, as shown by the Sun and Moon in the birth-chart, depends in great measure the discords and harmonies, the fortunes and misfortunes, of its life.

But Arcanum XIV treats of a plane above that indicated by Arcanum VII. It reveals the mysteries of regenerate love.

Regenerate love does not consist of any physical act, nor does it consist of refraining from any physical act. Instead, it is a blend and exchange of finer forces. This blend and exchange can take place between husband and wife even while they are far distant in space from each other. In fact, when properly established, there is a continuously consciousness of each other on the part of both, and the fusion is more or less continuous. It is the beautiful ecstatic union between two who are devoted to each other, and who feel the most tender emotions toward each other.

It is a pure and holy relation, and has nothing in common with the practices of certain mediumistic individuals who leave their body to dissipate themselves and express unrestrained passion while thus on the astral plane. All such practices are destructive, and once were features of the witch's sabbat. They are much more destructive, because more intense and less subject to control, than physical dissipation; and are harder to break off because of the magnetic bondage established.

Nor is the regenerate union a matter of forced celibacy; for this often stimulates to unnatural desires, and always leads to an unbalanced magnetic condition which is undesirable.

Instead, it is merely the complete fusion of the finer forces of two purified souls who are working together in loving harmony, and in tender sympathy, for the advancement of the race. This fusion may be broken at times through intruding discords from without, but is again established at the first opportunity, and is maintained as completely as possible.

Initiation

In the soul's initiation, Arcanum XIV indicates that state of advancement in which there is spirituality enough so that the animal desires and passions are transmuted into tender expressions of love which establish and maintain, with the matrimonial partner, a constant exchange of the finer energies. At this state of the soul's pilgrimage there still may be occasional physical expressions; but the chief and most satisfactory avenues for manifesting love are now purely in the ecstatic and devoted exchange of invisible forces.

Occult Science

Practical Occultism is the application of the knowledge concerning astrology, concerning psychology, concerning alchemy, and all other invisible properties and energies to the affairs of everyday life. As such it corresponds to Arcanum XIV.

The Solar Spread

The Solar Spread is based upon the 50 posts, or gates, of initiation. It thus depends upon correspondences to the seven active principles of nature which penetrate the seven departments of human endeavor, for its revelations. The spread as a whole constitutes the jubilee, or fiftieth factor.

The cards are shuffled and cut as usual, and then they are dealt from right to left in 7 rows of 7 cards each as illustrated on page 176.

The cards should be turned over as read, starting at the bottom row and reading from right to left.

When the birth-chart of the consultant is known, each row of 7 cards reveals those things that the planet ruling the row governs in his birth-chart. And in all cases the three cards to the right of the middle card in any row govern the past of the department of life, the middle card represents the present condition, and the three cards to the left of the middle card reveal the future developments concerning this department of life.

When the birth-chart is not at hand, or, if the reader is unfamiliar with astrology, each row is read as referring to the department of life generally signified by the planet in front of the row.

Thus the bottom row, as ruled by the Moon, governs the home, the domestic life, the public, and if the querent is a man, his wife.

The second row from the bottom is ruled by Mercury, and has rule over studies, travels, writing, papers, brethren and the fruits of intelligence.

The third row from the bottom is ruled by Venus, and relates to love, society, friends, partners, cash and art.

The fourth row from the bottom—the middle row—is ruled by the Sun and signifies the honor, health and vitality, and if the querent is a woman, indicates her husband.

The fifth row from the bottom is ruled by Mars and relates to accidents, antagonisms and enemies.

The sixth row from the bottom is ruled by Jupiter and refers to business, occupation, employment and religion.

The seventh row from the bottom—the top row—is ruled by Saturn and relates to elderly people, real estate, sickness, losses, sorrows and secret things.

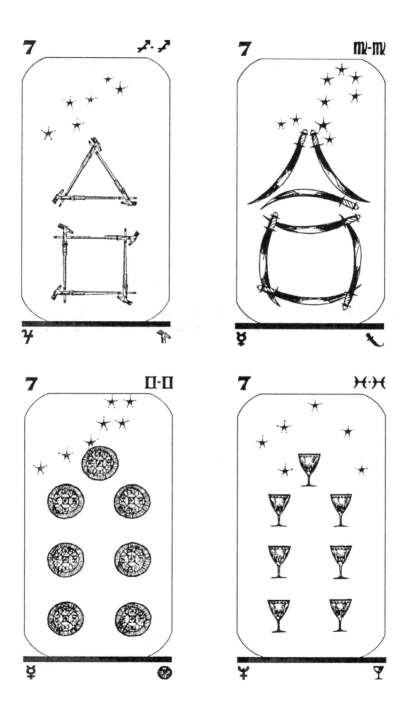

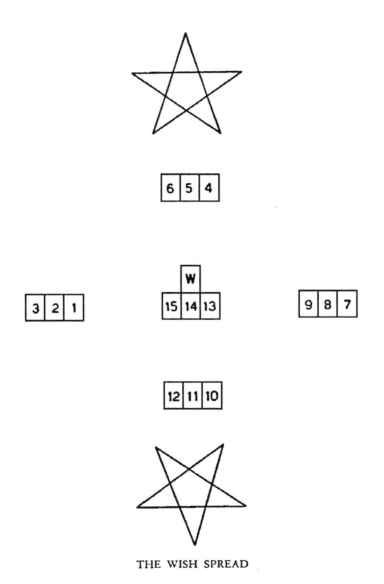

THE WISH SPREAD

Chapter 10 _____

Natural Talismans
and Artificial Charms

_____

O F THE three types of invisible energies which have a power to influence human life and destiny, I have already given consideration to those thought vibrations emanating from names and numbers. Trains of thought are more specifically treated, in their effect of changing the organization of the astral form and thus attracting certain types of events into the life, in Course 9, *Mental Alchemy*. Thus, in this and other courses, I have quite fully explained the use and effects of thought vibrations. And in Course 10-1, *Delineating the Horoscope*, I have gone into the subject of astrological vibrations. There remains yet to consider, therefore, only character vibrations.

The character vibrations of localities, climates, and types of environment are set forth in Chapter 5 of Course 8, *Horary Astrology* and Chapter 2 of Course 12-1, *Evolution of Life*; the character vibrations of plants and minerals are stated in connection with the various Arcana in this course; and the character vibrations of colors are explained more specifically in chapter 9 of this course.

Now, of course, the subject of character vibrations is as wide as the universe itself; for every object and condition has its vibratory rate, which may influence those associated closely with it. We, therefore, can not hope to exhaust this subject; but I feel that some mention, at least, should be made of the vibratory quality of musical tones; and that, because of their unusual potency, both artificial charms and talismanic gems should receive special consideration.

Musical Tones

Music has two influences. The first is that which influences the mind through its suggestive power, reaching it through the physical sense of hearing. The rhythm, harmony and melody thus reaching the consciousness stir up emotional states and physical responses. Whether certain music is beneficial or not depends upon the individual. If it stimulates gross and selfish, or destructive, thoughts and feelings, it is detrimental to the individual. But if it engenders feelings of tenderness, the desire for helpful service, and aspirations to a noble life, it is beneficial.

But the tones of a musical composition have an astral vibratory rate as well as a physical one. The chief vibratory rate, and the one that thus has most influence directly upon the astral body, is that of the Key in which the composition is played. This key is itself a musical tone; for instance, the Key of C. The Key of C has an astral vibratory rate which is the same as that radiated by the planet Mars, or by the letter O. The direct astral effect of a tone, or of a musical composition played in the Key of that tone, may be known by referring to the tone associated with each Major Arcanum.

Talismanic Gems

Talismanic gems differ from artificial charms in that the influence of a talismanic gem is that of its character vibration, while the influence of a charm is almost wholly due to the thought vibration imparted to it.

Gems are particularly active crystals which have been attracted about lively and energetic souls occupying the evolutionary plane of the mineral kingdom. The active life of the astral form of the soul occupying a gem reflects itself somewhat in the brilliancy of the gem. And due to the high degree of astral intelligence possessed by certain kinds of gems, and due to the powerful character vibrations which they radiate, they become among the most important of all character influences with which we can associate, in their power to impart energy to the structure or zone of the astral body of a person closely associated with them.

Now a birth stone is merely a gem ruled by the zodiacal sign occupied by the Sun on the day of birth. And because the dynamic thought structure in the astral body mapped by the place of the Sun in the birth chart is a very powerful thought group, a gem ruled by this sign, when worn, through adding energy to the structure mentioned, undoubtedly is rather powerful to influence the life.

But, as pointed out when discussing other things which add

astral energy to structures and zones of the astral body, whether this
rather powerful influence will increase the power to attract good
fortune or will increase the power to attract misfortune, depends
upon whether or not, as shown by its aspects, the Sun structure thus
given power is harmoniously or discordantly organized.

The rising sign, also, corresponds to very strong thought cells
within the astral body. Consequently, a gem ruled by the rising sign
in the birth chart has a powerful influence upon the person. The
intensifying of these thought cells lends itself to a more energetic
personality. This may have its advantages. But whether such a gem
will attract harmonious or inharmonious events through the greater
energy of the personality depends on whether or not the rising sign
in the birth chart is harmonious or discordant.

Furthermore, because certain stellar structures and zones of the
astral body, as shown by the house positions of the birth chart, tend
more to influence certain departments of life, and other structures
and zones to influence other departments of life, either a gem or a
person taken into close association adds energy to the thought cells
of the astral body in that zone which accentuates a given department
of life. That is, either a gem or a person adds energy to the astral body
of the one associated with it chiefly in that compartment ruled by the
dominant astrological influence of the gem or person. Therefore, in
selecting a talismanic gem, or any associate, this should be kept in
mind, and such should be chosen as will add energy to the particular
department of life where help is most desired.

If the gem is desired, for instance, as an aid to business success,
it should have the same character vibration as the sign or planet in
the birth chart most harmonious to business. If the gem is desired as
an aid to matrimonial harmony, one should be worn having the same
character vibration as the sign or planet in the birth chart most
harmonious to matrimony. But for general purposes, a gem may be
selected that has the same character vibration as the best planet or
sign in the birth chart.

A word of caution should be inserted here; for jewelers who are
not occult students, and have only a desire to push the sale of
whatever gems they may have in stock, sometimes get up a list of
birth stones according to their fancy and their particular need for
sales. That is, having heard of birth stones, but having no actual
knowledge of astrology, they give certain stones to certain months
with no real information on the subject.

The gem given to each zodiacal sign, in association with the

Major Arcana, is the one which, according to the ancients and according to competent occult students who have checked as to accuracy, has been found most potent as having the character vibration of that sign. To these gems listed under the Major Arcana should be added these other available gems which most powerfully have the character vibrations of the planets:

Sun—Sunstone.
Moon—Moonstone.
Jupiter—Chinese Jade.
Mars—Hematite.
Venus—Red Coral; also Amber.

Artificial Charms

Charms do not owe their potency to their character vibrations, but to the thought vibrations imparted to them in their preparation. Therefore, the substance used in the making of charms should be mediumistic, in the sense of receiving and retaining thought influences.

We all know that a piece of iron, a knife blade or a nail, for instance, if rubbed repeatedly with a magnet, takes on the magnetic condition and itself becomes capable of attracting and holding other objects. In like manner certain other metals—chiefly gold, silver, copper and tin—have the ability to take on, retain, and exert the influence of, a thought vibration imparted to them. That is, whatever thought influence is imparted to them with proper ceremony and at proper time, becomes a part of the charm, and the charm henceforth radiates this thought influence, whatever it may be.

Metals, unlike gems and stones, are very negative, and radiate almost no character vibrations; but they readily, for this reason, absorb thought vibrations that may be imparted to them. Organic substances, also, may be used in the manufacture of charms, if pains be taken to select only those which, like the young sprouts of peach, willow and witchhazel, are negative in quality.

The black magician usually makes his charms of organic substances of revolting character and in grotesque form, the symbolism thus tuning him in on the type of invisible force he wishes to attract and use. To this inversive image—as in voodoo rites—he attaches a diabolical thought form by means of ceremonies and invocations to the spirits of evil; the hideousness of the rite exciting the mind to fever pitch and releasing emotional energy of sufficient volume and intensity to impregnate the charm with the sinister thought and attach to it elemental forces. The fate of those who make such charms as this is well depicted in Arcanum XVI.

Evil charms, however, are not always the outcome of design; for mediumistic substances often absorb the mental images unconsciously impressed upon them. Houses in which there has been great mental anguish, or terrifying emotions associated with tragedy, sometimes become so permeated with these thought forms as decidedly to be uncomfortable, and even unlucky, for subsequent occupants. For this reason rooms in which there has been much sickness and suffering should not be occupied, without special purification and ceremony, by sensitive persons.

Certain famous jewels, though not in themselves especially mediumistic, and therefore not particularly suited to becoming charms, nevertheless, through tragedies associated with them, have come to exercise such an evil function. The emotional activities accompanying the tragedy have attached to the gem a vicious elemental, which is not the astral counterpart of the gem, but an added intelligence of malignant potency which guards it and brings misfortune to all who possess it. Such is the Hope diamond. And as probably bearing a more deliberate curse, are the treasures taken from the tomb of the Egyptian, Tut-Ank-Amen.

For ordinary purposes of making a fortunate charm, 14k gold or sterling silver is excellent. For special purposes a charm for a man may be made of 21k gold, 1k silver, 1k copper and 1k tin; and a charm for a woman may be made of 21k silver, 1k gold, 1k copper and 1k tin. The silver in the gold charm and the gold in the silver charm are responsive to the feminine element in man and the masculine element in woman; while copper and tin exercise the functions denoted by the planets Venus and Jupiter, the love element and the devotional.

Such a charm should be made only for some constructive purpose which can injure no one. The thought the charm should carry should be imparted to it with due ceremony and with as much high emotional intensity as possible, at midnight (completing the ceremony just before that time) of the full moon (the midnight that occurs just previous to the Moon making its opposition to the Sun). If the Moon is in a negative sign, so much the better.

Whatever thought is thus imparted to the charm, it will carry, and impart to the wearer. And it is potent to bring good luck, or any certain type of event into the life of the wearer, in proportion to the clearness and the intensity of the thought thus imparted to it.

The Black Magician—Arcanum XV

Letter: Egyptian, Xiron, Hebrew, Samek; English X. Number, 15. Astrologically, the planet Saturn. Color, blue. Tone, G. Occult science, weather predicting. Human function, the physical body. Natural remedy, naturopathy. Mineral, lead.

X—15, expresses in the spiritual world, predestination.
In the intellectual world, mystery.
In the physical world, unseen fatality.

Remember, then, son of earth, that the most unprofitable thing in the world is selfishness. Pride and rebellion but enchain the soul to lower spheres; but all trials and misfortunes accepted with resignation to the supreme Will are an accomplished progress bringing an eternal reward. If Arcanum XV should appear in the prophetic signs of thy horoscope, cease to rely upon thy own power and wisdom and labor to disengage thyself from pride and selfishness, which but bind thee to matter, mortality and evil Fate.

In Divination, **Arcanum XV** may be read as **Fatality** or **Black Magic.**

Arcanum XV is figured by Typhon, genius of evil, standing triumphantly over the ruins of a temple. In his right hand he holds a scepter surmounted by a circle resting between two divergent bars. These spreading bars signify the inversive forces that hem in and hamper the influence of spirit, represented by the circle. It is the emblem of hatred and division.

In the other hand this creature holds the torch of destruction, whose blaze has been applied to the ruins of the temple. He is crowned with flame to indicate he is not of this world, and he has the wings of a bat, to indicate he is a denizen of the realm of darkness. The horn on his nose signifies stubborn rebellion.

He has the breasts of a woman and the organs of a man, and is thus hermaphrodite, emblem of self centeredness and a being devoid of love. The body is that of a hog, to denote greed. The feet are those of a goat, to indicate the sign Capricorn, the home sign of Saturn, or Satan; the sign most devoted to material ambitions. And the beings chained at the feet of this master of chaos also have goat heads, indicating that their intelligence has been used exclusively to further material and selfish ambitions.

This malignant entity has the head of a crocodile, symbol of cruelty. The snake emerging from his body, instead of from his brow, indicates the use of the creative energy, not for enlightenment, but for physical gratification. It also represents mediumship, rather than conscious control; for the chief center of power in disintegrative mediumship is the solar plexus.

The two men with goat heads chained by the neck at the monster's feet represent the certain fate that awaits all who use magical powers to attain selfish or purely material ends. Sooner or later they become slaves of the very forces they have used, and are finally completely destroyed in body and mind; and even after passing to the next life, are chained by their evil deeds in the underworld.

All such evil entities, of this plane and the next, survive by preying on the ignorance and credulity of others, as shown by the sign of sorcery they make with their hands. They are racketeers and gangsters of both planes; and the ensemble, taken as a whole, indicates both the bondage and the fate of those who follow the inversive path and become dominated by the spirit of selfishness.

Number

Numerically, 15 is the second decave of 6. Arcanum VI represents Trial and Temptation, and Arcanum II, being negative, may bring a yielding to such temptation to use invisible energies to gain personal ambitions at the expense of others. 15, therefore, in this sense, is the number of black magic. 5 is the religious hierophant, indicating the intellect dominating the elemental world. But adding 10 brings a change in fortune; and if this change of fortune precipitates the master from his height, the 5 is reversed, and the elemental world dominates the intellect. Thus the higher the station the farther the fall, and when such fall occurs, the exalted priest becomes a prince of evil, and is then represented not by 5, but by 15.

Astrology

I suppose, from a very extensive study of birth charts and the influence of progressed planets in the lives of people, that the influence of the planet Saturn coincides with at least one-half of the total of all human suffering and misfortune. He is the planet of crafty selfishness, and, more than any other planet, seems to represent inexorable fate. He well corresponds to Arcanum XV.

Human Function

The physical body is man's universe of matter. It is the external vehicle through which the soul gains experience and manifests its developing attributes. It should always be governed by consideration of what actions, thoughts and feelings contribute most to universal progression. But, alas; all too often it is made merely the seat of animal gratification and the organ by which to gain purely selfish ends. As the most external of man's forms, and thus the least spiritual, the physical body corresponds to the planet Saturn, and to Arcanum XV.

Alchemy

Arcanum XV is the impure ingredients which must be eliminated in any type of alchemy. In mental alchemy they are the discords which are annulled. In spiritual alchemy they are the material effects as distinct from the influence on the character. And in general this Arcanum represents the dross which rises to the surface of the fluxed mixture as a skum, or excess slag, which must be skimmed off and cast aside.

Bible

All the various references to Satan give us the picture of Arcanum XV. Thus, Math. 8:31; "So the devils besought him, saying. If thou cast us out, suffer us to go away into the herd of swine." So the forces obsessing these men passed into swine, or were symbolized by swine, because of their greed. And their dashing down a steep place to perish in the sea well depicts the condition and the end of those who are ruled by selfishness; their affinity for evil forces precipitating them into frightful practices that are supported by abandoned emotions, and which, sooner or later engulf them in an ocean of misery.

Arcanum XV is also the star of religion inverted: Rev. 8:10; "And a third part of the waters became wormwood; and many men died of the waters, because they were made bitter." That is, the emotions of men became corroded by selfishness.

Rev. 9:1; "And the fifth angel sounded, and I saw a star fall from heaven unto the earth; and to him was given the key of the bottom-less pit, as the smoke of a great furnace; and the sun and air were darkened by reason of the smoke of the pit." Thus is described in accurate symbolism the slums and hells of the astral region, and the works that emanate from these regions.

Some maintain that the inversive brethren can have no organization, but they are certainly misinformed. These entities are, in truth, the racketeers and gangsters of the life after death. Even on earth bandits and gangs have their organizations and their leaders. And such parasites on society when they pass to the other side retain all their evil propensities and their cunning. They are human beasts of prey, that hunt down and try to destroy the defenseless.

Their chief method of getting victims is through having ideas widely accepted that are untrue and which place people in their power. To get these ideas thus widely accepted, they have recourse to thought dissemination, to the suggestive power of repetition, to insinuations, to platitudes, and to inversions.

Inversion is a method of presenting some idea in a manner that the lie is deeply and inconspicuously concealed amid much truth. The more real the facts, and the more widely they are recognized as facts, the better they afford cover for some cunning lie. The inversive twist, by which the whole matter is made to appear to have a meaning exactly the opposite of its true purport, is made to occupy so small a portion of the whole presentation, and is so cunningly concealed by sophistical handling, that it escapes the notice of all but the most acute. And this inversive twist—the misinformation or misinterpretation—is so worded as to be subject to no direct and simple test of accuracy. It is left as full of loopholes as possible, so that when one presentation of the matter is proved to be a lie, it can be said that, after all, something else was meant.

These inversions, having their origin in the astral hells by those who would prey upon the credulity of the human race, are well symbolized by smoke arising from the pit to darken the sun and air. And St. Paul recognized this invisible influence when he says, Eph. 6:12; "For we wrestle not against flesh and blood, but against principalities, against powers, against the rulers of the darkness of this world, against spiritual wickedness in high places."

Masonry

In the Past Master's degree, the power of the forces indicated by Arcanum XV are represented by a riot when the candidate attempts to preside over the lodge and is dethroned. The Secret Master's degree is represented by Arcanum XIV. But the Master's Elect of Fifteen degree is indicated by Arcanum XV, in which the ruffians who assassinated Hiram Abiff are overtaken and captured. They attempted to take passage to Ethiopia, the dark underworld region, but were overtaken and paid the penalty.

Magic

In Magic, Arcanum XV indicates all those methods by which the selfish and evil strive to gain control of others, to exploit them, and to make them their slaves. This subject is elaborated in detail in Chapter 6 of Course 18, *Imponderable Forces*.

But here it is convenient only to point out that as soon as some religion, some political doctrine, or some philosophy gains a goodly following, that the common course is for it to fall into the hands of those who use it for their own selfish interests.

There are those on both planes who have powerful intellects, but no spirituality. They are intelligent beasts of prey, having no sympathy, and no kindly feelings for others. They are dominated by a greed for power, and permit nothing in heaven or earth to stand in the way of their ambition.

By means of thought diffusion—by sending out powerfully charged thoughts, they dominate weaker thoughts, and thus collect them as a snowball gathers in size as it rolls down hill—they gain acceptance of certain ideas, which are utterly false, but which are advantageous to themselves. They worm themselves into the highest positions of authority by showing power of leadership. And as soon as they reach a position where they can do so they begin to betray their trust by warping ideas and twisting truths, so that doctrines which were once spiritual and pure become the very reverse of this.

Christianity at start boldly set out to renounce the sword, and to be purely socialistic in its regard for money and property. But as soon as it gained sufficient following those came into control who made it a religion whose followers are noted for seeking power and worldly goods, and who carried, by means of torch and sword, their religion into every land. With rifle bullets to back them they thrust the Christian religion down the throats of weaker and less organized people the world over, and made them trade for their merchandise, greatly to Christian profit. The missionaries have been pioneers of trade, backed by soldiers, and later have been instruments for keeping the doors of trade open.

The bloody crusades were for the purpose of establishing the religion of peace and good will by means of the sword. And Christianity, as witnessed by the world wars, continues to tolerate the murder of one nation by another. I am not commenting on whether war is necessary, or whether the preachers did right in praying that God would help their soldiers kill the enemy. I am merely pointing out, that right or wrong, the original teachings of Christianity, as soon as the religion grew strong, were twisted to mean just the opposite of their original intent.

Confucianism was originally merely an interpretation of the Tao, but it degenerated into a political lever used to persecute those who followed other doctrines. Mohammedanism was to abolish priests and rituals, but in after times these returned. Buddhism now, having been practically driven from India, teaches many things diametrically opposite to its early doctrines, and like Brahmanism in India, is a great political power.

Perhaps no doctrine was ever concocted and forced on a people quite so successful in keeping them servile and in despoiling them as Brahmanism and its caste system, based on the doctrine of human reincarnation. Through investing the priesthood with the authority to say what acts give good karma and what acts bad karma, and the belief in its followers that bad karma is responsible for all the ills of life, and that doing anything the priests forbid condemns the individual to suffer in the next human incarnation, it places an absolute power in the hands of the priests which they use to enslave the people while themselves living in luxury.

The effort is made also, in certain quarters, to discourage a belief in a self conscious, progressive, enjoyable life after death. It is taught we must return to earth to gain experience, over and over again. But the evidence of this inversion is too strong. Thousands are proving for themselves that their loved ones still live in full consciousness, and can, under specific conditions, yet communicate with those on earth.

But behind all these inversions, stands the cunning, destructiveness and selfishness of those on both planes, who, in some manner, profit by confusing and deluding men.

Initiation

In the soul's pilgrimage Arcanum XV represents the meeting with the Dweller on the Threshold.

This threshold dweller is Selfishness, and can only be overcome by a rigid determination to live for the good of the whole and its progress, rather than for self. When the individual decides, no matter where the path leads, to step only in the direction of universal progress, to work only constructively, he meets the grim dweller of the threshold.

You may be sure that racketeers and gangsters on either plane resent with tremendous venom the rescue of victims from their clutches. Those who attempt to enlighten their brethren, consequently, often suffer vile persecution.

Savanarola and other noble martyrs, were liberators of mankind from dark ignorance, and paid for it with suffering. Martin Luther was not dreaming when he threw his ink well at the devil; and he meant vastly more than appears on the surface when he announced he married to please himself, to vex the Pope and spite the devil. For where love is not, selfishness rushes in to fill the void; and ascetism, through extinguishing the finer emotions, prevents the building up of spiritual strength. Intellect alone can not build a spiritual body. It is feeling that creates. And the ascetic crushes out the very emotions of sympathy and kindness, of love and devotion, which otherwise would build an immortal vehicle for his soul.

Occult Science

Weather predicting is the science of forecasting, chiefly by means of astrological charts and positions, what weather will prevail on a given date. As influencing weather, especially weather of severe character, the planet Saturn seems most important. Therefore, this science corresponds to Arcanum XV.

Youth Court Cards

The Youth of Scepters signifies a person ruled by the sign Sagittarius: benevolent, free, jovial, quick tempered, energetic and fond of outdoor sports. Right way up it denotes a Sagittarius man; reversed it indicates a Sagittarius woman. The dominant idea is I SEE.

The Youth of Swords signifies a person ruled by the sign Capricorn: crafty, subtle, reserved and avaricious. Right way up it denotes a Capricorn man; reversed it indicates a Capricorn woman. The dominant idea is I USE.

The Youth of Coins signifies a person ruled by the sign Aquarius:

witty, argumentative yet amiable, artistic, humanitarian and fond of refined society. Right way up it denotes an Aquarian man; reversed it indicates an Aquarian woman. The dominant idea is I KNOW.

The Youth of Cups signifies a person ruled by the sign Pisces: negative, timid, listless, harmless, and much influenced by those about him. Right way up it denotes a Pisces man; reversed it indicates a Pisces woman. The dominant idea is I BELIEVE.

The Lightning—Arcanum XVI

Letter: Egyptian, Olelath; Hebrew, Ayin; English, O. Number, 16. Astrologically, the planet Mars. Color, red. Tone, C. Occult science, Stellar Diagnosis and Stellar Healing. Human function, the animal soul. Natural remedy, thermo-therapeutics. Mineral, iron.

O—16, expresses in the spiritual world, the chastisement of pride.

In the intellectual world, the exhaustion of the mind which attempts to penetrate the mystery of God.

In the physical world, the ruin of fortune.

Remember, then, son of earth, that only God is absolute. If Arcanum XVI should appear in the prophetic signs of thy horoscope, reflect on the old oaks that have defied the ravages of time and have finally been brought down after a century of immunity; and think that thou too mayst be brought low at the very moment of thy great arrogance by some unexpected blow.

In Divination, **Arcanum XVI** may be read as **Accident** or **Catastrophe**.

Arcanum XVI is figured by a pyramid decapitated by a thunderbolt. A crowned and uncrowned man are precipitated from a platform built of seven stages, falling down with the rest of the debris.

A pyramid is the most stable of solids, is the symbol of the earth, and also represents the climax of earthly security. As composed of four trines, which are its sides, corresponding to the houses of a birth chart, it symbolizes the horoscope of physical life. From mineral up to man there are seven degrees of mundane life, the seventh, or last stage of incarnation, being that of man. After one incarnation of man, and thus gaining self consciousness, the soul continues its progress in higher-than-physical spheres. Thus the platform on which the men were standing represents the last incarnation in matter.

That the pyramid has been struck by lightning to the disaster of both a crowned and an uncrowned man, symbolizes that Nature is no respecter of persons, and that she strikes down both the high and the low, kings as well as subjects, who transgress her law. It is also the symbol of those rivalries which are so common among men, which divert energies into channels that result in ruin for all. It signifies sterile projects, ill considered enterprises which are doomed to failure, ambitions which are frustrated, and death by catastrophe. And it represents the false security which results from material success and the reliance upon purely material science, as well as the sure punishment which is attracted ultimately by all those who use magical forces in the attainment of selfish ends.

Number

Numerically, 16 is the second decave of 7, and thus represented by Arcanum VII, or complete physical union, used on the negative plane of Arcanum II. In this aspect it indicates the power of sex to destroy, when actuated by any motive other than love. Lust, selfish gratification with no care for the feelings of the other, union actuated by desire for gain, and union in the practice of magic, all generate a force, but this force is destructive in quality. Sex magic, in particular, generates a frightful force, but, as indicated by 8 plus 8, in the end reacts on the user and brings to him a violent punishment.

Astrology

Astrologically, Mars is the planet of passion, of war, of violence, of accident, of sudden destruction. As such it is well portrayed by Arcanum XVI.

Human Function

A great deal is said in condemnation of the animal propensities that so frequently crop out in the actions of men. But these animal propensities are merely men's most valuable assets in a state of undevelopment. They should not be encouraged to express their animal activities, it is true, yet without them to furnish energy, still higher functions would have no power.

Nature has been at great pains to develop those qualities which lead to self preservation and race preservation. These qualities are selfish, having been developed through the struggle with other forms of life, for survival. But even though they are, on the animal plane, self centered, and dedicated largely to the destruction of enemies and the gaining of sustenance with no thought as to the consequence to others, nevertheless, in order thus to preserve and provide for self and family, creatures have developed initiative and an energy supply. This energy supply and aggressiveness is the force behind the animal soul of man, to which Arcanum XVI corresponds.

Yet without this animal energy man would have no force, would be able to accomplish nothing. The animal propensities are the sole source of his energy, they are the reservoir from which he must draw for any spiritual accomplishment. Intellectual force may be on the plane of the animal, seeking selfish ends, or on the plane of the spiritual, seeking good for all. But while man is still in the flesh, even spiritual energy must draw its force from the volume of energy developed by the animal; transmuting it merely, that is, diverting it from a selfish to an unselfish, purpose. Therefore, before there can be a vigorous divine soul, or a vigorous spirituality, there is usually present a vigorous and active animal soul.

Alchemy

In Alchemy, Arcanum XVI represents the heat of the reverberatory furnace. This, on the mental plane, is supplied by feeling, the feeling of pleasure or pain. On the spiritual plane it is supplied by a still higher type of feeling, by aspiration and inspiration; and in its highest manifestation it arises from an insatiable longing to assist to the highest possible degree in the advancement of the universe and the happiness and joy of all forms of life.

Bible

Elijah built an altar of twelve stones, represented by the four triangular sides of the pyramid of life shown in Arcanum XVI. Kings, 18:38; "Then the fire of the Lord fell, and consumed the burnt sacrifice, and the wood, and the stones, and the dust, and licked up the water that was in the trench." The fire is seen thus falling in the Arcanum under consideration.

Sex magic also is mentioned in Revelations, and the destruction of all those who follow such practices: "Mystery, Babylon the Great, the mother of harlots and abominations of the earth." And, Rev. 16:18, "And there were voices and thunders, and lightnings; and there was a great earthquake, such as was not since men were upon the earth, so mighty an earthquake, and so great."

The great pyramids of Mexico, and those of the Mound Builders of the Mississippi Valley, had a flat place on top, where a fire was built by a priest. Atlantis is reputed to have been sunk in a single night by volcanic action and earthquake. Sodom and Gomorrah perished by fire and brimstone, and the Tower of Babel, according to Bible tradition, was never completed. And to still further clarify Arcanum XVI, it may be repeated that those who take up the sword perish by the sword, that those who seek to destroy others, themselves meet destruction.

Masonry

In Masonry, the Master's Elect of Nine degree is based upon Arcanum XVI. We find that Joabert steals ahead of the other pursuers, and discovering one of the assassins of Hiram Abiff asleep, stabs him in the head and in the heart, then cuts off his head and carries it home.

The 15 craftsmen who conspire to murder Hiram are represented by Arcanum XII. Tubalcain represents the constructive attributes of the planet Mars, while Cain represents the destructive side. Thus the three assassins of Hiram, and their punishment, as well as the act of Cain, are symbolized by Arcanum XVI.

Magic

Arcanum XVI illustrates one of the most certain principles of magic, that any destructive force sent against another, when the period of its orbit has been completed, will return to inflict punishment upon the sender.

To send out an evil, or destructive, thought or force, a corresponding center, or point of projection must be formed in the astral body. This nucleus of evil, or discord, itself attracts influences of like quality, and thus ultimately brings misfortune upon the one who projects such a force.

To fight an invisible force is but to increase its power, unless the source of it is completely destroyed; for thinking about it in the act of fighting it keeps the person tuned in on its vibratory rates. One can, of course, build a protection of cold deflective armour about oneself, which will prevent the entry of such a force. Still better, one can tune in on some entirely different interest so strongly that the invisible energy is cut off, the receiver hung up. This is the safest of all methods.

But to start in to fight any individual, on any plane, by means of mental force, is dangerous, and nearly always brings punishment. I do not mean that injustices should be permitted. But that thought force, or magical energies, sent against another, usually do as much damage in the long run to the one sending them, as to the one against whom they are sent. Truth must be upheld, and the weak protected. But not by using mental magic as a weapon.

Evil influences can not exist in an atmosphere of love and constructive effort, nor can they penetrate into such a region. Therefore instead of sending out other discordant vibrations in combat, evil forces should be ignored, and only constructive thoughts built up and sent out. Such constructive efforts, together with the high energy supplied by love, paralyze any force of evil; for it can accomplish nothing in such an environment.

Initiation

In the soul's pilgrimage, Arcanum XVI indicates that stage of development where the neophyte finds himself called upon to protect those weaker than himself from the influence of destructive psychic forces. But whether these forces are such as arise from the practice of disintegrative forms of mediumship, or are those directly from the inversive magi, either on earth or in the astral, he should obey the admonition of the Bible to overcome evil with good. If he builds the things he desires, if he constructs love and harmony, destructive forces can find no point of contact or influence.

Occult Science

Stellar Diagnosis and Stellar Healing is the science of diagnosing from the birth chart and progressed positions of the planets the nature of the disease, and of applying the appropriate energies to the physical and astral bodies which will restore harmony; for all disease is caused by discord. Such a discord is depicted by Arcanum XVI.

The Wish Spread

The wish spread, pictured on page 198, is used to determine if some wish will be realized. First a card to represent the one making the wish is selected and placed face up in the center of the spread.

The cards of the deck are then spread out, face down, and fifteen of them to be used in this spread are selected at random. The other cards are then discarded.

The fifteen are shuffled and cut in the common routine manner, and dealt, one at a time, face downward. Three go to the left of the central card, three above it, three to the right of it, three below it, and three in the center on it.

To read, turn those over to the left—1—2—3, saying, "This is what surrounds you."

Then turn over and read those above—4—5—6, saying, "This is your wish."

Next turn over and read those at the right—7—8—9, saying, "This is what opposes you."

Following which turn over and read those below—10—11—12, saying, "This is what comes to your home."

And finally turn over and read those in the center—13—14—15, saying, "This is what you will realize."

If the wish card—the 9 of cups—appears anywhere in the reading except in "This is what opposes you," it is a sure sign that the wish, at least in part, will be realized. The place where it falls will determine how soon it will come, the closer it is to card 1 the sooner the matter will come to pass. But if the wish card—the 9 of cups—falls on 7, 8, or 9, the desire will not be gratified, and the cards will show why.

When the wish card—the 9 of cups—fails to appear, if the cards are very favorable the wish will come true, but if unfavorable, it will be denied. In either case the cards by their different stations will indicate the details and show why the result is as denoted.

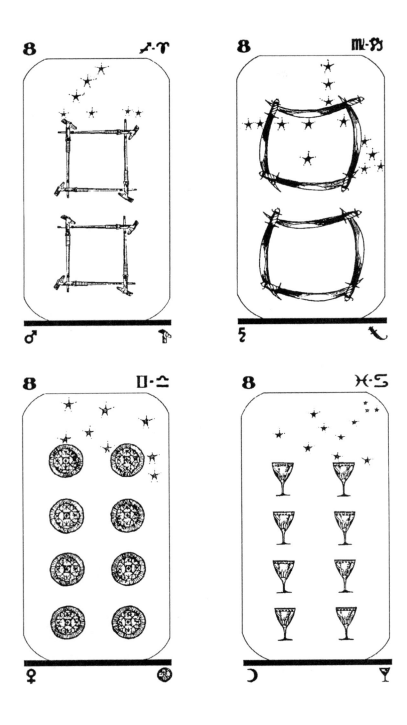

36	35	34	33	32	31
30	29	28	27	26	25
24	23	22	21	20	19
18	17	16	15	14	13
12	11	10	9	8	7
6	5	4	3	2	1

The Spread of 36

Chapter 11

Chronology of the Tarot

S the tarot is a pictorial synthesis of the universe, not only must it correspond to astrological influences, but also to the various divisions of time which are measured by these influences.

Already I have pointed out in some detail the strict correspondence between the 22 Major Arcana and the 10 planets and 12 zodiacal signs, that the 12 common Court Arcana describe people born under each of the 12 signs of the zodiac, and that the 4 horseman Court Arcana signify thoughts that relate to the 4 departments of life.

Now, as fully explained in Chapters 1 and 2 of Course 10-1, *Delineating The Horoscope*, each zodiacal sign is divided into three equal sections, called decanates. Each of these decanates embraces 10 degrees of the zodiac and has an influence distinctly its own. Thus in each quadrant of the zodiac there are 9 decanates. These decanates of the zodiac, however, each belong to one of the four elements; that is, to the triplicity of fire, of water, of air or of earth. The 10th, or transitional influence, therefore, represents the element to which the 9 decanates belong; for the 9 decanates are distributed among the three signs which make up one of the zodiacal triplicities. Thus the Minor Arcana of any one suit do not belong to one quadrant of the zodiac, but to signs in three quadrants; the triplicity to which they belong being designated by the suit, and the 10th Minor Arcanum of each suit, representing the completion of the cycle of that element and a transition to some other, more conveniently being placed adjoining the fixed sign of the element to which its suit belongs.

The astrological relationship of each card of the tarot is given in the key on page 21 of chapter 1. This key contains vastly more than is apparent at first glance, and is well worth careful study followed by deep meditation. The ring of the key shows the rulership of each decanate and each triplicity of the zodiacal circle in relation to each of the 40 Minor Arcana of the tarot. The stem of the key shows the relation between each planet and sign to one of the 22 Major Arcana. The wards of the key turn in the three worlds; physical, astral and spiritual. And the people who exert an influence in these three worlds, and the four types of their thoughts, are shown on these wards as the 16 Court Arcana.

Here, however, we are more interested in chronology. The 12 common Court Arcana which represent people born during each of the 12 months, of course, correspond to the 12 months of the year. The 4 Horsemen, who represent the type of influence each person exerts through his thoughts, correspond to the distinctive influence exerted by each of the four seasons. If we include the 40 Minor Arcana, giving to each suit 13 cards in addition to the Horsemen, they then correspond to the influence of the 4 seasons, which contain 13 X 4, or 52 weeks. And the 22 Major Arcana then represent the 22 astrological influences that cause the weeks and seasons.

The numerical value of the Minor Arcana of each suit, obtained by adding their numbers, is 55; or 220 for all 40 cards. The value of the Horsemen is one each, or 4 for all; and as each Major Arcanum represents a single principle, if we omit the no-numbered tarot for the present, it gives us for the value of the whole tarot pack, 220 plus 120 plus 4 plus 21, or 365 The value of the 12 common Court Arcana is 10 each, or 120.

Yet the no-numbered tarot does not represent exactly zero, but any indeterminate quantity, which in this case may be taken as a trifle more than 1/4. This no-numbered tarot, which here is given an arbitrary value of slightly more than 1/4., represents both the unknown factors of astronomical calculations and of human endeavors. It recognizes that both people and stellar bodies have the power to deviate slightly through the use of their own volition from any orbit defined for them by environmental influences. It thus signifies the inherent power of action known as Free Will. But in the Chronology we are considering it becomes something more than 1/4 day in excess of 365, such as is found in a year.

The Birth-Chart

Turning now to a more practical application, it is found that the Major Arcana can give the astrologer additional information, when it is required, about a birth-chart or a progressed chart. The chart may be completely read, if desired, by placing each of the Major Arcana on the place occupied in the chart by its corresponding astrological sign or planet. Then it should be noted what might be expected, in the houses where the influences fall, from such combinations of forces as are shown by the tarot cards when united, either discordantly or harmoniously, as indicated by the astrological aspects.

The chief value of the tarots to the astrologer, however, is their use in this manner when he is in doubt, or needs additional information. When, in natal astrology, horary astrology, mundane astrology, stellar diagnosis, or in any other branch, he finds some difficult problem, such as determining what will transpire under a certain progressed aspect; if he will combine the cards according to the aspects and conditions in the chart, they often will shed an illuminating light that makes the answer clear.

Talismans Other Than Gems

Although stones and gems are more durable than others, they are not the only substances that can be used as talismans. Plants, for instance, have a temporary talismanic value when worn by those in whose birth-charts the sign ruling the plant is harmonious. And because some plants may be quite antagonistic to an individual, it is much better to select plants for the home and garden, not indiscriminately, but with the end in view of obtaining such as have a strengthening quality of astral vibration, and the aromas of which furnish subtle essences harmonious to the soul.

For talismanic purposes the young growing shoots or the parts bearing the flowers and seeds should be used. A good time to gather plants, either for talismanic or medicinal purposes, is during the hour just before the Moon rises in the sign ruling the plant, the best time being just at moonrise while the moon is in the sign ruling the plant.

Animals also sometimes have an influence similar to talismans, this being particularly true of domestic pets, such as cats, dogs and horses. When the attachment between the pet and its master is pronounced there is a keen desire on the part of the animal to afford protection and benefit. This desire stimulates its unconscious mind. And the unconscious mind, even of a creature much lower in the scale than man, through its psychic senses, has a very wide scope of perception. Not being inhibited by reason, the things that it thus senses psychically may make quite a strong impression upon it, and cause it to behave in such a way that it warns its master of approaching evil.

Even after the animal dies, its strong attachment to its master may cause it to linger in the astral realm quite close to him. Its unconscious mind, thus free from physical limitations, has a scope of intelligence far beyond what we expect of such an animal on earth. It perceives, from the astral plane, the events that affect its master. And it keenly senses his wishes, and desires that these wishes shall be granted.

It may thus, from time to time, be able to convey to him, through dreams and impressions, a knowledge of such conditions as are about to affect him. Or it may follow him to the seance room, and if this be of a certain low order, assist in manifestations there.

I am not assuming that an animal, just because it passes to the next plane, acquires human intelligence. But an animal which has had much human association while on earth, has little difficulty in sensing just what its former master wants. Just as, while on earth, a dog will fetch a stick that its master throws, so on the next plane will it try to do that which will please. It has not acquired human intelligence, but because it is free from the body its unconscious mind has a wide scope of perception, and it is more responsive than ever to its master's thought. And it sometimes finds opportunity to manifest an intelligence of a not very high order in the seance room.

But aside from talismans and exceptional types of influences, the various objects of our environment each radiate a characteristic energy. If an object vibrates to the frequency of an astrological influence which is beneficial in our birth-chart, through increasing the strength of the harmonious vibration in us it renders us assistance. But the association with either objects or people which stirs up in us consciously or unconsciously, a feeling of discord, should be avoided as much as is practicable; for we attract events into our lives that correspond to the discords or harmonies we harbor within.

Response to Healing

This same principle explains why some people respond readily to one type of healing and some to another. By inspecting the birth-chart and the progressed chart the astrologer quickly can determine which planet's vibrations are chiefly responsible for the trouble.

Then by referring to the Arcanum ruled by the planet he can find the Natural Method of treatment which is commonly most efficacious in correcting the discords caused by the planet.

Thus if Mercury causes the affliction, mental healing is particularly applicable. If Neptune is the chief disturber, the disease is more susceptible to spiritual healing. Jupiter brings ailments that need a corrective diet. Venus tends to depletion that may be treated with rest and recreation. Uranus produces peculiar disturbances in the electromagnetic body that often yield readily to electricity and mesmerism. The discords of Pluto yield quickly to stellar healing. Water is the natural remedy for the afflictions caused by the Moon, and light for those caused by the Sun. If Mars is the disturber there is usually a temperature to be reduced, and if Saturn is back of the discord you may be sure that the vitality is low and needs earth-baths and outdoor life to build it up.

The affliction shown by a planet, due to the sign it is in, may manifest its discord in any one of the twelve zones of the body. In this course certain herbs ruled by each sign are given under the Arcanum corresponding to the sign. This will enable you to select those suitable for temporary talismans, or those that, through a corresponding vibratory rate, most readily affect the part of the body ruled by the same sign. For more details of the rulership of specific diseases you are referred to Course 16, *Stellar Healing*, on Stellar Diagnosis and Stellar Healing.

Herbal remedies are administered according to two different schools of thought. The homeopathic system is that like cures like. From the occult point of view this means that an herb belonging to a certain sign, if taken into a healthy organism in excessive amounts, tends to cause a diseased condition of the corresponding part of the body. But if that part of the body is already diseased, the taking of the herb corresponding to this part of the body in very small amounts, builds up and strengthens this part of the body with its similar vibratory rate. In other words, the remedy is applied in such quantity as will give the diseased part the vigor to overcome the disease.

But this system can not be successfully applied to all diseases. Hence we have the allopathic system, which works on the principle that contrary cures contrary. From the occult point of view this means that the disease itself is attacked and an attempt made to annihilate it by means of something violently antagonistic to it. Instead of building up the vigor of the diseased part of the body, the attempt is made to destroy the disease and eliminate it from the body. Fire is thus fought with water, earth with air, and Mars with Saturn. This method seemingly is necessary to combat certain virulent diseases, but, through the violence of the remedies used, is much more apt to impair the constitution.

Here, of course, no attempt is made to discuss the relative value of medicines, or to give instructions in the specific cure of diseases through the administration of herbs. Instead, I merely give such hints as to the relative principles of underlying cures as I hope will prove of value to those who specialize in healing. From these hints they should be able to work out, in connection with their experience, the application in detail. And when the nature of the disease is obscure and the method of treatment in doubt, the use of the tarot as a divinatory instrument, by one who has some skill, can be used both in diagnosis and in determining the most effective treatment to secure a speedy recovery.

The Star—Arcanum XVII

Letter: Egyptian, Pilon; Hebrew, Pe; English, F—P—Ph. Number, 17. Astrologically, the zodiacal sign Gemini. Color, the lighter shades of violet. Tone, high B. Occult science, cosmic alchemy. Human function, the sense of sight. Natural remedy, such herbs as madder, tansy, vervain, woodbine, yarrow, meadow-sweet, privet and dog-grass. Mineral, the talismanic gem beryl, and such stones as are striped.

F—17 expresses in the spiritual world, immortality.

In the intellectual world, the interior light which illuminates the spirit.

In the physical world, hope.

Remember, then, son of earth, that hope is the sister of faith. Shed thy passions and thy errors in order to study the mysteries of true science and the key will be given thee; then a ray of divine light will break from the occult sanctuary in order to dissipate the shadows of thy future and show thee the way of happiness. If Arcanum XVII should appear in the prophetic signs of thy horoscope, whatever may happen in life, never injure the flower of hope and thou wilt gather the fruits of faith.

In Divination, **Arcanum XVII** may be read as **Truth, Hope** or **Faith**.

Arcanum XVII is figured by a blazing star of eight rays in the center of which is a white trine with point upward joined at its base to a black trine with its point downward. This star is surrounded by seven other stars. It hovers over a nude young girl who has one foot upon the sea and one foot upon the land, and who pours the fluid of universal life from two cups, one of gold, the other of silver. Near the girl is a flower of three blossoms, and above the upper one a butterfly opens its wings.

This young girl is the emblem of truth. She is nude, signifying that truth can be perceived only when stripped of the preconceived ideas and dogmatic opinions with which it has been clothed by the artificialities of civilization.

She rests partly upon the land and partly upon the sea to denote that truth is dual, the truth of reality and the truth of appearances, the truth of the practical and the truth of the ideal. The fluid is poured from a silver cup into the sea to indicate that the loving, emotional side of man's nature must be nourished if he is to grasp the inner truth. And it is poured from a golden cup upon the land to denote the necessity of cultivating the positive, reasoning intellect if he is to possess the external truth.

The fluid flowing from the golden cup represents the forces of man, and that from the silver cup the forces of woman; together revealing the truth of soul-mate-hood, and indicating how the finer energies of man rejuvenate woman and how the finer energies of woman rejuvenate man; their forces mutually sustaining each other and making a joint immortality possible.

The eight-point star symbolizes the Law of Equilibrium, the balance between spirit and matter, male and female, the inner and the outer. It is the book of the apocalypse sealed with seven seals, and thus represents the inner realization and the outer realization, the birth of the soul and the birth of the body, under the influence of the planets, represented by the 7 surrounding stars, or seals.

Each of these smaller stars, or seals, has four points, to signify that man should recognize the nature of its influence and realize how to direct it into channels of his own choosing.

The two trines of the larger star symbolize the Hermetic Axiom, "As it is below, so it is above," and reveal that evolution implies a preceding involution. It also indicates the necessity of experiences with both good and evil for soul progression.

The flower of three blossoms represents the three planes of existence from which the soul sips the nectar of wisdom, gaining thereby the strength to attain immortality, symbolized by the butterfly.

Number

Numerically, 17 is the 2nd decave of 8, denoting the crystallized condition of Arcanum VIII polarized to the frequency level denoted by Arcanum II. It is involution followed by evolution, for, after all, matter is but polarized spirit. In the universe there is but one Principle, which manifests under two modes of motion as force and will. There is but one LAW, and this is sex, manifesting as male and female. There is but one Agent, which manifests as spirit and matter. And there is but one Truth, which manifests as appearance and reality. This is the truth represented by the star of Arcanum XVII.

Astrology

The most pronounced symbolism of Arcanum XVII pertains to its duality, and the most dual sign of the zodiac is Gemini. This sign, pictured among the constellations as the Twins, representing Reason and Intuition, belongs to the first degree of emanation of the airy triplicity, and therefore represents the most interior and free use of the intellect. It corresponds to the day house of Mercury, the planet of mental expression, and thus is a fitting symbol of Truth. Better than any other sign, Gemini typifies the duality that sustains all worlds and alone makes life and consciousness possible.

Human Function

The first step toward truth is perception. This perception should embrace both sides of the situation. And while knowledge requires also an inner comprehension of the meaning of things seen, the necessity for correct sight is implied in the vernacular expression, "I see," used to signify comprehension. Mercury rules both Gemini and the eyes, and as Gemini corresponds to the day house of Mercury, it is more closely allied with the external vision. And if additional testimony were required to show the correspondence of the sense of sight with Arcanum XVII, it could be found in the restless activity of the eyes, and of the natives of Gemini, in their unceasing search for new information and new experiences.

Alchemy

Arcanum XVII pictures the finding of the fountain of eternal youth. Gold and silver have been completely purified and the dross removed. Each, united to a proper flux, has been reduced to the first matter in the reverberatory furnace. And as a result of their transmuted union they are no longer merely gold and silver, but a delectable fluid, the coveted elixir of life.

Many have sought, but few have found, this precious draught. Some who have had it ready to their hand, have failed to recognize it. Others have discovered it accidentally, and while deeply awed by its wonderful properties have never perceived its real use and partaken of its life giving properties. More have been poisoned by drinking that which they hoped would prove to be the elixir, a fluid somewhat resembling it, but in reality quite destructive. Yet Arcanum XVII pictures its preparation in unmistakable terms to those who do not discard the simple and plain in search for the intricate and complex.

Bible

The first pointed reference in the Bible to Arcanum XVII is Gen. 1:27; "So God created man in his own image, in the image of God created he him; male and female created he them."

Thus is revealed the great truth exemplified in still more detail by the duality shown in Arcanum XVII. For not only does it point out that man is formed in the image of God, that the microcosm is a miniature copy of the macrocosm, but that both are, when complete, male and female. Whatever exists in the starry firmament above, according to both the Bible and this Arcanum, must have its correspondence in the constitution of man. But in addition thus to formulating the relation of the soul to the stars, it states positively that the macrocosm is both male and female; and implies that souls to persist must retain their sex; for when this attribute is destroyed man ceases to be an image of God, and no longer partakes of the divine nature.

John 8:32 reads; "And ye shall know the truth and the truth shall make you free." Now freedom implies a previous bondage. The bondage here considered is that imposed by the restrictions of the physical. But these restrictions are removed when the truth is perceived of man's relations to the universe, and that the soul, educated for a definite mission in the cosmic scheme, survives physical death.

Rev. 5:1 mentions Arcanum XVII: "And I saw in the right hand of him that sat on the throne a book written within and on the back side, sealed with seven seals." This, of course, is the book of nature, under the dominion of the 7 planets; and through a knowledge of it immortality is gained, for it enables the soul to partake of the tree of life mentioned in Gen. 3:22.

Just how this book of nature is to be opened and its contents made plain is quite distinctly stated; "Behold, the Lion of the tribe of Juda, the Root of David, hath prevailed to open the book, and to loose the seven seals thereof." As the lion is the zodiacal sign Leo, which rules the house of love, it is clear that the affections are used. But this is not the only factor; for next we read that the Lamb took the book. This is the zodiacal sign Aries, ruling the head. And this explains to us, in the language of universal symbolism, that neither love nor reason alone is sufficient, but that truth can be grasped completely only when there is a union of head and heart. And thus does the Lamb here typify the soul which has triumphed over Arcanum XIII, or death, through the combined activity of its intellect and its affections.

Masonry

The degree of Provost and Judge is based upon Arcanum XVII. The duality of truth is symbolized in this degree by two keys. One is the key to the small ebony box containing the plans for building the temple, that is, the key to understanding the Divine Plan. The other is the key to the ivory box containing the temple keys, that is, the laws which govern the universe and the progress of the soul. The ivory box and the ebony box clearly indicate that both positive keys and negative keys are required, and that man and woman complement and complete each other.

Magic

In Magic, Arcanum XVII is the perception of both the external and the internal truth. Such perception is made possible through the cultivation of the soul senses. But, because, through the principle that like attracts like, even a slight desire to deceive others attracts deceiving influences, care should be exercised here. The desires of the unconscious mind, also, have a tendency to warp such information to coincide with them, as it is raised from the astral brain to the physical consciousness. When one becomes unusually sensitive an idea through its sentiment may exert so strong an appeal that the emotion may easily be mistaken for soul response. Then, again, the thought images projected by other powerful minds are sensed by the psychic faculties, and those not fully initiated are apt to respond to these as if they were soul-responses to truth, when they, in fact, are merely being dominated by thought-forms.

Therefore, while the pure intuitions of the soul, when sufficiently freed from various other influences, are reliable guides to truth; for those who have not attained a very high degree of spiritual initiation, they can not be relied upon too implicitly. Consequently, in the search for truth, and in its apprehension, one set of faculties is used to test the accuracy of the other; intuition is used to check the reports of reason, and reason is applied to determine the reliability of intuition. Thus the initiate grasps both the exoteric and the esoteric aspects of truth.

He perceives that every atom of physical life is but the symbolic expression on the external plane of an indwelling spirit-atom. With his psychic vision he notes that every living form is a collection of these indwelling spirit atoms controlled by a central soul monad. This monad furnishes the conditions for their progress, as they do for it, dominating them by virtue of its labors in past incarnations.

That is, every plant and animal, as well as gem and stone, is but the material vehicle through which some soul is evolving and elaborating its powers. These astral entities that mold the form of crystals, plants and animals, causing them to assume the shapes they do, are the realities; for they continue to occupy new and higher forms, while the material forms they inhabit are transitory and unenduring, and consequently but an appearance.

The initiate recognizes the truth of appearance at its true value. He does not deny the existence of matter and its properties; for to those occupying the physical plane misery, disease and sin are as real as are spiritual verities to those occupying interior realms. It is as great a mistake to deny the qualities expressed by material form as to deny the reality of the spiritual ideals causing their expression. To one living entirely upon the physical plane the mere denial that a substance is a poison will not prevent it causing the death of the body. But to suppose that the material particles are the real cause of the fatality is to observe but one side of the truth; for these particles are but the material vehicles of spirit atoms that have a violent antipathy toward human life. They are really the physical expression of a spiritual ideal, or idea, and this idea can be sensed psychically.

If the spiritual development of the person is such that he realizes his own source and destiny, that he belongs to a higher spiritual state than the destructive forces of the poison, and that by virtue of his function in the cosmic scheme he should and can dominate all submundane atoms of life; in other words, if his spiritual nature is active, he can partake of the most violent poisons, or pass through fire as did Shadrack and his companions, unharmed, because his spirituality enables him to compel the obedience of the spirit atoms of the poison or the elementals of fire, preventing them from acting as usual.

Again, let us glance about us. The initiated see in all our great cities, slums and hotbeds of vice. It is useless to deny their existence, or the many contributing factors in external life that supply them with victims, the chief of which, perhaps, is the mental and magnetic inharmony of the parents at their conception. But even this is only a portion of the truth; for the clairvoyant vision reveals the existence of cities within cities, the lower astral world permeating the physical. The inhabitants of these astral slums are usually as unconscious of the people of the physical world as the latter are of them; yet the desires of the inhabitants of each realm react, through unconscious thought impression, upon the other, and the slums of the astral world stimulate the evil of external life. In fact, it might be said that the external slums are imitations of the inner hells to which they correspond.

Initiation

In the soul's initiation Arcanum XVII represents the attainment of divine illumination through the perfect rapport of the soul and the ego. The ego is not some mighty angelic power, but an eternal, scintillating atom of Deity, pure and innocent, depending on the soul-monads which are the positive and negative attributes of itself for knowledge of external life. The soul monad becomes closely associated with the brain of man, and when the spirituality is sufficiently active a conscious rapport is established between this monad and its ego. This brings the brain directly in touch with the soul's center of deific life, enabling it to grasp the cosmic idea and realize what portion of that idea it is progressing to express. What God is the soul can never know, but it does grasp its own relation to God, and this truth leads it to freedom. This freedom is not that of annihilation, or a dreamy nirvana, but the ability through increased knowledge consciously to direct its own progression in harmony with the laws of cosmic evolution. Instead of being subject to the stars, it rules them. This illumination brings the conscious knowledge of its missing soul mate.

Occult Science

Cosmic alchemy is the science of transforming the energies of society as a whole into those types of action that are most beneficial to it, that most effectively assist the highest development of its members, and that most completely cooperate in the fulfillment of the divine plan.

Horseman Court Cards

The Horsemen do not represent people, but thoughts or unseen intelligences. As thoughts are ruled by Arcanum I, each Horseman has a numerical value of 1. In divination they are read as thoughts or intelligences that have an influence upon the life of the client. The one who thinks the thoughts is indicated by the Court Card nearest whom the Horseman is found in the spread.

The Horseman of Scepters denotes thoughts concerning business. Right way up, it indicates thoughts advantageous to the client; reversed it signifies thoughts opposed to his business interests.

The Horseman of Cups denotes thoughts of love or affection. Right way up they are sincere and to the client's advantage; reversed they indicate deceit or opposition to the true affectional desires.

The Horseman of Coins denotes thoughts relating to health or money. Right way up, they tend to the prosperity of the client; reversed they are plots to unfairly obtain money from him.

The Horseman of Swords denotes thoughts of enmity, strife or sickness. Right way up, it indicates thoughts devoted to the defense and protection of the client; reversed they are plans and desires for his ruin.

The Moon—Arcanum XVIII

Letter: Egyptian, Tsaidi; Hebrew, Tzaddi; English, Sh—Ts—Tz. Number 18. Astrologically, the zodiacal sign Cancer. Color, the lighter shades of green. Tone, high F. Occult science, mediumship. Human function, spirit communion. Natural remedy, such herbs as water lilies, rushes, cucumbers, squashes, melons, and water plants generally. Mineral, the talismanic gem, emerald, and such stones as are soft and white, including selenite and chalk.

Sh—18 expresses in the spiritual world, the abyss of the infinite.

In the intellectual world, the shadows which envelop the spirit when it has submitted itself to the rule of the instincts.

In the physical world, deception and hidden enemies.

Remember, then, son of earth, that whosoever braves the unknown, does so at his peril. Hostile minds, figured by the black dog, will surround him with ambushes; friendly, servile minds will offer him flatteries; and treacherous minds, like unto the scorpion, will plan to attain their ends through his ruin. If Arcanum XVIII should appear in the prophetic signs of thy horoscope, observe and listen, but know how to be silent.

In Divination, **Arcanum XVIII** is **Deception, False Friends,** or **Secret Foes**.

Arcanum XVIII is figured by two pyramids at the edge of a road. The Moon above, half obscured by clouds, sheds a pale twilight. One of the pyramids, symbol of the twelve houses of the horoscope, is black, representing an ignorant and unspiritual life. The other pyramid is white, symbolizing a life enlightened by science and spiritual wisdom. In front of it is shown a door, or exit, indicating that those thus enlightened are not earth-bound, but pass freely, when their earthly life is completed, to a life in the higher spheres.

In the road before the pyramids are two dogs, one white and the other black; while between them, in a circle of white, crawls a scorpion. This dim, moonlight scene represents a seance room, the hidden perils of which are more redoubtable than those to be seen. The false radiance of the moon indicates the glamor that surrounds such an occasion. The good and the bad, the ignorant and the learned, symbolized by the pyramids, are gathered there at the edge of the road into the beyond. To such a place there may be attracted lying spirits, as signified by the black dog; friendly spirits, as denoted by the white dog; or treacherous and dominating spirits who have much knowledge, as indicated by the white circle in which the scorpion moves, but who use it to deceive and attain their selfish ends.

Number

Numerically, 18 is the 2nd decave of 9, or wisdom polarized. Arcanum IX operating on the plane frequency of Arcanum II implies the exploration of secret realms. Such exploration is not without its perils, and should be attempted only by one who has made marked spiritual advancement, or under the guidance of a competent master. Under these conditions the negative and disintegrative states are not permitted, and then 18 becomes True Wisdom regarding the Science of Occultism.

Astrology

Cancer is ruled by the Moon, and is the zodiacal sign most susceptible to influences from other planes, and most pronouncedly affected by its associates and its environment. The mediumistic quality correlates it to Arcanum XVIII.

Human Function

Cancer is the most interior degree of emanation of the watery triplicity, and most readily receives and interprets the thoughts of entities occupying the interior worlds. What appears to be intuition often, with people born under this sign, is in reality the prompting of a discarnate entity. This ease of spirit communion corresponds to Arcanum XVIII.

Alchemy

The true elixir of life has the peculiar power of absorbing and transmitting the energies of the surrounding magnetic atmosphere. If the elixir is pure it absorbs and transmits only the finer, higher, life giving energies. But if impure, it attracts grosser energies. Arcanum XVIII may represent either the true elixir or the false elixir.

The majority who seek this fluid of eternal youth fail to recognize the need for purity, or are unable to discern whether or not the elixir is truly pure. They thus prepare the draught by dissolving in the Water of Pythia whatever metals may be at hand, without precaution as to their purity and proper proportions. They deceive themselves, and drinking the false elixir thus prepared, are drugged into a semiconscious state in which they are unable to perceive even the approach of their own ruin.

Bible

Saul, in his extremity, consulted a medium at Endor. Sam. 28:8; "And he said, I pray thee divine unto me by the familiar spirit, and bring up whom I shall name unto thee."

The power of spirits to obsess is mentioned as a matter of course in Math. 10:1; "And when he had called unto him his twelve disciples he gave them power against unclean spirits, to cast them out."

Paul speaks of deceiving spirits, I Tim. 4:1; "Now the Spirit speaketh expressly, that in the latter times some shall depart from the faith, giving heed to seducing spirits, and doctrines of devils; speaking lies in hypocrisy; having their conscience seared with a hot iron: Forbidding to marry, and commanding to abstain from meats."

Masonry

The degree of Initiate Secretary is based upon Arcanum XVIII. Its lower aspect is the spy who listens at the veil and is captured, condemned by Hiram King of Tyre, and finally freed through the intercession of King Solomon. Its higher aspect represents that eminent saint, John the Baptist, to whom modern Masons dedicate their lodge; for the sun is baptised in the Holy Ghost when it enters the watery sign Cancer and reaches the highest, and symbolically the most spiritual, point in its annual journey.

Magic

Arcanum XVIII explains the process of mediumship. The passive ever becomes the medium of the active, hence matter is the medium for the expression of mind. Broadly speaking, in the sense that it receives and transmits force, everything is mediumistic. Because the energies of the interior planes are more active than those external, the physical is mediumistic to the astral, and thus astrological forces influence the life of the material world.

Carrying the same thought further, the astral world must be passive to, and the medium of, energies from the spiritual world. Thus may we consider God as the great central controlling spiritual force of the universe, and that from Him down to the densest mineral atom there is a complete, graded scale of mediumship; each higher plane transmitting the One Universal Force to the plane next below, until finally it reaches and energizes the lowest realm.

Even the adept is but the medium for the expression of spiritual ideas upon the physical plane. The spiritual truths externalizing in his life are taught by schools on the interior planes and subsequently verified by his own experiences. The true adept never claims to originate the teachings he gives out; for he recognizes the fact that whatever truth man grasps on the physical plane is due to his reception of it from exalted souls whose interior plane of life enables them to dispel illusion. The truth these exalted beings realize is transmitted to them from still more interior worlds, and so on, to the very throne of God, Who is the absolute source of all truth. But there is a great difference between such conscious and controllable mediumship and that of the person who trusts to some controlling spirit guide, or permits a discarnate entity to use his body as a means of communication.

In the first place it should be understood that under proper conditions it is possible, and frequently happens, that people who have crossed the boundary of physical life do return and talk with their loved ones through the organism of some medium. But the soul world closest to earth is the lower astral, in which dwell earth-bound souls, vicious elementals, depraved elementaries, and a host of other entities, some of which are harmlessly mischievous, some of which are inimical to man, and some of whom desire to use him for their own ends. To abdicate the rulership of the body in favor of whatever unseen entity happens to be present, and that may claim to be anything that suits its purpose, is to court the domination of the soul by entities which may use their advantage to deceive, demoralize, obsess; and which always weaken the will.

Of all places, the public seance room seems to be one least likely to furnish anything of value, for the mixture of the thoughts and magnetisms attracts all sorts of questionable entities. Such conditions favor physical manifestations; for the beings responsible for them belong to the realm of force. Where the electromagnetic energy is present, phenomena can be furnished through an irresponsible medium as readily and as genuinely as can be produced by an adept. But the mediums can not control them.

Much psychical phenomena is faked, because the genuine is so great a drain on the medium that he can not generate the force to produce it often. Yet he feels that he must keep his patronage at any cost. Irresponsible mediumship is fraught with great peril.

Initiation

In the soul's pilgrimage Arcanum XVIII denotes the neophyte's work in the astral, freeing earth-bound souls from their fetters, assisting those deceived to realize their errors, and encouraging them to strive for a new and better life.

Occult Science

Mediumship is the science of reception and transmission, embracing the law of affinity and its application in the production of phenomena.

Spread of 36

This spread is used to give a general reading of conditions and events. After the customary preparatory shuffling and cutting, the cards are dealt one at a time face downward in a square of 36, starting at the bottom right-hand corner.

To read this spread, turn the cards over, from top to bottom, one at a time, in the order of their sequence as given in the diagram on page 220. Read each card as it is turned either as something conditioning the card just preceding it, or as a subsequent event, as the case may be.

The bottom row represents the past, the next row above represents the present conditions, and the cards of the four rows above, each row in its proper sequence, as conditions in the future.

Then, for additional information, after the spread has been read in this manner, start picking the cards up in pairs, reading each pair as some incident of the future. The first two to be picked up and read in this manner are 1 and 36, the next are 2 and 35, and so on until all 18 pairs have been read. This pair reading starts with the immediate future, as denoted by 1 and 36. It is not meant to supplant or contradict the first portion of the reading, but through revealing incidents of the future to shed additional information.

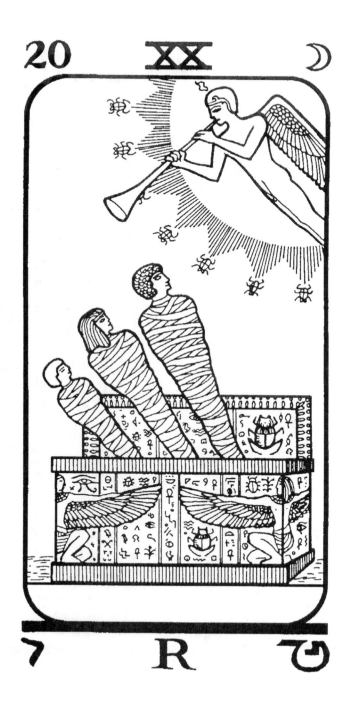

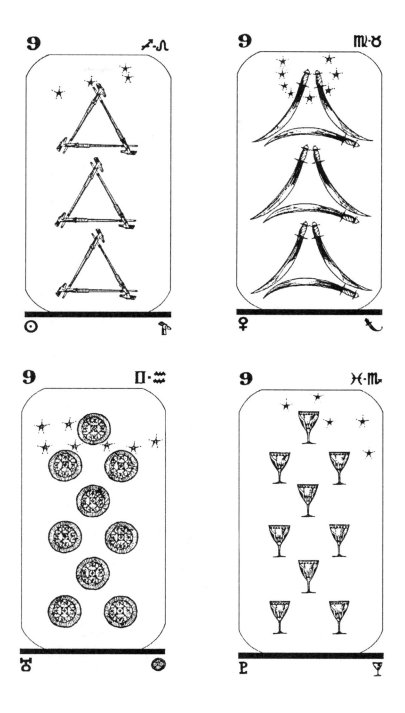

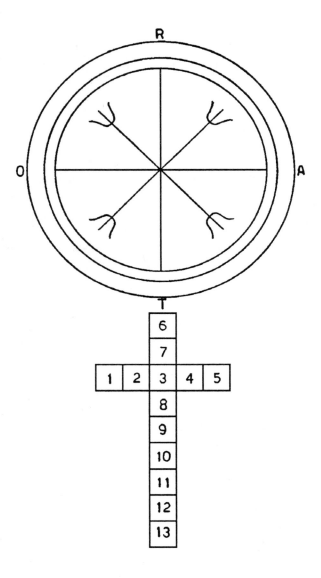

The Magic Cross Spread

Chapter 12

The Solution
of Ancient Cycles

I HAVE designated under Arcanum VII that completion and perfection of form, in so far as the three-dimensional plane is concerned, is expressed by the number 7, and under Arcanum IX that the number of astral manifestation is exemplified by the number 9. We are now ready, therefore, to apply these two numbers to the law of cycles.

The cycles man can understand pertain to the physical plane and to the astral plane. He should first, of course, have some knowledge of the completion of form as seen on the physical plane, such as is to be found, for instance, in the septenary grouping of chemical elements. And for this purpose the number 7 is a valuable tool. But behind all such physical expression is the realm of ideas, the realm of astrological vibrations, the realm of the character-vibrations of things. And for the purpose of investigating this inner-plane region, the number 9 should be employed to aid the understanding.

Man, formatively considered, for instance, possesses a sevenfold constitution. Yet viewed from a higher scale, his interior potencies are not properly manifested until he has developed two additional factors, which we call reason and intuition. This adding of an evolutionary positive and negative factor to the outer-plane 7 gives us the inner-plane viewpoint, in which 9 aids the proper explanation.

Or, let us say, the 7 colors of the spectrum give formative expression to light on the earth-plane. But to understand the more essential nature of light, its inner-plane relations must be included. Black and white, the polar opposites, must be added to the physical 7, to get the necessary inner-plane comprehension.

The chemical properties of an element, to consider matter, are subject to the same law, being a periodic function of its atomic weight. But to reveal the thought-quality of the element it must be considered also as possessing a positive and negative, bringing the factors up to 9.

Yet as 10 is the cyclic number, the orbit of the cycles based either on 7 or 9, or both, expand and contract in this manner: Ideal cycles, those which measure intellectual and spiritual force, are solved by applying number 9. Practical cycles, which measure magnetic and vital force and the planes of manifestation, are unlocked by number 7. 10 closes the cycle. And by using 7 and 9 in connection with the cyclic number, 10, it is possible to solve every cycle in nature below the spiritual plane, from the intra-atomic cycle of the electron up to the orbital movement of a universe.

Why are there 360 degrees in a circle? We can not say it is merely chance. A circle is obviously a cycle, therefore embraces the number 10. It is also in nature the measure of intellectual and spiritual force, as can be observed in the study of orbital motions either of planets or of atoms.

Such orbits always express through four phases, which are well recognized in the moon's orbit as its four quarters, and in the earth's orbit as the four seasons, but are none the less present in all orbital motion. Therefore an orbit, or circle, is the cyclic number 10 multiplied by 4, or Realization (Arcanum IV), giving 40, which indicates any cycle as measuring the Realization of effort.

This number 40, which is the number of Minor Arcana of the tarot, explains all reference to 40 in the Bible as periods in which Realization was accomplished.

But an orbit, as a measure of ideals, or intellectuality and spirituality, is a function of the inner-plane number 9. 9 evolved to the 40th decave is 360, meaning Wisdom (9) Realized (4) in a cycle (10). Thus it is that any point on the earth's surface passing through 360 degrees, or a day and night, is a measure of intellectual and spiritual force as applied to those born at different hours. It causes them to express, not merely the mental activity and repose which humanity at large does each 24 hours, but different Personalities.

In expressing cycles in terms of time, round numbers are used because often there are variable factors, such as are spoken of in connection with the no-numbered Arcanum of the tarot. The most apparent of these variations is that the relation of the Day to the Year is not exactly 1 to 360, but 1 to 365 ¼.

There is a good reason for this, but suffice it here to point out that the ancients overcame this discrepancy by making their year measure 360 days, and then at the winter solstice cutting out 5 days. Those five "Dies Non" were given over to festivity and were not counted in their calendar. The year, or orbital motion of the earth through 360 (3 plus 6 plus 0 equal 9) degrees, measures to humanity at large not only the variation in light and heat, but the quality of mental and spiritual influx. People born at different times of the year thus express different Individualities.

Furthermore, the yearly return of the Sun by transit over its place in the birth-chart is the measure of spiritual energy received by individual man.

Now if we wish to find the operation of the practical forces in life, we divide the number of days in the year by 7. This gives us 52 weeks. As 5 plus 2 equals 7, we know these weeks relate to practical affairs rather than to spiritual influences. And as a matter of fact, man regulates his physical existence by a week of 7 days.

The Moon, as it passes through the zodiac, by its phases, or relations to the Sun, measures out to man the magnetic expansion and contraction which govern intellectual activity. This cycle is a little more than 29 days. 2 plus 9 equals 11, therefore the 4 quarters of the Moon measure the Realization of Magnetic Force (Arcanum XI), the practical operation of which depends upon each phase of the Moon of a little more than 7 days. People born with the Moon in different parts of its orbit have different kinds of capacities.

But there is another cycle of the Moon of greater import to the Soul of man. It is the cycle of a little over 27 days during which the Moon traverses 360 degrees of the zodiac. 2 plus 7 equals 9, therefore this cycle relates to intellectual and spiritual forces, and we find actually that this cycle of the Moon from one transit of the Sun to another such transit in the birth-chart, measures the germination of spiritual powers and psychic possibilities.

By virtue of the function of 9, the movements in the heavens during the earth's diurnal motion through 360 degrees measures out the Major events of life to man while the earth moves in its orbit 360 degrees. And the Moon's orbital motion of 360 degrees measures out to man the Minor Events occurring during the earth's orbital motion of 360 degrees. In other words, in natal astrology, whose influences come from the inner plane, the chief events of life are measured to man at the rate of a day for a year, and the minor events of life at the rate of a month for a year; both measures being functions of the number 9.

The Equinox is observed to move at the rate of 1 degree in 72 years (7 plus 2 equal 9). This makes the place of the Sun at the beginning of the astronomical year appear to retrograde through the zodiac 1 degree in 72 years, or through 360 degrees, completing the circle in about 72 x 360 equal 25,920 years. 25,868 to be exact. This period measures unto man all the different mental and spiritual forces possible during one Precessional Cycle.

This cycle of 360 degrees is divided by 12 into sections corresponding to the zodiacal signs, each section containing 30 degrees. Divide 25,868 by 12, and we get 2,156 years as the duration of one sub-cycle, or Age, as it is called. The equinox passes through the 30 degrees corresponding to each zodiacal sign, and this gives rise to the Age of that sign. It is the measure of the intellectual and spiritual force received by humanity, and determines its general trend.

The equinox, or place of the Sun at the beginning of the astronomical year, retrograded by "Precession" back from the first of constellated Aries, which is the beginning of the circle of stars, 30 degrees, and therefore into the space corresponding to the sign Aquarius, in 1881. The exact date is January 19, 1881. The chart for the hour and minute as well as the date, and a discussion of it, are given in *Astrological Lore of All Ages*. This is the time of the commencement of the Aquarian Age, and because the mental and spiritual force received by humanity is different when the Sun's place among the stars at the beginning of the year corresponds to the place of different zodiacal signs, the student can get some idea of the type of civilization that, past or future, exists while the equinox is in any sign by multiplying 2,156 years by the number of signs removed from Aquarius, and adding to or subtracting from, the year 1881.

History thus records that during the time the Equinox moves by Precession through each sign there is also a change in the practical trend of the mental force and dominant interest about every 308 years. That is, the movement of the equinox through one sign is divided into seven equal periods, the number 7 signifying this formative trend. The duration of this period within the Sub-Precessional Cycle is obtained by dividing 2,156 years by 7, the result being 308 years.

Each of these formative periods is apparently under dominion of one of the seven planets. The Equinox always backs into a sign, entering the end of the 30th degree and moving back to 29, 28 and so on. And by reference to historical events we find that the first period after the Equinox enters a sign precessionally is ruled by the Sun, that the next period is ruled by Venus, the next by Mercury, then the Moon, Saturn, Jupiter and finally Mars as the last period in any sign. Anyone conversant with history can verify the influence of these periods.

From this information, which was first given out by Abbot Trithemius, it is possible to determine in a general way the trend of the intellectual forces as practically applied during any period of 308 years, past or future. If the period was ruled by the Sun the energies were applied to the engrandizement of State or Empire; if by Mars, they were devoted to mechanics and war; if by the Moon, it was a period of intellectual slumber; if by Venus, the energies were given over to art and luxury; if by Mercury, to intellectual culture; if by Saturn, to subtlety and superstition; if by Jupiter, to expansion and benevolence. The Sun started his rule of 308 years on December 23, 1880. Mars ceased to rule Dec. 21, 1880. Or, to be more precise, the solstice of 1880 in December is the point of reckoning from which the student can trace the influence of these periods either forward or backward.

Now we come to a very interesting theory which probably has no valuable practical application. That the obliquity of the ecliptic is constantly changing was observed by ancients as well as by moderns. That is, the Pole of the earth is moving in an orbit at right angles to the earth's diurnal rotation at the rate of about 1 second every 2 years, or 1 degree in 7,200 years. If, therefore, the earth should continue this motion it would turn completely polarwise in 7,200 x 360 equal 2,592,000 years. And as turning around completely equatorwise is called one common day, so turning completely around polarwise is called one polar day.

According to modern astronomers, however, the earth does not thus turn completely over polarwise, but after moving through 3 or 4 degrees starts to swing back, according to known laws, which cause it thus to wobble. But because the time involved to observe this swinging back was so great some ancient concluded this polarwise motion continued uniformly on around the circle, and he based his larger periods of duration on this false Polar Day of 2,592,000 years. The days of creation mentioned in Genesis refer to these Polar Days of immense duration.

The Polar Day was known in Egypt, and its duration is incorporated in the Great Pyramid; although just because the amount of average movement of the earth Polarwise is included in this monument does not warrant us to conclude that they believed the earth thus completely to turn over, as this movement over a few degrees, even though it swings back, is really one of the most important astronomical movements, having profound effects upon the climate and other matters on the earth. And it is this average movement of 1 degree in 7,200 years which the pyramid records.

It should be understood that there is both geological evidence and archaeological evidence as well as modern knowledge of astronomical movements which all indicate that the earth does not turn over Polarwise and that the races which have been assumed to exist never have existed on the earth in physical forms. But because the theory was developed to a fine degree in India, and is the basis of the various sacred cycles there recorded, as well as being linked up with their accounts of races which once inhabited the globe, it is valuable to know it, even as a theory which modern science seems completely to have refuted.

The theory is that the Polar Day is the exact duration of the life-wave on the earth, and that this is the average time of the life on each planet. Therefore for the life-wave to travel once around the chain of 7 planets, and thus give formative expression to and develop 1 Round of Humanity, containing 7 Root-Races, takes 7 x 2,592,000 equal 18,144,000 years. Then to produce 7 Rounds of humanity requires 7 x 18,144,000 equal 127,008,000 years or 49 Polar Days. Then comes the Jubilee of Nirvana during which Nature sleeps for 7 Polar Days while the life-wave goes once around the septenary chain.

Then, according to this Eastern theory which archaeology quickly disproves, commences the Second Series, and the 7 Families, or Rounds of 7 Root-Races, each ascending to Angelic Spheres to become the parents and Guardians of the new series of humanity.

The number 360 was used by the ancients of the East to veil their sacred cycles, 360 Common Years being called One Divine Year. The Hindus, in their studies, also made use of the cyclic number 10. Thus we are informed that the Divine Maha Yug is composed of 10 Great Ages or Cali Yugs. A Cali Yug is 1,200 Divine Years, or 360 x 1,200 equal 432,000 common years, during which the earth's pole, according to their theory of polar motion, was supposed to pass over 1/6 of its orbit of 2,592,000 years, making the sextile aspect to its own place.

A Dwaper Yug is two Cali Yugs, or 2,400 Divine Years, or 864,000 common years, during which the pole is supposed to pass over 1/3 of its orbit, making the trine aspect to its original place. A Treta Yug is 3 Cali Yugs, or 3,600 Divine Years, or 1,296,000 common years, during which the earth's pole was supposed to pass over 1/2 of its orbit, making the opposition to its original place. A Satya Yug, according to these Hindu cycles, is 4 Cali Yugs, or 4,800 Divine Years, or 1,728,000 common years, during which the earth's pole is supposed to pass over ⅔ of its orbit, making the second trine to its original place.

Furthermore, a Maha Yug is composed of 1 Cali Yug plus 1 Dwaper Yug plus 1 Treta Yug plus 1 Satya Yug, or the equivalent of 10 Cali Yugs, 12,000 Divine Years, or 4,320,000 years, during which, according to the Hindu theory, the earth's pole is supposed to pass 1⅔ times around its orbit. A Maha Yug is thus composed of 4 aspects bearing the relation 1-2-3-4 to each other, completing the number 10. And a Manwantares is 1,000 times 1 Maha Yug, during which portion of the Great Kalpa the planetary chain has been disintegrated and reorganized several times.

In some sense, for tradition so wide spread is seldom without adequate foundation, there doubtless was a Golden, Silver, Copper and Iron age. Astrological influx combined with climatic conditions at some time in the dim past of the world. We are not justified, however, in believing these ages were dependent in the strict sense upon the hypothetical Polar Day. Yet an account of this theoretical linking up, as derived from Hindu sources, is not devoid of interest.

It was supposed that these ages referred only to the first Round of humanity, and as a matter of scientific fact, the evidence all points that humanity has not been upon the earth longer than the periods embraced within one or two Polar Days. But it is supposed, according to the theory, that these ages recur again as the life-wave leaves the planet, developing the highest states of the round, although they are not strictly called by the same names.

It was supposed that with the pole at right angles to the ecliptic, or sun's path, there was an ideal climate in the temperate zones, and that the climate does not become excessively severe until the pole moves through 4 x 9 equal 36 degrees. As the pole moves through 1 degree in 7,200 years, this period of the Golden Age was supposed to have lasted 36 x 7,200 equals 259,200 years. Then while the pole passed through 3 x 9 equal 27 degrees, giving the Sun a maximum declination of from 36 to 63 degrees, there were hot long days in summer and cold long nights in winter. This Silver Age lasted 27 x 7,200 equal 194,400 years. While the pole passed through 2 x 9 equal 18 degrees, the Tropics reached an angle of from 63 to 81 degrees, and there were tropical summers and arctic winters on all portions of the globe. This Copper Age is supposed thus to have lasted 18 x 7,200 equal 129,600 years.

Then while the pole was passing through 1 x 9 equal 9 degrees, the Sun was approaching its vertical position once a year to both North and South Poles, and the climatic conditions were frightful. This Iron Age was supposed to have lasted 9 x 7,200 years or 64,800 years. These 4 Ages, related to each other by this theory as 1-2-3-4, are embraced in the time the Pole passed over one quadrant of 10 x 9 degrees, or 90 x 7,200 equal 648,000 years. And according to this Eastern theory the place in evolution of our present Great Western Race is that of one branch of the Fifth Root-Race of the 4th Round of Evolution.

Not the slightest evidence has been found to date that man existed on the earth so long ago as is thus implied. The records in the rocks indicate that one round of 18,144,000 years ago takes back to the end of the Oligocene Period of Geology, in which horses were the size of coyotes with three toes in front and three behind, camels were the size of sheep, bison, deer and the ox were small hoofed mammals, dogs were soon to develop to the size of bears, and the claws were developing on what later became lions, tigers and cats. And if we go back 4 such rounds, geology indicates there were no mammals, that it was a time when reptiles dominated the earth, and the first primitive birds, and the marsupials, forerunners of the mammals, were just developing. Or, if we wish to call the little rat-size marsupials mammals, which later they developed into, we can say they were beginning to develop along the lines we now recognize as mammals, about 4 such rounds ago.

But if we consider the length of time covered by the Golden, Silver, Copper and Iron Age, that is, 648,000 years, there is plenty of evidence that man was on earth that long ago. Also that the earth once had, but not due to polar motion, a mild and fruitful climate, followed by increasing cold, which about a million years ago ushered in an ice age, with intervals of warmth for thousands of years, followed by more glaciers. Racial memory undoubtedly preserves a consciousness of times which were mild and bountiful, followed by times in which there was tremendous cold and hardship. Eden on earth, and the Age of Horrors are dreams which record actual conditions that transpired since men are known to have inhabited the earth.

The Sun—Arcanum XIX

Letter: Egyptian, Quitolath; Hebrew, Quoph; English, Q. Number, 19. Astrologically, the zodiacal sign Leo. Color, the lighter shades of orange. Tone, high D. Occult science, organic alchemy. Human function, inspiration. Natural remedy, such herbs as camomile, daffodil, cowslip, anise, eglantine, fennel, eyebright, dill, lavender, poppy, yellow lily, marigold, St. John's wort, mistletoe, pimpernel, parsley and garden mint. Mineral, the talismanic gem ruby, and such stones as the chrysolite, hyacinth and soft yellow minerals.

Q—19 expresses in the spiritual world, the supreme heaven.

In the intellectual world, true happiness.

In the physical world, sacred union.

Remember, then, son of earth, that the light of the mysteries is a redoubtable fluid, put by nature at the service of the will. She lights those who know how to direct her; she strikes down with a thunderbolt those who ignore her power or who abuse it. If Arcanum XIX should appear in the prophetic signs of thy horoscope, happiness awaits thee in domestic life if thou knowest how to strengthen the conjugal circle and guard its sacredness in the sanctuary of the heart.

In Divination, **Arcanum XIX** may be read as **Happiness** and **Joy**.

Arcanum XIX is figured by a young man and a young woman holding each other by the hand. About them a circle of 20 flowers springs from the earth. Above is a radiant Sun of 21 rays, in the center of which is the symbol of conjugal union. This sun is the symbol of perfect union expressed on all three planes; perfect harmony of physical desires, intellectual interests, and spiritual aspirations.

The young man and woman are plainly dressed, indicating simplicity of life, moderation of desires and purity of thought. The flowers springing up about them symbolize the joy and happiness of the domestic circle which more than compensate them for material hardships. The 20 flowers signify the potency of domestic harmony to Awaken and Resurrect the spiritual flora of the soul.

This ensemble personifies the fact that when the sexes are truly wed, and the triple laws of harmony are obeyed, that their lives are a constant round of happiness and joy, even amid adversities and privation.

Number

Numerically, 19 is the third decave of 1; or Arcanum I, Creative Energy, operating on the plane of Arcanum III, or Marriage. Consequently, Arcanum XIX is the application of the Divine Fire, controlled by Will and Intelligence, to the elaboration of domestic bliss. It is not only the perfect nuptial union of 7, but denotes added Sacrifice and Devotion (7 plus 12 equal 19).

It may, or may not, indicate the union of soulmates. But it certainly indicates the union of souls harmonious on all planes, not merely for the purpose of spiritual advancement, but also for the production and rearing of children and to experience the joy of a home. Yet in fact, the harmonious vibrations set in motion, and the sacrifices necessary in the rearing of offspring, are most potent factors in developing the spiritual nature.

Astrology

Astrologically, the house governing pleasure, joy, happiness, children and love affairs, is ruled by the zodiacal sign Leo. Leo governs the heart and its sympathies. It is the significator of such love as springs unselfishly into existence as the result of natural harmony, rather than the artificial marriages that today are all too common, which are prompted by material advantages. This "Lion of the house of Juda," as it is called in Revelation, corresponds to Arcanum XIX.

Human Function

Inspiration means the indrawing of the spirit. The source of all life and energy and spiritual power is the Sun, and He is the true source of inspiration. Leo is the home of the Sun, the heart center of man through which the Sun exerts its strongest inspirational power. Leo, therefore, corresponds to the capacity to receive inspiration. Love, which is ruled by Leo, is acknowledged to be the power which opens the inspirational gates. This is symbolized by the Sun overshadowing the lovers in Arcanum XIX.

Alchemy

In alchemy, Arcanum XIX represents the quaffing of the true Elixir of Life. This does not bring instantaneous perpetual youth, for perpetual youth is the result of the gradual changes which the Elixir sets up in the finer forms.

This Elixir is really a love potion, and the result of quaffing it is a general and complete harmonizing of all the internal vibratory rates, so that they sound a sweet and powerful chord, the pitch of which gradually rises as the body and desires are refined, and in time thus results in youthful vigor added to perpetual life.

Bible

In the Bible, Arcanum XIX represents the increase of oil by Elisha: 2 Kings, 4:6. "And it came to pass, when the vessels were full, that she said unto her son, Bring me yet a vessel." Again in Kings 2nd, 4:17; "And the woman conceived, and bare a son at that season that Elisha had said unto her, according to the time of life."

In the New Testament we find, Math. 5:9, "Blessed are the peacemakers; for they shall be called the children of God." And Rev. 22:17, "And the Spirit and the bride say, Come. And let him that heareth say, Come. And let him that is athirst, Come: and whosoever will, let him take the water of life freely."

Masonry

In Masonry, Arcanum XIX is the basis of the Intendant of the Building degree in which the vacancy left by Hiram, the lost soul-mate, is filled. As the third decave, or marriage function of the creative 1, it is mentioned in the first Masonic degree: "Behold how good and how pleasant it is for the brethren to dwell together in unity! etc." Furthermore, Arcanum XIX is the Lion's paw grip by which Hiram Abiff is finally raised.

Magic

In Magic, Arcanum XIX represents the sanctity of the home circle, within the protection of which, when it is harmonious and pure, there is utmost safety from any and all forces of evil.

Where there is complete harmony, the forces of discord, and all evil tends to discord, can not intrude. The harmony between two who love devoutly is repellent to pernicious thoughts and pernicious entities. It is a hallowed circle of invisible influence which they can not penetrate.

For this reason, and because the unselfish feelings developed in the rearing and care of children tend powerfully to raise the dominant vibratory-rates far above any which can be reached or influenced by pernicious entities, these do their utmost to discourage domestic life and the rearing of children.

It is even taught in some quarters that a woman who bears children forfeits her chance of spiritual attainment in this life; and not until she reincarnates again and lives a non-child-bearing life can she expect to make much spiritual progress.

This is patently an inversion of the real truth; because spiritual progress depends upon love, unselfishness, and the refinement of the thoughts and emotions, and nothing develops these soul qualities faster than the love and care of a parent for children. The love of parents for their offspring is often the saving grace of their lives, keeping the inward affectional fires burning, whose warmth transmitted to the soul, keeps it from sinking into the icy death of self-centeredness.

The bearing of children on earth corresponds to sacred functions in the spiritual world. And while it is true that economic conditions, as well as pronounced discords in the fifth house of the birth-chart, may be severe enough that it is the wiser course not to bring children into the world, as they could not be given proper support and proper vigorous bodies, yet such conditions contravene nature, and occasion the loss of valuable experience to the soul.

The very fact that childlessness is always indicated in a birth-chart by severe discords, shows that such a condition is in the nature of an affliction rather than a benefit. Such a childless life can only be compensated for, in its effect upon the soul, by some marked and continuous effort, to benefit and care for some section of mankind, or some work for mankind as a whole.

There is a great amount of foolishness taught concerning the possibilities of eugenics. In order that men should profit as does domestic stock, through proper breeding for results, it would be necessary to place a practical breeder in charge of the whole human race, with the power to prevent the mating of all humans except a few superior individuals whom he would select, and to be able to compel the union of any man and woman, regardless of their desires in the matter. Such power, which is the secret of a stock-breeder's success, is not likely to be given any man.

It is possible, within limits, however, to select the birth-chart of a child and thus determine many of the characteristics which the child shall possess. It is possible, also, through proper environment, to encourage characteristics which otherwise would not develop. And the ancient magi believed that an ideal image of characteristics of the future child, held by both parents before and at the time of conception had a powerful effect in determining the kind of soul attracted to the form thus conceived. They held also, as elaborated in Course 4, that the mental plane in general of the parents, as indicated by their daily thoughts, and their harmony or discord in relation to each other, had a still further influence in shaping the destiny of the future child.

Initiation

In the soul's pilgrimage Arcanum XIX represents the reunion of true soul-mates into a single soul-mate system. So far as common require-ments are concerned the marriage of harmonious souls is sufficient to afford those harmonies which aid spiritual progress. And, because this inner union is of spiritual bodies, only the few are highly enough developed to recognize it when it does take place. The majority mistake magnetic affinity for this inner blend, and consequently all too many discard one partner for another in the belief that the soul-mate has been found.

This is a deplorable situation, but does not mitigate against such relations when they exist in truth. In fact, this abuse is just another inversion of something holy to gratify sensuality.

The real union of soul-mates, to which Arcanum XIX cor-responds, is purely spiritual, and does not of necessity require carnal contact. The blend may even take place in the spaces while the individuals are asleep, all, or nearly all recollection of it often vanish-ing when they awaken. Yet once this bond is formed, its power is never lost, and ultimately the two become conscious of the bond, either in this world or the next, and they begin to function then as a single system.

Occult Science

Organic alchemy is the science which embraces all life-forms in the universe, and the changes in their characters which are produced by their experiences, and the processes by which they develop along special lines, each to become a valuable function in the body of the universal organism. Such processes are indicated as taking place by Arcanum XIX.

The Sarcophagus—Arcanum XX

Letter: Egyptian, Rasith; Hebrew, Resh; English, R. Number, 20. Astrologically, the Moon. Color, green. Tone, F. Occult science, the next life. Human function, the Divine Soul. Natural remedy, hydro-therapy. Mineral, the metal silver.

R—20 expresses in the spiritual world, the immortality of the soul.

In the intellectual world, the judgment of conscience.

In the physical world, unexpected elevation.

Remember, then, son of earth, that all fortune is changeable, even that which appears most stable. The ascension of the soul is the fruit that it should draw from its successive trials. Hope in suffering, but mistrust thyself in prosperity. If Arcanum XX should appear in the prophetic signs of thy horoscope, fall not asleep, either in idleness or forgetfulness; for thou hast a mission to accomplish which providence will reveal when thou art prepared to receive it.

In Divination, **Arcanum XX** may be read as an **Awakening** or **Resurrection**.

Arcanum XX is figured by a sarcophagus on whose side is pictured a scarab. Above this tomb a genie sounds a trumpet, whereupon it opens and a man, woman and child rise from it, still dressed in their winding sheets.

The sarcophagus is the tomb through which man ascents to a higher life. The scarab is symbol of the immortality of the soul. The genie blowing the trumpet is the call to ascend to higher spheres. A man, woman and child arise together to indicate that immortality depends upon the trinity of positive and negative soul-monads united about their Deific ego. The innocence of the ego is represented by the child.

The real tomb is the physical body which confines and envelops the soul while it develops its powers through the functions of social life; its relations to other life-forms. After one life in human form it has acquired self-consciousness and has no need to return to earth. As indicated by the trinity rising from the grave, there are opportunities for family life and other experiences on the next plane, the total ensemble symbolizing this entering into a new and active life in a realm above matter.

Number

Numerically, 20 is the third decave of 2, and thus represents Arcanum II operating on the plane of Arcanum III, occult science manifesting in marriage. In the King's chamber of the Great Pyramid in Egypt is found a lidless sarcophagus, symbolizing the soul's flight out of matter, and out of the physical body; but significant enough, no sarcophagus is found in the Queen's chamber, for those who devised this great monument of occult science recognized that man and woman were but the two immortal portions of one Deific spiritual ego.

Astrology

The Moon governs all periods of gestation, and is the magnetic mother of all life. Life on earth, in a physical body, is but the period of gestation which precedes a more vivid and active life in higher-dimensional realms. The Moon thus corresponds to Arcanum XX.

Human Function

The ego is a spiritual spark of Deity, and as such is eternal; but the soul alone is immortal. What the Moon is to the Sun, that the soul is to the ego. It is the divine soul which, having evolved through countless life-forms, attains self-conscious immortality. Its effort in this direction is shown in Arcanum XX.

Alchemy

In alchemy, Arcanum XX represents the Consciousness of the changes in himself, or the changes in other things, as the case may require, that take place as the transmutations proceed. It is the recognition of the new vibratory rates.

Bible

The trinity rising from the sarcophagus of Arcanum XX is referred to in John 21:14; "This is now the third time that Jesus showed himself to his disciples, after He was risen from the dead." Then Luke 24:51; "And it came to pass while he blessed them, he was parted from them, and carried up into heaven." Such ascensions are mentioned still further in Rev. 20:6; "Blessed and holy is he that hath part in the first resurrection: on such the second death hath no power."

This signifies that those who attain adeptship, and in the process build a spiritual form, not only voluntarily translate to the inner plane when life's work is over, but that, instead of requiring still more arduous experience in the astral realms, they move at once to sojourn on the spiritual plane, thus escaping the so-called second death. Voluntary ascension is plainly indicated for both Elijah and Jesus, and may be inferred for Moses; Deut. 34-6; "But no man knoweth of his sepulchre unto this day. And Moses was an hundred and twenty years old when he died; his eye was not dim, nor his natural forces abated."

The birth into the next life may be accidental, natural, or surgical, depending on the circumstances. The natural method is that indicated in the lives of Jesus, Elijah, Moses and certain of the Indian tribesmen of the North. That is, they go voluntarily, and need no assistance from others on either plane.

The accidental method of birth into the next life occurs frequently on the field of battle, in sudden accidents, where there are explosions, and other places in which the death of the physical comes without warning and with considerable shock. In such cases not infrequently the individual does not realize for some time that he is dead. These cases, however, which represent a temporary inability to make the proper adjustment to the inner plane, are not the same as those in which, through the strong and unbreakable attachment to some earthly thing the individual is earthbound: Rev. 20:5; "But the rest of the dead lived again until a thousand years were finished."

Masonry

In Masonry, Arcanum XX is the basis of the Perfect Master degree. It is symbolized by the sprig of cassia, sign of immortality, that was found on the grave of Hiram Abiff. Still more is it exemplified by the coffin with a five-point star on the lid, and leaning over it the immortal sprig of cassia.

In the ritual of raising Hiram Abiff from the grave, there are three attempts made, as signified by the three persons rising from the tomb of Arcanum XX. The first two efforts are unsuccessful; and the resurrection is finally accomplished only when the soul-union method of the Lion's paw grip of Arcanum XIX is employed.

Magic

In many magical practices the assistance of those who have once lived on earth is invoked. More commonly than not those who control mediums are, or pretend to be, those who have once lived on earth.

It is true that a medium can tune in on a thought-form, or record left in the astral substance about our planet, so thoroughly as to be dominated by it. This is especially true of thought-forms to which, through mental magic, elemental life-forms have been attached. More commonly, however, mediums are actually controlled by those who once lived on earth, or they tune in on the thoughts and desires emanating from the unconscious minds of those in their circle.

The electromagnetic body of a person never moves far from the corpse after physical death, and it has no intelligence, or special power that can be utilized. The astral body of an individual can only be used through control of it, and an astral body is not a shell. The only spooks and shells of human origin are the powerful thought-forms left by people under great emotional excitement, the astral bodies of souls which are earth-bound, and the electromagnetic bodies of those whose corpses have not yet disintegrated. One might delude oneself into thinking any one of these was a departed loved one; but the discriminating would not make this mistake; and such spooks and phantoms can not be made successfully to impersonate loved ones who have passed to the next plane. The teaching that such is the case is merely the inversive use of a fact in the effort to disparage the belief in the immortality of the soul and to create a disbelief in the possibility of spirit communication.

Initiation

In the soul's pilgrimage Arcanum XX represents the awakening of the soul to its angelic state as the result of entering into the soul-mate system.

Occult Science

The Next Life, is the science of those conditions which surround the life-form after it passes from the physical plane, and embraces a consideration of inner-plane properties, and the means by which the soul continues its advancement in the realms beyond the tomb.

The Magic Cross Spread

In this spread the cards are shuffled and cut as usual. Then five cards are dealt in a straight line from left to right; and eight more cards are dealt in a vertical line crossing the horizontal row at right angles, as illustrated on page 242. Thus while there are really only 13 cards in the spread, there are 5 in the horizontal line and 9 in the vertical line, making 14, the double 7 of regeneration. This explains the mystery of the cross; for 13 is the cross of death and 14 is the rosy cross of life.

The cards marked on the diagram 1 and 2 are to be read as the past. Cards marked 6 and 7 are the hopes and expectations. 4 and 5 represent the opposition and the adversaries. Then 3 is the present, where all factors meet to give birth to the future. And cards 8, 9, 10, 11, 12 and 13 represent the future so conceived.

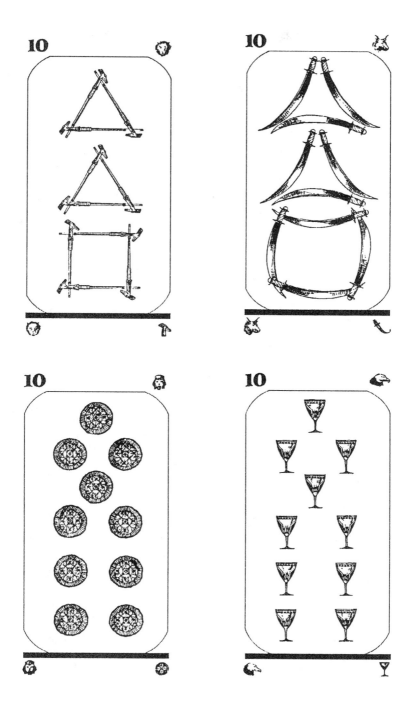

THE LIFE SPREAD

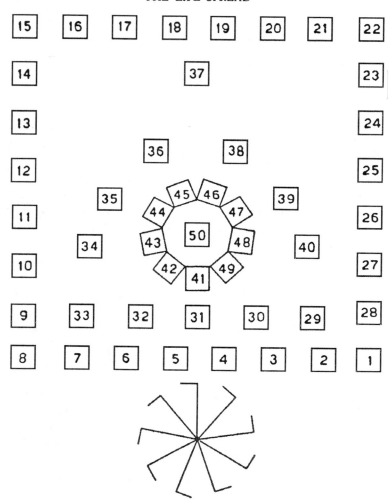

Chapter 13

How to Read the Tarot

ROFICIENCY in any art, physical or psychical, depends largely upon system and method; and this is true of acquiring proficiency in tarot reading.

The first thing to adopt in formulating such a system is a rule in which, except when another shuffles them for the purpose of receiving a reading, no other person is permitted to handle the cards. The more the tarot reader handles the cards the better, for they thus the more completely become impregnated with his magnetism and are able to respond to the subtle thought-vibrations of his unconscious mind. But the magnetism and thought-emanations of others tend to impair this responsiveness through mixing the influences.

For this reason new cards are not so good as those which have been used repeatedly in card reading. And in order that they may the more fully retain the reader's influence they should not be left lying around in contact with the household furniture and thus become contaminated with the magnetism of others; but for best results they should be kept in a special box. This box should not be too large, and a wooden box lined with silk, which is a non-conductor, is preferable; a small box of soft white pine being excellent for the purpose.

If the reader expects to devote much time to tarot practice, and to the spiritual aspect, it is better to have two different tarot packs. The magnetism, or mental emanations, with which the cards become saturated in giving personal readings belongs to one basic vibratory level, while philosophical and spiritual research belong to another. If the cards used for the higher lines of thought are also used in personal readings they may become so influenced by the lower trend for which they are used that they do not properly respond to the desire to obtain information about spiritual things. So it is well to have a separate pack for each type of use, and not to use either pack for gaining information except on its own vibratory plane.

As a table on which to lay out the cards, any surface will do. A sewing table is excellent and easily handled; but where the amount of time devoted to the subject warrants, a light, unvarnished and unpainted table of soft white pine is still better. A new table imparts no extraneous thought-vibrations to the cards, and if unvarnished more quickly absorbs the thought emanations of the reader and gives the best conditions for the psychic intelligence to manifest itself.

A room which is the scene of constant discord and strife is not suitable for any kind of psychic work, as the vibrations left disturb the tranquillity of the unconscious mind and tend to impair the action of the psychic intelligence in its manifestation through the cards. Of course, good results can be obtained when the conditions are not ideal. I have here merely outlined the best conditions. But if these are not to be had, diligent practice will yield good results with the cards even under very unfavorable circumstances.

I have in an early chapter of the course indicated that a definite system in shuffling and cutting should be followed, and only departed from when there is a very urgent impression to do so. Thus the unconscious mind of the reader, and such other psychic intelligences as may be present, will have a clear idea of how the cards are going to be handled. Knowing how the cards will be handled facilitates giving them the proper arrangement by which accurate information may be conveyed through them.

The person to whom the reading is given should be seated on the opposite side of the table facing the reader; and if the arrangement permits, it is better that the reader sit on the south side of the table and the person to whom the reading is given sit on the north side. The natural magnetic flow is from north to south, and this seating aids the establishment of a relation of positive to negative between the client and the reader.

Before the cards are touched the reader should ascertain just what it is that the client wishes to know, so that he will have a clear idea of what the cards are expected to reveal. Then he should ask the client to clear his mind of all desires and thoughts other than the desire to receive a true and correct reading, or answer to the question. A trivial attitude will cause the reading to take a frivolous turn. And if there is a strong desire in the mind of the client or reader to receive a certain answer, it will tend to cause the cards to give that answer.

But if the desire is only for the truth, and there is earnestness, the cards will mirror this attitude and respond with a clear and accurate reading.

Holding their minds to this unbiased attitude to know the truth, the client is then instructed to pick up the cards and shuffle them in such a manner that the ends of some will also be reversed. He is then told to cut them at random into three separate piles, and to collect them again into one pack in a manner giving them a different position than they had before cutting. This process is gone through a second time, and then a third time, all the while the minds of both being occupied with the desire to receive a truthful answer. When they have been thus shuffled, cut, and recollected the third time by the client, the reader takes the cards and deals them from the top, face downward, in the form of the spread he chose to use before the shuffling started.

Then the reader starts by taking the first card by the top and turning it over from top to bottom so that it lies face upward on the table. He looks at this card and notes any impressions he receives in connection with its usual divinatory significance and states them to the client. But in reading the interpretation he is merely to be guided by the common meaning, and is not to be restricted to it.

For the sake of facility the brief divinatory meaning of each card as given in these lessons should be memorized. Yet the real artist will recognize that every card is the symbol of some astrological influence, and his intuition often will select some phase of this astrological rulership to indicate the events which are to transpire.

The Broader Significance of Each Card

On each Major Arcanum is given its corresponding number, at the upper right-hand corner is the symbol of its astrological planet or sign, below is the English letter, at the lower left-hand corner its Hebrew and Chaldean letter, at the lower right-hand its Egyptian letter, and if it corresponds to a zodiacal sign, the stars of the constellation picturing the sign are traced on the card as they appear in the sky. Outstanding things relating to each Major Arcanum are given in the text accompanying its description; and further things ruled by the corresponding sign may be learned from Chapter 5 of Course 5, *Esoteric Psychology* and Chapter 3 of Course 4, *Ancient Masonry;* and further things ruled by the corresponding planet may be learned from Chapter 7 of Course 8, *Horary Astrology* and Chapter 5 of Course 10-1, *Delineating The Horoscope.*

The scope of interpretation of each arcanum is thus vastly increased through the application of the law of correspondences. For instance, should Arcanum XVI be turned up it might read as an accident, which is the common meaning. But this arcanum is really an expression of the energy of Mars, so that if there were cards preceding it which indicated sickness, it should then be read as a surgical operation; for surgical operations only occur in people's lives when there is a Major Progressed Aspect involving Mars in their birth-charts.[1]

The Kings, Queens and Youths

On each of the court cards which represents a type of individual, in addition to the corresponding playing card symbols to be found above and below on the left-hand side of the card, and the emblem of the suit to be found at the lower right-hand corner, the symbol of the zodiacal sign it represents is given at the upper right-hand corner, and on the card the stars of the constellation picturing that sign are traced as they appear in the sky. If the picture on the card is that of a man, it represents a man when right way up, and represents a woman when reversed. If the picture is that of a woman, it represents a woman when right way up, and represents a man when reversed. Then the suit alone indicates one of the four general temperaments, and the complexion of the individual thus designated, if such is all that is required.

The brief description and the Key-phrase given in association with each card representing a person, adds further information about the designated individual. But the student, as he advances will desire more details about such persons as are indicated in the spread; and on occasions will wish to know their spiritual leanings as well as their more common characteristics. The description of people born under each zodiacal sign, as set forth in Chapter 2 of Course 2, *Astrological Signatures* and Chapter 3 of Course 10-1, *Delineating the Horoscope*, will give full details of their characteristics; Chapter 4 of Course 8, *Horary Astrology*, will give their personal appearance; and the allegorical story and its spiritual teaching given in Course 7, *Spiritual Astrology*, as relating to the sign, will reveal their spiritual possibilities.

The Horsemen

The Horsemen are mounted to signify the carrying power and astrological significance of thought. The suit, as shown by the symbol at the lower right-hand corner indicates what the thoughts are about. They represent the thoughts of other people in relation to the client; usually being the thoughts of the person nearest whom found in the spread. If a Horseman is found right end up, it indicates that the thoughts and plans so signified are favorable to the client; but if the Horseman is reversed, the thoughts and plans are detrimental to the interests of the client.

The Minor Arcana

In astrology the Sun or a planet is considered not only in its relation to the point where the observer stands, but also in relation to its position in the zodiac. In relation to the diurnal rotation of the earth, when the Sun is on the M.C. at noon, it corresponds to Jod of the divine word, and to the suit of scepters; yet in relation to the Sun's apparent annual journey through the zodiac, scepters correspond to the fiery signs.

When the Sun sinks below the western horizon its position corresponds to the first He of the divine word, and to the feminine suit of cups; yet in relation to the zodiac, cups correspond to the watery signs.

When the Sun is on the nadir at midnight, where one day joins another and the power of darkness is greatest, this position corresponds to Vau of the divine word, where Jod and He unite, and to the suit of swords. Yet in relation to the zodiacal circle, swords correspond to the earthy signs.

Finally, when the Sun rises on the eastern horizon, bringing new life to an awaiting world, its position corresponds to the suit of coins; yet in relation to the whole zodiac, coins correspond to the airy signs.

The common divinatory interpretation of the Minor Arcana considers the suit according to the positions relating to the diurnal rotation of the earth; that is, in reference to the M.C. (business), the Desc. (affections), the Nadir (affliction) and the Asc. (life and money). But the inner interpretation is derived from the correspondence of each card to a ten degree section of the zodiac.

Each Minor Arcanum has its number placed at the upper left-hand corner, and the symbol of its suit at the lower right-hand corner, the emblem being repeated the proper number of times in the symbolic design. The nine arcana of each suit correspond to the nine decanates of each zodiacal triplicity, the tenth arcana, both embracing the whole triplicity as a completed circle and marking a transition to a new cycle, being summarized by the triplicity's Key-word.

The Movable signs of the zodiac are the starters, the PIONEERS, hence the true point of departure in any triplicity is not where it first appears in the zodiac, which with the earthy triplicity, for instance, would be Taurus, but with its first appearance in a movable sign. Thus the fiery triplicity commences with Aries, the watery triplicity with Cancer, the Airy triplicity with Libra and the earthy triplicity with Capricorn.

If you will turn to the illustrated key on page 21 of chapter 1, it will be plain that the first three decanates of the earthy triplicity, corresponding to the suit of swords, are there shown numbered 1, 2, 3, in Capricorn at the top of the key; that the next three decanates occur in Taurus and are numbered 4, 5, 6; while the last three decanates of the earthy triplicity appear in Virgo, numbered 7, 8, 9. A little study of this key will indicate the astrological position and correspondence also of the decanates of the other triplicities corresponding to the other suits.

Each of the Minor Arcana below 10 thus corresponds strictly to one of the 10 degree section of the zodiac. And as each of the 36 decanates is pictured in the sky by a constellation, the stars of the constellation corresponding to each Minor Arcanum are traced upon it. In the text, in addition to the common divinatory meaning of each Minor Arcanum is given its inner interpretation, which is revealed by the Key-word of the decanate to which it thus belongs.

As the student advances, however, he will wish still more detailed information as to the significance of these Minor Arcana. The symbols indicating the decanate to which each belongs are given at the upper right-hand corner of the card, and the planet ruling the decanate is placed, for ready reference, at the lower left-hand corner. Full details of the physical significance of each decanate, and thus of its Minor Arcanum, may be learned by consulting Chapters 1 and 2 of Course 10-1, *Delineating the Horoscope*, while the allegorical story relating to each, which reveals its spiritual significance, can be had by looking up the decanate in Course 8, *Horary Astrology*.

Interpreting The Cards

Beginners should restrict their interpretation closely to the common divinatory meaning; but it will be seen that as all events, thoughts and circumstances have astrological correspondences, every possible combination of events and conditions may be indicated in a tarot spread if the wide astrological interpretation is used.

If all the cards are turned over before the reading starts the mind spontaneously wanders all over the spread and it detracts from the ability to draw correct conclusions from the card under consideration. Therefore, the cards should be turned over, one at a time, as read. After reading the first card, which usually indicates some event or condition in the past, the next card should be turned over and read as a subsequent condition or event modifying the first, and the third card as a circumstance modifying all that has preceded. Thus proceed from past through the present into the future, each card like a single petal of the opening bud of events, which alters in shape as it expands, yet all required to represent the full blown flower of the future.

Some of the cards will be found right end up, and some reversed. But this reversal of ends does not reverse the meaning, as is sometimes thought. Instead it makes the card somewhat less fortunate than it is when right end up, just as a planet is less fortunate when it receives a bad aspect, or as a sign is less fortunate when its ruler receives an inharmonious aspect. For instance, Saturn can hardly be considered a benefic planet when well aspected, and Arcanum XV is never a good card, even when right end up; but when reversed it is more like Saturn afflicted by a discordant aspect. On the other hand Jupiter, even when much afflicted, is never very malefic; therefore Arcanum V, even when reversed can signify very little evil, although it is then not so good as if right end up. The same principle applies also to the minor arcana. Thus except for the court cards, the significance of which when reversed has already been explained, any card right end up is more fortunate than it is when reversed.

To determine the influence upon the life of the client of any Court Arcanum, consider the card just preceding it in the spread. To determine what action will be taken, or move made, by a person represented by a Court Arcanum, consider the card that next follows it in the spread.

One may read the cards for himself; and one may read the cards successfully for an absent person, both shuffling and reading the cards. And as in any art, proficiency is acquired only by much practice and observation of results.

When using the tarot cards for spiritual and philosophical problems, in which the life of no person is involved, the Major Arcana become of great importance, and at times may be used apart from the other cards. In such considerations the 12 Court Arcana represent the 12 zodiacal signs, and the things to which they correspond, such as the 12 types of intelligence. The Horsemen then represent the 4 elemental kingdoms, and also the four principles related to the word Jod-He-Vau-He. The Minor Arcana become useful to designate the various numerical relations.

In using the tarot for philosophical and spiritual problems, the Court Arcana, other than the Horsemen, may also be taken to signify the influence of their corresponding zodiacal signs to modify conditions.

And in the use of the cards for such purposes, it should be carefully borne in mind that the reading of the Major Arcana should always occupy the same plane as the problem to be solved. Thus if the problem concerns the physical plane, such as the destiny of a nation, its success in war or commerce, the geological epochs of the earth, the growth of plants and animals—physical relations—the reading given for the physical world should be used. But if the problem is concerned with the soul world, with mental action, with the intellectual development of life, or with the interaction of magical forces, the reading should follow the interpretation of the Major Arcana given for the Intellectual world. Furthermore, if the thing about which information is sought has to do with universal principles, with spiritual conditions, with eternal verities, or with the working of God's Great Plan, the interpretation given in connection with each Arcanum in the spiritual world should be employed. The idea is always to have the premises and conclusions on the same plane.

The Major Arcana of the tarot are only surpassed as subjects for meditation by the spiritual texts of astrology. One such card can be used thus on one day, and another card on the following day, its symbolism and meaning in the three different worlds receiving undivided attention. After thus thoroughly covering the entire 22, they may be variously joined in twos, the interaction of the two principles being meditated upon, in different arrangements. If, for instance it is desired to know the value of good and evil, conjoin Arcanum V and Arcanum XV; or if the effect of controlling desire would be known, meditate upon the union of Arcanum I with Arcanum VI.

Because everything which exists has an astrological correspondence which is also associated with a tarot card, by selecting the proper factors, any physical or occult problem may be solved by the use of the tarot. Thus, taking something crude, if you wished to know the possibilities of gasoline, ruled by Neptune, for power, you would select Arcanum XI. If you wished to know more about the alternating current of electrical science, you would combine X, ruling electricity and sudden changes with VI ruling the copper transmitter. Arcanum XVI thus would give you something definite to think about.

In an astrological chart, to get a clearer view, you can substitute the admonition which starts, "Remember, then, son of earth," for the dominant planet, or for the significator of the thing asked about. And if the correspondences of the factors in the problem are unknown, you can take the pack of cards and lay out a suitable spread as in other divination by cards, to get the answer. What the tarot can be made to reveal is limited only by the capacity of understanding of the person using it.

The Adept—Arcanum XXI

Letter: Egyptian, Sichen; Hebrew, Schin; English, S. Number, 21. Astrologically, the Sun. Color, orange. Tone, D. Occult science, personal alchemy. Human function, the ego. Natural remedy, light and color. Mineral, the metal gold.

S—21, expresses in the spiritual world, angelhood.
In the intellectual world, the triumph of adeptship.
In the physical world, the highest possible attainment.

Remember, then, son of earth, that the empire of the world belongs to the empire of light and that the empire of light is the throne which God reserves for the sanctified will. If Arcanum XXI should appear in the prophetic signs of thy horoscope, thou wilt gather the fruit of the knowledge of good and evil, and drink of the eternal fountain, if thou art sufficiently master of thyself to approach it without coveting; obstacles will disappear from thy path, and thy destiny will have no limit save those of thy will.

In Divination, **Arcanum XXI** may be read as **Success** or **Attainment**.

Arcanum XXI is figured by a kneeling young girl playing on a harp of three strings. Above is a wreath of twelve flowers, each flower having three blossoms. At each of the four angles of the wreath is a head; the two below being the head of an eagle and the head of a bull, the two above being the head of a lion and the head of a man. The man's head has the sacred serpent at its brow to indicate mental fertility. In the center of the wreath is a phallus and a yoni conjoined. This sacred lingha is soaring upward through the wreath, sustained by two wings.

The young girl symbolizes purity of life. She is modestly clothed to indicate simplicity of living and moderation in desires. She kneels as she plays the harp to indicate absolute devotion to the higher laws, and prayerful aspirations to live a spiritual life.

The harp has three strings, signifying harmony of body, intellect and emotions.

The twelve flowers of the wreath above are the twelve zodiacal signs in which all experience is gained. The three blossoms of each flower indicate that both souls, as represented joined in the winged linga, have garnered the flowers of zodiacal experience on all planes, physical, astral and spiritual.

The head of the Lion signifies the creative forces of the solar sign, Leo, and the courage which is necessary to all real attainment. The head of the Bull represents the fructifying agent of nature and points out the necessity of labor in all progress. The Eagle signifies that sex, as signified by the sign Scorpio, has been turned into channels which lead to spirituality. And the head of the Man indicates that both intuition and intelligence are necessary guides in unfolding the highest spiritual possibilities.

These four emblems ranged around the zodiac typify the processes of evolution. They are the four forms of the Egyptian sphinx, and also symbolize the passage of the Sun through the four zodiacal quadrants. As applied to adeptship they point out that the neophyte must have energy and courage to sustain his efforts, must have knowledge to direct his energies properly, must labor ceaselessly for the realization of his aspirations, and must gradually tune his emotions to a higher, more spiritual vibratory level. Those four attributes, Wisdom, Perseverance, Courage, and Love are usually rendered in occult circles as: "To Know, To Do, To Dare, To be Silent."

The winged linga in the center of the wreath of zodiacal flowers symbolizes the permanent union of soul-mates and their ascension into angelic worlds by virtue of the properties of the soul-mates system so formed. The girl kneeling by the harp denotes that this union was brought about by living the life of the spirit while on earth. Spiritual aspirations and devotion to furthering God's Great Plan, loving and unselfish endeavor to contribute the utmost to cosmic welfare, together with a clear conception of the laws of harmony, in time bring about the recognition across the spaces and the development of exchanging lines of force, which lead to this ineffable union. This harmonious reverberation of soul to soul is symbolized by the harp of three strings, for the union embraces all three planes.

Strength depends upon harmony, and the music of their souls sounding across the spaces endows both with a hitherto unknown power to overcome obstacles, to gain the blossoms of experience on all three planes, as signified by the three flowers related to each of the 12 zodiacal signs. As a whole the ensemble signifies the attainment of adeptship while on earth, and the crown of angelhood that awaits such perfect human beings when they have passed from the physical and function in the sublime vistas of the future.

Number

Numerically, 21 is the third decave of 3, representing Arcanum III operating on the plane of Arcanum III, hence marriage in its most perfect expression. It signifies the complete nuptial union of 7 carried through three planes to be developed into angelic expression. And it also signifies in its other aspects, the 3 x 7, or highest possible development of human functions and possibilities.

Astrology

As in truth the Sun is the source of all physical, mental and emotional power expressed on earth, the planets merely refracting its various attributes, and the signs acting as sounding-boards for such expression, so Arcanum XXI, signifying perfection, union and attainment on all three planes, corresponds to the Sun.

Human Function

Arcanum XXI pictures the ultimate reunion of soul-mates. And as such reunion enters into the formation of a new system in which the ego is the central nucleus, about which the magnetic and spiritual forces of both souls play, endowing the whole with properties which transcend even those of five-dimensional life, Arcanum XXI well corresponds to the ego.

Alchemy

In Alchemy, Arcanum XXI represents the final product, or successful transmutation, and more specifically it denotes the completion of The Great Work.

Bible

The Bible refers to the principle involved in Arcanum XXI as the Promised Land, on which Moses was permitted to look, but into which he was not able to enter. In this respect the Kabala states that Moses was able to pass 49 gates, but could not pass the 50th, or gate of jubilee.

Masonry

In Masonry, the Degree of Perfection is based upon Arcanum XXI. This Arcanum is symbolized in ancient masonry by a two-headed eagle. An eagle is the spiritual aspect of sex, and the two heads signify two intelligences, or souls, united and occupying one soul-mate system.

Magic

In Magic, Arcanum XXI represents the exercise of the functions of adeptship. Although not easily distinguishable, there are seven grades of humanity who live and move upon the earth, the seventh, and highest, state being that of the perfect man. The attainment of adeptship on the physical plane is the grand climax of physical evolution, the topmost point in the ladder of worldly ambitions.

The adept, commencing as an earnest neophyte, has undergone a system of study by which he has mastered the 21 different branches of occult science. He has entered upon a process of regular psychic training by which his inner faculties are made active and accurate, and thus he masters the 21 lucidic arts. Intuition is used to check reason, and the psychic senses are developed to a keenness that they can be depended on for far-reaching information not accessible in the outer world.

Furthermore, there are 7 states of consciousness which are developed, which constitute soul attainment. Those 49, then, are the 49 gates of attainment which Moses passed. And the 50th is that which relates to the union of true soul-mates.

The real adept, however, is not, as so many seem to imagine, a being who has attained wonderful power, but who resides in seclusion and lets mankind work out its own problems. Instead, if he is really an adept, and not merely a magician, he moves among men, and uses all his powers, in the manner that will be most helpful, to alleviate suffering and to aid the forward movement of universal progression.

Whatever the powers he has developed, you may be sure the adept is actively engaged in using them for human welfare. He realizes that the destiny of the cosmos depends upon each section of it advancing as rapidly as possible, and performing its own work. And he has striven to become an adept, not to have magical powers by which to amaze the multitude, but because such a high state of development gives him added usefulness in the general scheme of things. Constantly, and persistently, he works for human upliftment, and for everything that will aid in the proper development of God's Great Plan.

Initiation

In the soul's pilgrimage, Arcanum XXI represents the consciousness of the whereabouts of the soul-mate, and finally, due to spiritual work accomplished and spiritual faculties developed, the union in a soul-mate system. As such permanent union is a relation of spiritual forms, it is apparent there can be no permanent union until both have spiritual forms developed. Spiritual bodies are not something with which people are born, they are builded through living a spiritual life. Consequently, the effort to locate the soul-mate, until such finer forms have developed, is premature, and leads many people to grievous error.

Furthermore, as when the spirituality is sufficiently advanced, through living a truly spiritual life, it leads spontaneously to a recognition of the soul-mate, the most fitting effort toward such a state is not to set out on a soul-mate quest, but to set out with the determination to develop adeptship. When adeptship, or even its approximation, is attained, the knowledge of the soul-mate comes by virtue of the states of consciousness developed, and with no special endeavor required.

Occult Science

Personal alchemy, which embraces the various changes which the devotee of The Religion of the Stars must make in his manner of living as he ascends the spiritual ladder to become the perfect man, or adept, corresponds to Arcanum XXI.

The Materialist—Arcanum XXII or 0

Letter: Egyptian, Thoth; Hebrew, Tau; English T. Number 22. Astrologically, the planet Pluto. Color, ultra-violet and infra-red. Tone, harmony. Or the color may be black and the tone inharmony. In science it is either materialism or spirituality. Natural remedy, stellar healing. Human function, soul-mate system. Mineral, the soil of earth, or the element plutonium.

T—22 expresses in the spiritual world, annihilation; 0 expresses eternal progression.

In the intellectual world, 22 is atheism; and 0, devotion to The Religion of the Stars.

In the physical world, 22 is materialism, and 0 is ceaseless cooperation in the furtherance of God's Great Plan.

> *Remember, then, son of earth, that all things physical pass away; and that before the soul can pass to higher realms every debt to nature must be paid to the utmost farthing. If Arcanum XXII should appear in the prophetic signs of thy horoscope, imprudence threatens to encompass thy ruin, and thou wilt be called upon to pay for thy folly unless thou immediately changeth thy ways.*

In Divination, **Arcanum XXII** means **Failure, Folly,** and **Mistake;** (or **Spirituality**).

Arcanum XXII, or 0, like the planet Pluto, has a dual interpretation. As XXII, it is well represented by the letter T with its point thus down; but as 0, the circle being the symbol of spirit, it is represented by the reversed T, that is, having the point, or energy, directed upward, the cross-bar resting below on the earth, and thus indicating that the thoughts, emotions and actions, are directed exclusively toward spiritual endeavor. It is figured by a blind man carrying bags on his left shoulder. He leans on a black staff and walks toward a fallen obelisk behind which a crocodile with open mouth awaits to devour him. Above is an eclipse of the Sun. The eclipse signifies that the spiritual light from within has been obscured by material interests; or it signifies that dark forces from the inner plane try to shut away the spiritual illumination which guides the neophyte.

The bags over the left shoulder of the blind man indicate the material things of life he has spent his efforts acquiring; or it represents his ability to minister in physical ways to those in need.

The staff of experience with good and evil is black, indicating that prudence is subservient to the demands of the senses; or that the demands for uplifting and protecting others is so great that, though enlightened, he ignores all danger.

The fallen obelisk symbolizes the final overthrow of all temporal work and power. The crocodile indicates the ultimate fate of all who are blind to spiritual things, and also the persecution of those who work to spread the true facts of spirituality.

This blind man is the atheist, or materialist, and the man who is so absorbed in material aims that he neglects all thought of spiritual things. It is likewise the man who is a slave to his desires. And the ensemble thus symbolizes the inevitable suffering which follows sin. Or, it symbolizes the truly spiritual man, who is so enthusiastic in his effort to assist the race that he is completely blind to the consequences to himself. And thus, equally well, it symbolizes the law of universal compensation, which decrees that for all effort expended in a constructive channel there inevitably follows increased ability and real advancement.

Number

Numerically, 22 is the third decave of 4, and thus represents sex used to gratify the passions, or for magical and selfish purposes. 0, however, which is the alternate reading of the Arcanum, represents the cycle, and shows that there is a transition of character to a higher basic spiritual, or vibratory, level.

Astrology

In astrology it is found that the planet Pluto has two marked and opposite qualities. It rules the gangster and racketeer when its destructive side manifests; and it rules the highest type of spiritual effort, and the realization by the individual of his cosmic work, when the better side is manifest. These two extremes are symbolized by Arcanum XXII.

Human Function

On its destructive side Arcanum XXII corresponds to, and symbolizes, the disintegration of the vehicle on the inner plane occupied by the soul; and on the constructive side Arcanum 0 represents the infiltration to the soul yet on earth of information and instructions from adepts occupying the super-velocity spiritual plane.

Alchemy

In Alchemy, Arcanum XXII signifies failure in transmutation, and the regimes adopted in the hope of transmutation which lead only to repressions. Arcanum 0, on the other hand, represents the work in cosmic affairs which is undertaken after the Great Work has been accomplished.

Bible

In the Bible we read that the Fool has said in his heart that there is no God. Also, Math. 16:26; "For what is a man profited, if he shall gain the whole world, and lose his own soul?" Math. 12:32; "But whosoever speaketh against the Holy Ghost, it shall not be forgiven him, neither in this world, neither in the world to come." Speaking against the Holy Ghost is effort made to prevent the progress of God's Great Plan of eternal evolution.

Masonry

In Masonry, the Sublime Knight Elected is based upon Arcanum XXII, the Tau, or T, with the point down, instead of with the point up, and thus indicating that the creative energies are devoted exclusively to material ends.

Magic

In Magic, Arcanum XXII indicates that the individual has given himself over to the control of invisible intelligences who have no regard for his welfare, and who use him consistently to thwart any and everything which is true and progressive on the face of the earth. It symbolizes elemental affinities that are formed in the selfish endeavor to gain, through magic, material advantages over others.

Arcanum 0, the alternate interpretation, however, indicates that there is freedom from all control; but that the individual has contacted intelligences of a very exalted spiritual plane who direct him consistently in his efforts to give to those on earth new and higher teachings.

Initiation

In the soul's pilgrimage Arcanum XXII represents the failure of the soul to gain self-conscious immortality. It also represents the obstacles which, whenever the neophyte sets his feet resolutely on the path of adeptship he is sure to attract. The resolution to live in a different manner, by the law of affinity, causes the thinking about it to attract obstacles to the performance of the thing resolved upon.

Arcanum 0, on the other hand, indicates that the soul through its earthly experiences has developed in the building of its spiritual form far enough that it will not need to tarry in the astral world after the dissolution of the physical, but will go at once to undertake a higher mission for The Father, on the still more interior planes. And it represents that law of affinity which, when the aspirations are vivid, attracts spiritual entities and forces which enable it, through their help, to overcome the obstacles to its spiritual progress.

Occult Science

Arcanum XXII represents the soul-annihilating dogmas of materialism. But Arcanum 0, on the other hand, represents the soul uplifting teachings of THE RELIGION OF THE STARS.

The Life Spread

The Life-Spread requires a large table, or space, on which to lay the cards. After shuffling and cutting the cards in the usual manner, the cards are dealt, one at a time, face downward in the form of a hollow square of 28 cards. 4 is realization and 7 is perfection of form, and these 4 x 7 cards of the square, or 28 (2 plus 8 equals ten) involving to 10, symbolize the cycle of life in the physical form. Yet, as laid, there are 8 on each side, the number of crystallization. This square relates to the physical endeavors.

Within this hollow square of the physical, deal a triangle of 12 cards, so that there are 5 cards on each side of the triangle, always dealing from the right hand corner around to the left. 5 is the number of inspiration and 3 is the number of action. These 12 cards indicate the sacrifices (12) which have been made of the physical comforts for the sake of developing the mentality. This triangle, the triangle symbolizing mind, relates to mental attainment.

Then in this hollow trine, commencing at the bottom, deal a circle of 9 cards. 9 is the number of divine wisdom, and as it is in the form of a circle, which symbolizes spirit, it relates to spiritual attainment.

There are now 49 cards, or 49 gates to life, and there remains only to add the 50th card in the center to give the jubilee, which is the point where square, trine and circle are one. The spread is illustrated on page 264.

In reading this life oracle, start with the lower right hand corner of the square and read entirely around the square to the left, turning and reading but one card at a time. The cards in this outer spread are all to be considered as events relating to the physical life and material success; and not as having much direct bearing on intellectual pursuits or spiritual attainment. Each, in the order in which it occurs is to be considered as a subsequent event or influence.

After the material events and influences have thus been read, start at the lower right hand corner of the trine, and read around to the left; but consider these cards, as turned and read, to have to do with the mental processes, the intellectual attainment, and such studies and opportunities as have to do with acquiring knowledge.

Next start with the bottom card of the circle and read it around to the left. The conditions there found, and the opportunities shown, relate to the spiritual development, and the moral trend. Of course, material happenings and mental opportunities have an influence upon the spiritual life; but only such as are found in the circle of 9 cards are to be considered as really important factors in the spiritual life.

The events relating to each plane of endeavor, as shown in this spread, are to be considered as those of most importance throughout the whole of the life. And as a final revelation, indicating the event which, on the physical, mental and spiritual plane, will have most influence in shaping the client's life, the central card, or Jubilee, should be turned over and read.

Note

1. See *Astrology: 30 Years Research.*

Study Questions _____

Chapter 1, Doctrine of Kabalism

1. What is the most essential kabalistical doctrine?
2. When was the first Jewish Kabala placed in writing?
3. What does the Jewish Kabala teach relative to reincarnation?
4. What is the teaching of the Jewish Kabala in regard to soul-mates?
5. Just what is the mystery of the Shekinah, and how is it related to the doctrine of the Tree of Life?
6. What light is thrown upon the mystery of the fruit of the Tree of Life by the knowledge that Kether, at the head of the tree is represented in the planetary chain by Pluto, and represents both differentiation and reunion?
7. Of what does the Sephir Sephiroth treat?
8. What is the meaning of Sephir Yetzirah, and who is supposed to have dictated it?
9. What are the four divisions of the Dogmatic Kabala?
10. What does the word kabala mean?
11. What is the significance of the statement that he who can rightly pronounce the Divine Name causeth heaven and earth to tremble?
12. To what elements do the four kabalistical worlds correspond?
13. What are the Ten Emanations of the Sephiroth?
14. What is the most studied of the Jewish kabalistical works?
15. How many single letters are there in the Jewish alphabet, and to what in a general way do they correspond?
16. What do the fourth and fifth chapters of the Sephir Yetzirah represent in the universe?
17. Of what does the Practical Kabala treat?

18. What is the kabalistical teaching regarding the relation of God to the universe?
19. What is the kabalistical trinity which is the commencement and the end of the student's researches?
20. Of what does Asch Metzareph treat?
21. How many double letters are there in the Hebrew alphabet, and in a general way to what do they correspond?
22. Trace the kabalistical doctrine from its origin to the present time.
23. What is the method of the Literal Kabala?
24. What is the Unwritten Kabala?
25. What is Mr. Waite's opinion as to the nature of the one secret doctrine of the Jews?

Chapter 2, **Foundation of the Science**

1. How does the science of vibration, as interpreted by numbers, differ from numerology?
2. What was Caruso's experiment by which he demonstrated the power of the vibration of his voice?
3. Is the sound of a name effective in influencing the person wearing it; and, if not, what is it?
4. What is the really important influence of a name, number, tone, color, talismanic gem, thought, or character on a person closely associated with it?
5. What is meant by divination by numbers?
6. Is either divination by numbers or divination by cards a strictly scientific and positive process?
7. Give the origin of the 22 Chaldean square-formed letters.
8. In what manner, in olden times, were verified spiritual facts associated with the constellations, with the pictured tarot plates, and with numbers?
9. What are the results to an organism when it can no longer make successful adaptations?
10. Why is earnestness and a strong desire to know the truth essential if the tarot is to give reliable answers?
11. In laying out the tarot spreads for divination, is there any force present which tends to arrange them in a manner to give a correct answer?
12. What season is represented by the rose, by the cup, by the trefoil

and by the acorn?

13. To what celestial influences do the 22 Major Arcana correspond?
14. Give the Egyptian meaning of the word Tarot.
15. Why is a spiritual science so essential to man?
16. What shapes the ethical standards of a people?
17. To what do the four Court Arcana of each suit correspond?
18. What relations did the square-formed Hebrew letters have to numbers?
19. What is the nature of the Book of Soul Knowledge?
20. What is the nature of the method of mystical procedure so carefully guarded by certain Secret Occult Schools?
21. What must lie at the foundation of any real spiritual science?
22. Indicate the origin of the Holy Trinity of Christianity.
23. To what do the ten Minor Arcana correspond?
24. Explain the general method of shuffling and cutting the cards previous to laying them out in a spread.
25. Should the cards be laid face up or face down as they are dealt?

Chapter 3, Scope and Use of Tarot

1. From what course do we gain an accurate and authentic description of the Egyptian Tarot as it was explained to candidates in the process of ancient Egyptian initiation ceremonies?
2. Where can accurate pictures of the Egyptian Tarot cards be found at this time?
3. How can the admonition which follows each Major Arcanam be used in a practical way?
4. How have the various packs of European tarot cards been influenced by Christian mysticism, and are they more suited to revealing the beliefs of Christian mystics than the Egyptian Tarot?
5. What is symbolized by the veil falling over the face of Isis?
6. What stage of the soul's pilgrimage is represented by Arcanum I?
7. What is the significance of the cup of Arcanum I?
8. What is the symbolical significance of the Magus?
9. Explain how creative energy must be present to accomplish anything worthwhile on any plane.
10. What is the Philosopher's Stone which converts all it touches into gold?

11. In magic, what is meant by the principle of formulation?
12. In what way is the significator of the Minor Arcana determined from the significance of the Major Arcana of similar numerical equivalence?
13. What is the significance of the statement, "I am the Alpha and Omega?"
14. What portion of Solomon's Temple is represented by Arcanum II?
15. What does the science of Esoteric Psychology embrace?
16. From whence comes the Virgin Mary of Christianity?
17. What is the inner meaning of the immaculate conception?
18. In what way is man dependent upon woman for his spiritual birth?
19. What is meant by the astrological signature of a thing?
20. To what does Arcanum II correspond in Alchemy?
21. Why is the book on the knees of Isis half hidden?
22. What is the symbolical significance of the standing attitude?
23. What is symbolized by the tiara on the head of Isis?
24. How many cards are laid out in the pyramid spread?
25. In the pyramid spread what is represented by the four cards to the right of each of the keys?

Chapter 4, **Involution and Evolution of Numbers**

1. What is a root number?
2. What relation to 9 has any number above 9?
3. Indicate how adding the digits of a number is but a short-cut way of dividing by 9.
4. When a physical tone has been raised to a higher level so that it there repeats itself, what is it commonly called?
5. When a thought-vibration has been raised to a higher level so that it there repeats itself, what is it called?
6. How many root-tones are there in astral vibrations?
7. What functions have overtone effects in determining the number of key-tones of astral vibrations?
8. How many key-tones are there in astral vibratory rates?
9. What is meant by a Decave?
10. How is the Key of a number above 22 found?
11. How is the Key of the Decave found?

12. How is the second decave of any number obtained?
13. What is symbolized by a helmet?
14. How is a card read when it is found with the top reversed?
15. Why are cards, in preparing for a tarot reading, always dealt face down?
16. In what way is barrenness a crime?
17. Why is sex so important in the development of spirituality?
18. What Masonic story is depicted by Arcanum III?
19. What is symbolized by a cube covered with eyes?
20. What truth is there in the idea that one must be miserable to be holy?
21. What is the significance of a serpent pictured at the brow of a human being?
22. What do the 12 stars above the woman in Arcanum III symbolize?
23. What is the alchemical significance of Arcanum III?
24. What relation has the hawk of Arcanum IV to the Masonic letters: H-T-W-S-S-T-K-S?
25. In the spread of the Sephiroth, if the question relates to honor or business, at what point does the reading start?

Chapter 5, **Reading the Meaning of Numbers**

1. From what 3 sources may astral tones arise?
2. What is meant by the Key to which a character vibrates?
3. What is meant by the Key to a train of thoughts?
4. How does the astral tone, or thought-vibration of a certain Key, affect us when radiated to us by many people?
5. Why is the key-tone of the name we use as signature usually important in influencing our lives?
6. Upon what does the importance of some name or number associated with us depend?
7. Is the chief influence of a name or number due to the sound produced in speaking it?
8. How is the numerical equivalent of a name found?
9. When the numerical equivalent of a name is found, how is the Key to which it vibrates determined?
10. How are the character vibrations determined?
11. How can a name be charted on a staff of 11 lines and 11 spaces?
12. How can it be determined how associating with a certain astral

vibratory-tone emanating either from character-vibration, from astrological-vibration, or from thought-vibration, will affect the life and destiny of a given individual?

13. Upon what does the carrying power of the will upon the physical plane depend?

14. What is represented by gold, frankincense and myrrh?

15. What is symbolized by the triple tau?

16. To what do the two women in Arcanum VI correspond?

17. What is the magical significance of the pentagram?

18. Why is the astral body sometimes called the desire body?

19. What do the two men at the feet of the Hierophant symbolize?

20. What is the dross of mental alchemy which must be removed from the metals and cast aside?

21. Why did the wise men of the East return to their land by a different way?

22. Why was the great star which fell from heaven, as related in Revelation called wormwood?

23. What is the nature of the two mantrams set forth in the tarot, and how can they be used to greatest advantage?

24. Does the innocence of the meaning of the use of a rite or symbol prevent the force or entity to which it corresponds being attracted?

25. Why, when the neophyte decides to take some definite spiritual step, is he so often confronted by unseen obstacles in carrying out his decision?

Chapter 6, **Making an Astrological Chart of a Name**

1. What is the one positive and reliable way of determining how any invisible vibratory tone, or any combination of such tones, will affect a certain person?

2. What is the chief influence of a name or number upon a person?

3. If the Mars center in a person's astral body is very harmonious will he attract additional misfortune through association with the number 16?

4. If the Key-tone of a number or name is the same as that of a planet in the house of money in the birth-chart, in what department of life will the vibration have most influence?

5. When there is a planet in a sign in the birth-chart, and the sign is

given additional stimulation through association with a name, number, or other thought, is the influence upon the individual to be judged chiefly by the influence of the planet or by the influence of the planet ruling the sign?

6. When there is no planet in a sign, how is its power to attract harmony or discord when stimulated to be judged?
7. How can we estimate the magnitude of the influence that stimulating a certain vibratory tone in his astral body will have, in the case of an individual whose birth-chart is known?
8. How can a name or number be converted into an astrological chart?
9. Does a name alone, without additional data, permit of the giving of a reading to the individual wearing it?
10. What is the individual element to be added to a name which enables a divinatory reading to be given?
11. Why is it that the sound of the name is unimportant in the system we are considering, and that the spelling is the thing from which the vibratory rates are determined?
12. What is the significance of Solomon's Seal used as a magical pentacle?
13. What relation do the 7 fat kine and the 7 lean kine of Pharaoh's dream bear to the sphinxes of Arcanum VII?
14. What is meant by, "Render unto Caesar the things that are Caesar's, and unto God the things that are God's?"
15. What is symbolized by the two loops of the Figure 8 as joined in that number?
16. What is the numerical meaning of Bel?
17. Should there ever be any thought of vengeance or mercy in repelling any evil influence?
18. Why are the eyes of Justice represented as blindfolded?
19. What does the Egyptian deity, Ra, symbolize as revealed by number-divination?
20. What is the divinatory significance of Arcanum VII?
21. What is signified by a winged globe?
22. In what way is the Royal Arch degree of Masonry symbolized by Arcanum VII?
23. The relation between what forces makes the practice of horary astrology possible?
24. What is the significance of Lot's wife being turned into a pillar of salt?

25. In the Magic Seven Spread, what is the significance of the 7th card dealt?

Chapter 7, Influence of Changing the Name

1. Can there be more than one correct interpretation of the vibratory force exerted by a certain name?
2. Can there be several systems of divination by numerology, and all give quite accurate results?
3. Why is the signature so important as a vibratory influence?
4. What is the influence when different groups of people think of the same individual by different names?
5. Give common instances of a change of name being coincident with a marked change in fortune.
6. Show that it is common for an individual to be known in business by a name other than the one with which endowed soon after birth.
7. What is the positive and scientific method by which it can be known just how a name or number will influence the life of a given person?
8. In selecting a name for the purpose of benefiting some particular department of life, what is the principle followed?
9. In selecting a name which will be most fortunate in general, without special reference to any one department of life, what is the method followed?
10. What is the significance of the scriptural passage: "Unto Adam also, and to his wife, did the Lord God make coats of skins, and clothed them"?
11. What is the significance of the scriptural passage: "Be ye, therefore, wise as serpents and harmless as doves"?
12. In what realms do the emanations of the Sephiroth manifest?
13. Why does a blessing or a curse always affect the one sending it?
14. What is signified by there being 8 spokes in the wheel of Arcanum X?
15. Why is number 9 called the Deific number?
16. What planets form the Tree of Life in the Kabalistical diagram of the ten emanations of the Sephiroth?
17. What planet gives the most abrupt changes of fortune?
18. What are the two methods of obtaining information from higher realms?

19. Which of the two methods of gaining information from higher realms is safest?
20. Is innocence of the meaning of magical symbols a protection to those who dabble in ceremonial magic?
21. Of what does mental alchemy treat?
22. Why, as the soul advances, must the life-form it occupies become more sensitive; and what quality should be developed with equal rapidity to prevent the added sensitiveness leading the individual into danger?
23. Why does the soul, when it has reached a certain state, look upon the conditions brought by astrological squares and oppositions as opportunities for progress?
24. What letter has the form of a double 7?
25. In divination by the Spread of the Kabala, what significance have the cards found upon the Tree of Life?

Chapter 8, Reading Names in Detail

1. What is meant by the Birth Path?
2. How is the number of the Birth Path obtained?
3. How is the Divinatory Number of a person's name obtained?
4. How is the Key of the Divinatory Number of a person's name obtained?
5. How is the Key of the Decave of the Divinatory Number obtained?
6. After the Key of the Divinatory Number and the Key of the Decave of the Divinatory Number have been found, how is a chart formed to give a reading of the person's life?
7. In giving a reading of a person's life, what function has the Key of the Divinatory Number?
8. In giving a reading of a person's life, what function has the Key of the Decave of the Divinatory Number?
9. In giving a reading of a person's life, what is represented by each letter of the person's name?
10. In giving a reading of a person's life, how long a period is represented by each letter in the name?
11. What is signified by Sampson breaking his bonds three times?
12. What is symbolized by the honey Sampson took from the carcass of the lion?
13. What planet is usually prominent in the birth-chart of a genius?

14. What is the divinatory significance of the King of Cups?
15. What is symbolized by a cross above a triangle?
16. Why do each of the Warrier Court Cards have a numerical valuation 1?
17. What is the only thought-form persistently launched by the white magician?
18. Explain the magic chain produced by thought-diffusion.
19. What is the meaning of Sampson slaying the lion?
20. What is symbolized by the twelve cut branches of Arcanum XII?
21. What do bees signify and why?
22. What planet denotes the ability to receive mental messages from others?
23. What is symbolized by the eyes of Sampson being put out by his enemies?
24. What is symbolized by the angry lion, the jaws of which are easily closed by the girl of Arcanum XI?
25. Explain briefly the principles of the Horoscope Spread.

Chapter 9, **The Color of a Name**

1. What did Paracelsus mean when he said, "If I have manna in my constitution I can attract manna from heaven"?
2. What activity in the astral body causes money to assume much importance in the life?
3. How can this activity in the astral body which causes money to be important in the life, be increased?
4. What are the three sources of invisible energies that have the power to stimulate the centers and positions of our astral body into exceptional activity?
5. What determines whether such stimulated activity within the astral form will attract additional fortune or additional misfortune?
6. How is the color of a name determined?
7. Which one of the disciples of Jesus is represented by Scorpio and why?
8. What is symbolized by a rainbow?
9. Why was Jacob required to work 14 years for Rachel?
10. What is the divinatory significance of Arcanum XIII?
11. What is the origin of the idea that the number 13 is unlucky?
12. In the blessings of Jacob how is the sign Sagittarius signified?

13. How may the color of any number be found?
14. What zodiacal signs correspond to the light shades of the 7 colors of the solar spectrum?
15. What will determine the effect upon a given person of the letter N, the number 14, and the color dark yellow?
16. What is the divinatory meaning of the Queen of Scepters?
17. What is symbolized by a scarabaeus?
18. Is regeneration simply a matter of celibacy?
19. Just what is the nature of regenerate union?
20. In the blessings of Jacob, how is the sign Capricorn signified?
21. What is the divinatory significance of the Queen of Swords?
22. What zodiacal sign is represented by Simon and Levi?
23. In the blessings of Jacob, in what way is the sign Aquarius signified?
24. In the Solar Spread what relation has each row or cards to the birth chart?
25. In the Solar Spread what do the three cards to the left of the middle card of each row signify?

Chapter 10, **Natural Talismans and Artificial Charms**

1. What are the three types of invisible energies which have the power to influence human life and destiny?
2. Under which of these three classifications belong musical tones?
3. Under which of these three classifications belong talismanic gems?
4. Under which of these three classifications belong artificial charms?
5. What particular department of life does a birth-stone chiefly influence?
6. What particular department of life does a gem ruled by the rising sign in the birth-chart chiefly influence?
7. What determines or not if a gem is beneficial to a certain individual?
8. How is a gem selected which will be most beneficial for general purposes?
9. Why are gold, silver, copper and tin especially suitable for the manufacture of charms?
10. How is a charm made, and on what depends its potency to bring good or evil fortune?

11. What is symbolized by the scepter of the two divergent bars held by Typhon?
12. What do the wings of a bat symbolize?
13. What does a pyramid symbolize?
14. How is victory gained over the Dweller on the Threshold?
15. What is symbolized by the head of a crocodile?
16. What is meant by the inversive method of presenting an idea?
17. In the inversive method of presenting an idea is there any direct and simple test of accuracy that can be applied?
18. What is the motive behind the inversive presentation of ideas, and from whence do they often originate?
19. What is meant by thought-diffusion?
20. What planet has special significance in weather predicting?
21. Of what value, in human life, are animal propensities?
22. Why, without a vigorous animal soul upon which to draw, is it usually impossible on the physical plane to develop a vigorous spirituality?
23. How can constructive effort and love be used successfully in combating any force of evil sent against a person?
24. For what purpose should the wish spread be used?
25. When the wish card appears in the cards, 1—2—3—, at the left of the wish spread, what does it signify?

Chapter 11, Chronology of the Tarot

1. Why should the soul response to an idea be accepted only after close analysis?
2. What is the Truth that gives Freedom?
3. What does a butterfly symbolize?
4. Why is the young girl of Arcanum XVII pictured nude?
5. In a general way how may the method of treatment for illness be determined from the birth-chart?
6. How should the plants and flowers for the home be selected to produce the most harmonious results?
7. Explain in what way the Tarot symbolizes the 12 months of the year.
8. What constitutes a barrier that spirits of iniquity cannot pass?
9. What is the divinatory significance of the Warrior of Cups?
10. What is the data that must be supplied an astrologer to enable him to erect a correct chart of birth?

11. To what state of the soul's initiation does Arcanum XVII correspond?
12. Why is it a mistake to deny the existence of matter and its properties?
13. In Masonry what does the small ebony box containing the plans for the temple and the ivory box containing the keys symbolize?
14. What is the most dual sign of the zodiac?
15. What is symbolized by an eight-pointed star?
16. What is the divinatory significance of Arcanum XVII?
17. When is the best time to gather a plant for a particular purpose?
18. How may an astrological birth-chart be read by the Tarot?
19. Explain in what way the Tarot symbolizes the 52 weeks of the year.
20. What is symbolized by a dog?
21. What is the divinatory significance of Arcanum XVIII?
22. What is the divinatory significance of the Warrior of Swords?
23. What is the bondage from which Truth frees man?
24. Why does the girl in Arcanum XVII rest partly on land and partly on the sea?
25. In what way may pet animals affect the life?

Chapter 12, The Solution of Ancient Cycles

1. On what date did the Aquarian Age start?
2. What is it that retrogrades through the stars at the rate of 30 degrees in 2,156 years, which gives rise to the different Ages?
3. What is the cycle which measures out to individual man the major events of life?
4. What is the nature of the force measured out to man by the phases of the Moon?
5. What is the cycle which measures out to man the minor events of life?
6. What number is the key to the practical expression of Cyclic influence?
7. What number is the key to the cycles that involve four-dimensional factors, such as astrological influences and the influence of thoughts and ideas?
8. What planet governs the period of gestation?
9. Do those who bring children into the world forfeit the right to spiritual progress in this life?

10. What is the nature of the force measured out to man by the Moon in its orbit about the zodiac in a little over 27 days?
11. Just what is the significance of the number 40?
12. According to the theories of the Hindus, what race of what round of evolution is the present Great Western Race?
13. What is meant by a Polar Day?
14. What is the energy measured out to man by the rotation of the earth on its axis?
15. What is a Divine Year?
16. How is the planetary period of the Sub-Precessional Cycle, 308 years, 208 1/2 days obtained?
17. What is the Solar Nirvana?
18. What is the truth about Shells, and do they actually control mediums, and why is it taught in some circles that they do?
19. What is meant by the second death?
20. What is signified in the Bible by the assertion that of Moses, "No man knoweth his sepulchre unto this day?"
21. What is symbolized by the tomb from which the man, woman and child of Arcanum XX arise?
22. What is the significance in Initiation of Arcanum XIV?
23. What are the conditions of the soul immediately following accidental birth into the next life?
24. What does geology, astronomy and archaeology teach regarding the probability of man having lived in a physical body on earth more than three rounds of 18,144,000 years each?
25. How many cards are dealt in the Magic Cross Spread?

Chapter 13, **How to Read the Tarot**

1. Why should no other than the reader be permitted to handle the tarot cards except when they are being used to give a reading?
2. Why is it desirable to have an extra pack of cards when considerable effort is devoted to solving spiritual and philosophical problems as well as giving personal readings?
3. What is the best seating arrangement between client and reader?
4. How can the astrological significance of any card be used to give an additional interpretation?
5. Why should the cards be turned over only one at a time as read?
6. In what manner does it change the significance of a card when it is found reversed in the spread?

7. In what way, when the King Court Card is turned, can it denote a woman?

8. How can much detail be learned about the people signified by the Court Arcana turned in a spread?

9. How, when the Horsemen are turned, is it denoted whether the thoughts so indicated favor the client, or are opposed to the client's interest?

10. How is the influence upon the life of the client of any person represented in the spread by a Court Arcanum determined?

11. What signifies the action a person indicated in the spread by one of the Court Arcana will take?

12. How can one read the cards for someone who is at a distance?

13. In what way can the admonition, "Remember, then, son of earth," be used?

14. Why is it that any problem is capable of solution by the method of the tarot?

15. What is signified in Arcanum XXI by the winged lingham?

16. What is signified by the harp in Arcanum XXI?

17. To what in alchemy does Arcanum XXI correspond?

18. What constitutes the basis of the various 50 degrees which constitute the steps to adeptship?

19. To what extent does the adept draw away from the world and ignore the suffering of humanity?

20. What are the alternate readings of Arcanum XXI and Arcanum O in the spiritual world?

21. To what planet does Arcanum O correspond, and what are the two aspects or influences of this planet, as indicated by the common T and the reversed T?

22. What is the divinatory significance of the highest aspect of Arcanum O?

23. What is the significance in magic of Arcanum O in its higher interpretation?

24. What does the higher interpretation of Arcanum O signify in initiation?

25. What does Arcanum O, in its higher interpretation, signify in occult science?

Index

listed, vi
memorizing, 56
Minor Arcana and, 56
number of, 36
pictures/symbolism of, 45
rulership of, 101-2
spiritual texts and, 272
Malkuth, 12-13, 149
Mantrams, 98-99, 143, 186
Manwantares, 249
Mark Master's degree, 80
Martyr, The, Arcanum XII, described,
167-71
Masonry, 47
G of, 74-75
universal principles of, 6
Master Mason degree, 74
Master Mason's lodge, 99
Master Mason's Word, 121
Master's Elect of Fifteen degree, 208
Master's Elect of Nine degree, 214
Mataloth, 180
Materialist, The, Arcanum XXII,
described, 278-81
Mathers, S. L. Macgregor, 32
on unwritten kabala, 1
Medicines, 223-26
Mediumship, 236-37
irresponsible, 215, 237, 238
Mem, 7, 8, 180
Mental forces, 246
fighting by, 215
tarot cards and, 272
Mesmerism, 225
Metals, negativeness of, 202
Method of the Sephiroth, 83-84
Method of Three Sevens, 106
Microposopus, 10
Middle card, importance of, 39
Minor Arcana, 48, 101, 221
interpretation of, 269-70
listed, vii
Major Arcana and, 56
number of, 36
numerical value of, 222
significance of, 270, 272
Minor Events, 245
Mohammedanism, 209
Moon, The, Arcanum XVIII,
described, 233-38
influence of, 67

phases of, 245
Moses, 258, 276
books of, 2
kabala and, 4, 5, 276
Most Excellent Master degree, 105
Mother (pillar), 11
Mother letters, 7
Mound Builders, 214
Movable signs, 270
Mu, 5
Mundane astrology, 188, 223
Musical tones, 68, 199-200
astral vibratory rates of, 200
corresponding, 47
influences of, 69, 200
Mysteries of Mysteries, 9
Mystical procedure, methods of, 34

Nain, 188
Names
changing, 133-38
color of, 177-80
deific, 17
as divinatory instrument, 133
influence of, 155
key of, 114, 134
reading, 114-17
thinking, 91
tone and, 112, 114
vibratory significance of, 116, 117,
133
Natal astrology, 223, 245
Natural Method, treating with, 224-25
Nature
self-preservation/race-preserva-
tion and, 213
transgressions against, 212
truths of, 58
Netzach, 12, 149
9 (number)
astral manifestation and, 243
peculiar function of, 68
Nine of Coins, 144, **241**
Nine of Cups, 144, **241**
as wish card, 216
Nine of Scepters, 144, **241**
Nine of Swords, 144, **241**
No, answering, 39
Noah, 5, 74
dogmatic kabala and, 4
No-numbered tarot, 222, 244

Purifying Fire. *See* Asch Metzareph
Pyramid Spread, **44**, 62

Quadrant of companionship, 102
Quadrant of home and end of life, 102
Quadrant of honor, 102
Quadrant of life, 101
Queen court cards, 188
Queen of Coins, 188
Queen of Cups, 188
Queen of Scepters, 188
Queen of Swords, 188
Queens, 166-67, 268
Quitolath, 250
"Quod Superius, Quod Inferius," 10
Quoph, 7, 8, 250

Ra, vibratory significance of, 115
Race-preservation, 213
Rachel, Jacob and, 191
Racial memory, 250
Radiation, types of, 94
Rasith, 255
Reading, 265, 266-67, 272
Realization, 96, 244
Reaper, The, Arcanum XII, described, 180-88
Reason, 58, 156
Reincarnation, teaching, 14
Religion of the Stars, The, 137, 278, 281
Resh, 7, 8, 255
Resurrection, 257-58
Reuben, 183
Reversed cards, 82, 271
Rising signs, 201
Rooms, 237
    for tarot readings, 266
Root numbers, 67, 68, 71
Rosy Cross, 191, 260
Round of Humanity, 248, 249
Rounds of Root-Races, 248
Royal Arch degree, 121
Royal Master degree, 125

Sacrifice, 168, 169, 170, 182, 185, 281
Sage, The, Arcanum IX, described, 138-44
    lamp of, 143
    square mantle of, 143

St. Martin, 32
Sameck, 7
Samek, 8, 204
Samson, story of, 163
Sarcophagus, The, Arcanum XX, described, 255-59
Satan, 204, 206
    vibratory significance of, 116
Satya Yug, length of, 249
Savanarola, 210
Scepters, suit of, 38, 56
Schin, 273
Science
    code of honor for, 33
    will and, 57
    See also Occult science; Spiritual science; Vibratory science
Scientific method, 134-38
Scientific thought, building, 28-29
Seal of Seven, 127-28
Second death, 258
Second Series, 248
Secret doctrine, 33, 34, 165
    guarding, 1
Secret of The Law, The, 9
Secret Master degree, 208
Select Master degree, 141
Self-Conscious-Immortality, 12, 97, 281
Self-consciousness, 105
    acquiring, 211, 256
Selfishness, 209, 210
Self-preservation, 213
Sephiroth
    method of, 82-84
    ten emanations of, 10, 11, 14, 148
    spread of, **66**
Sephir Sephiroth (The Book of Emanations), 3, 8-9
Sephir Yetzirah (The Book of Formation), 3, 5-8
Septers, suit of, 38, 56
Seven Active Principles of Nature, 11
Sevenfold constitution, 243
Seven of Coins, 123, **197**
Seven of Cups, 123, **197**
Seven of Scepters, 123, **197**
Seven of Swords, 123, **197**
Sex, 17
    destructive power of, 212
    mutual esteem and, 192

Other Brotherhood of Light Books _____

_____

The following pages present brief descriptions of the 21 Brotherhood of Light courses, written by C. C. Zain. The information contained therein represents the ancient wisdom of the Hermetic Tradition, transmitted orally in earlier ages only to initiates of The Brotherhood of Light. It was the life's work of Elbert Benjamine, under the pen name of C. C. Zain, to present this complete system of esoteric knowledge in an organized format, available for the first time to the public.

CS. 1, Laws of Occultism

Inner Plane Theory and the Fundamentals of Psychic Phenomena

$14.95   6x9   192pp

The word "occult" means hidden or unseen. *The Laws of Occultism* is the study of unseen energies and the subjugation of these energies, insofar as we are able, to human control. There are in existence undeviating natural laws that are yet unexplained by physical science. In this course various types of psychic phenomena are examined and explained. The nature of the inner plane and how it affects human life and activities is revealed.

1. Occult Data **2.** Astral Substance **3.** Astral Vibrations **4.** Doctrine of Nativities **5.** Doctrine of Mediumship **6.** Spiritism **7.** Phenomenal Spiritism

---

CS. 2, Astrological Signatures

Evolution and the Soul and the Nature of Astrological Energies

$14.95   6x9   256pp

This is our best book for those beginning their study of astrology. The Signs of the Zodiac, the Planets, the Mundane Houses and the Aspects are all discussed in detail. The philosophy of "The Religion of the Stars" concerning the nature of the soul, how it makes progress and why the experiences of life are necessary to prepare it for a higher destiny is presented. Of special interest are the chapters concerning the facts and fancies of reincarnation and the ancient ritual of Egyptian Initiation.

1. The Two Keys **2.** The Zodiac **3.** Mundane Houses **4.** The Mission of the Soul **5.** Physiology and Correspondence **6.** Doctrine of Signatures **7.** Facts and Fancies About Reincarnation I **8.** Facts and Fancies About Reincarnation II **9.** The Ritual of Egyptian Initiation

---

CS. 3, Spiritual Alchemy

The Hermetic Art of Spiritual Transformation

$14.95   6x9   144pp

The ancient alchemist sought transmutation and immortality. For the soul to be immortal it must build for itself an imperishable spiritual body in which it can function after the dissolution of both the physical and astral forms. The experiences of life are symbolized by the metals of alchemy. Through proper mental attitude we purify the metals, develop our character and create our destiny. The various states of consciousness available to man are set forth and analyzed.

1. Doctrine of Spiritual Alchemy **2.** Seven Spiritual Metals **3.** Purifying the Metals **4.** Transmutation **5.** Higher Consciousness

CS. 4, Ancient Masonry

The Spiritual Meaning of Masonic Degrees, Rituals and Symbols

$14.95   6x9   336pp

In this course the rituals and symbols of Ancient Masonry are revealed. For the modern Freemason this is an unprecedented work enabling him to perceive the esoteric and spiritual significance of the symbols and all things done in the lodge room. The astrological significance of the symbols and their relationship to soul-development are thoroughly discussed.

1. Ancient Masonry Introduction **2.** Entered Apprentice and the Planets **3.** Entered Apprentice and the Signs **4.** Numbers and Opening the Lodge **5.** Initiating a Member **6.** Fellowcraft **7.** Lodge Emblems **8.** Master Mason **9.** Mark Master Mason **10.** Royal Arch **11.** Degrees of the Cross **12.** Ineffable Degrees **13.** Historical Degrees

---

CS. 5, Esoteric Psychology

Success Through Directed Thinking and Induced Emotion

$14.95   6x9   320pp

Of all the energies that influence man none have a more powerful effect than his own thoughts. Directing one's thinking is the most potent of all forces to control one's life and destiny. Commonly, our efforts to exercise control are hindered due to faulty conceptions or repressions that result from environmental conditioning. Whether this conditioning expresses in a subtle way or in one that is more obvious, the consequence is a thwart to progress. Esoteric Psychology contains information which will assist in identifying and eliminating these obstacles to progress.

1. Doctrine of Esoteric Psychology **2.** Reason and Intuition **3.** Language and the Value of Dreams **4.** Desire and How to Use It **5.** Why Repression is Not Morality **6.** How to Rule the Stars **7.** How to Apply Suggestion **8.** Correct Use of Affirmations **9.** How to Think Constructively **10.** How to Cultivate Subliminal Thinking **11.** How to Develop Creative Imagination **12.** How to Demonstrate Success

---

CS. 6, Sacred Tarot

The Art of Card Reading and the Underlying Spiritual Science

$14.95   6x9   336pp

The Sacred Tarot is a favorite of metaphysical students everywhere and companion to the *Brotherhood of Light Egyptian Tarot Cards*. With this book, the student can readily determine the astrological correspondence of any number, name, color, gem or other object. In this course the "Religion of the Stars" system of numerology is set forth and divination by means of numbers is explained. It is also considered to be one of the most complete, detailed syntheses of the Tarot archetypes as they manifest spiritual truths in different areas of occult science. Each of the 78 cards is explained and 11 tarot card spreads are illustrated.

1. Doctrine of Kabalism **2.** Foundation of the Science **3.** Scope and Use of Tarot **4.** Involution and Evolution of Numbers **5.** Reading the Meaning of Numbers **6.** Making an Astrological Chart of a Name **7.** Influence of Changing the Name **8.** Reading Names in Detail **9.** The Color of a Name **10.** Natural Talismans and Artificial Charms **11.** Chronology of the Tarot **12.** Solution of Ancient Cycles **13.** How to Read the Tarot

CS. 7, Spiritual Astrology

The Origins of Astro-Mythology and Stellar Religion

$14.95   6x9   352pp

This course describes the outstanding attributes of those born under the influence of each of the 48 ancient constellations. Also revealed are the specific spiritual doctrines associated with each of the constellations. These spiritual doctrines, formulated by the most wise of prehistoric times, later found their way into ancient mythology, the Bible and other sacred writings. Course VII sets forth the most significant of these stories associated with these doctrines and reveals their true meaning.

1. Our Spiritual Legacy **2.** The Fountain of Youth **3.** Knights of King Arthur **4.** Story of the Three Bears **5.** The Ladder to Heaven **6.** Is There a Santa Claus **7.** Why Eve Was Tempted **8.** The Marriage in Heaven **9.** The Scorpion and the Eagle **10.** The Bow of Bright Promise **11.** News From the Summerland **12.** In the Reign of Aquarius **13.** The Tree of Life

---

CS. 8, Horary Astrology

How to Erect and Judge a Horoscope

$14.95   6x9   224pp

This course is often chosen by beginning students of astrology for its technical lesson, "How to Erect a Horoscope", as well as for its clearly organized system for judging any horoscope. More advanced students refer to this volume for horary chart interpretation. The section on horary astrology is of special interest for its explanation of how and why this branch of astrology can solve a problem relating to events past, present and future. Also included for beginning students are CC Zain's chart erection short-cuts, for which he designed the Church of Light #2 Chartpad.

1. How to Erect a Horoscope **2.** Strength and Aspects of the Planets **3.** First Seven Steps in Judging Any Horoscope **4.** The Doctrine of Horary Astrology **5.** Questions Relating to First Six Houses **6.** Questions Relating to Last Six Houses **7.** How to Select the Best Time for any Undertaking **8.** Chart Erection Short Cuts and Examples

---

CS. 9, Mental Alchemy

How Thoughts and Feelings Shape Our Lives

$14.95   6x9   224pp

The astrological energies mapped by a birthchart are not the cause of the conditions and events that come into one's life. It is the character of the individual that determines our destiny. Character is composed of thought cells built and organized on the inner plane. Course IX explains how these thought cell groups, which constitute man's unconscious mind, have been formed before his birth, and how they are modified after birth by experience. Of importance is an explanation of how these thought cells can and should be reconditioned to work for the things the individual desires.

1. The Inner Nature of Poverty, Failure and Disease **2.** Just How to Find the Thought-Cause of Any Condition **3.** How to Find a Mental Antidote **4.** How to Apply a Mental Antidote **5.** Just How to Heal Yourself **6.** Just How to Attain Realization **7.** Just How to Give Absent Treatments

CS. 10-1, Natal Astrology, Part One

Delineating the Horoscope

$14.95   6x9   224pp

As the Lessons on astrology emphasize, much is to be gained through a diligent application of the rules when interpreting a horoscope. In a step-by-step fashion, Delineating the Horoscope presents the Hermetic system of natal astrology along with the unsurpassed "Outline of a Complete Astrological Reading." Beginning and advanced students will enjoy the explanations of the 36 decanates, illustrated with examples of renowned persons having Sun, Moon or Ascendant in that decanate.

1. First Eighteen Decanates Analyzed **2.** Last Eighteen Decanates Analyzed **3.** Stature, Temperament, Disposition and Mental Ability **4.** Vitality, Health and Disease **5.** Business, Finances and Vocational Selection **6.** Friends, Enemies and Associates **7.** Love, Marriage and Partnership **8.** How to Delineate a Horoscope

CS. 10-2, Natal Astrology, Part Two

Progressing the Horoscope

$14.95   6x9   224pp

A technical manual on the Hermetic system of major and minor progressions. The progressed aspects of natal astrology reveal probable future events through indicating the manner in which an individual's thought-cells will work to attract events. With this information the individual can learn to take precautionary actions by reconditioning the energy so that a more desirable outcome can be achieved. To round out the study of natal astrology, a lesson on the Hermetic system of rectifying the horoscope is included for use in erecting a birthchart when the exact birth time is unknown.

1. Hermetic System of Progressions **2.** Major Progressions of Sun and Angles **3.** Major Progressions of the Moon **4.** Major Progressions of the Planets **5.** Minor Progressions of the Sun and Angles **6.** Minor Progressions of the Moon and Planets **7.** Transits, Revolutions and Cycles **8.** Rectifying the Horoscope

CS. 11, Divination & Character Reading

Tools and Techniques for Enhancing ESP

$14.95   6x9   192pp

Divination is a means for assisting extension of consciousness on the inner plane to acquire the information desired. It is then brought up into the region of objective consciousness. Clairvoyance, precognition, telepathy, the divining rod, teacup and coffee cup methods, among others, are discussed in detail. The last four lessons are devoted to learning to read character based on physical characteristics.

1. Doctrine of Divination **2.** Tea-cup and Coffee-cup Divination **3.** Divining Rod and Other Divination **4.** Instantaneous Character Reading **5.** Significance of Body and Head **6.** Instantaneous Reading from Profile **7.** Instantaneous Vocational Analysis

CS. 12-1, Natural Alchemy, Part One

Evolution of Life

$14.95   6x9   224pp

We live in kinship with all life forms, animate and inanimate. For man to understand his place in nature, and thus what his relation should be to other life-forms, to other people, and to God, he needs to know how the various life-forms, including man, have developed to the state they now occupy. Cs. XII-1 offers the unique interpretation of the Religion of the Stars on how natural selection and adaptation is influenced by psychokinesis, ESP and inner-plane influence.

1. Origin of the Earth **2.** Origin and Development of Plants **3.** Progress of Invertebrate Life **4.** Fishes and Amphibians **5.** Reptiles and Birds **6.** Development Among Mammals **7.** Development of Man **8.** Development of Knowledge

---

CS. 12-2, Natural Alchemy, Part Two

Evolution of Religion

$14.95   6x9   224pp

This course deals with the evolution of those ideas which constitute man's various religions. Cs. XII-2 begins with the most primitive religions and shows how these, and the cultures coincident with them, gradually developed into the more complex systems of belief of today. The tenets of each important present day religion are explained, and finally there is set forth the basic tenets of the Religion of the Stars.

1. The Foundations of Religion **2.** Early Religions of the World **3.** Religion in Historic Times **4.** Tao, Confucianism, Zoroastrianism and Mohammedanism **5.** Hinduism and Buddhism **6.** Judaism and Christianity **7.** The Stellarian Religion **8.** Astrology is Religion's Road Map

---

CS. 13, Mundane Astrology

Interpreting Astrological Phenomena for Cities, Nations and Groups

$14.95   5X7   272pp

Astrological energies influence the trend of world events. When a natal chart isn't available, these influences can be determined through the mundane cycle charts of nations, cities, groups, etc. This course is one of the few technical manuals on the erection of mundane cycle charts and their delineation. Such information is valuable because it enables one to take precautionary actions and arrange personal affairs to take most advantage of city, national or world conditions. It also helps one to foresee conditions and thus exert political influence in support of those measures which insure peace and give people freedom from want, freedom from fear, freedom of expression and freedom of religion.

1. Doctrine of Mundane Astrology **2.** Cycles of Pluto and Neptune **3.** Cycles of Uranus **4.** Cycles of Saturn **5.** Cycles of Jupiter **6.** Cycles of Mars **7.** Major Conjunctions of the Planets **8.** Cycles of the Sun **9.** Cycles of the Moon **10.** Precise Predicting: Eclipses

CS. 14, Occultism Applied

How to Increase Your Happiness, Usefulness and Spirituality

$14.95   6x9   320pp

Just how to use occult knowledge and occult energies in everyday life is considered in detail in Course XIV. It shows us that each soul is being trained for its own cosmic work and has its own kind of job to do in God's Great Evolutionary Plan, pointing out the advantage of living the completely constructive life. To gain the things we desire from life usually requires that some of our habit systems be changed. Changing habits is not easy, but the three fundamental principles given in Cs. XIV will give the quickest and surest success.

1. Finding One's Cosmic Work **2.** Living the Completely Constructive Life **3.** Diet and Breathing **4.** How to Keep Young **5.** How to Be Attractive **6.** How to Have Friends **7.** How to Get Employment **8.** How to Make Money **9.** How to Achieve Honors **10.** How to Be Successful in Marriage **11.** How to Have a Pleasant Home **12.** How to Be Happy

---

CS. 15, Weather Predicting

The Hermetic System of Astrological Weather Analysis

$14.95   6x9   192pp

Astrological energies have a profound influence over the weather conditions of earth. They indicate changes from the normal of a given locality in temperature, moisture and wind, quite precisely. This is particularly useful information for those involved in agriculture, aviation, travel or planning a social event. It is an aspect of the science that should not be neglected by anyone seeking a complete, working knowledge of astrology. *Weather Predicting* is a complete treatment of the subject and the only text available entirely devoted to astrological influences on the weather.

1. Astrological Weather Predicting **2.** Reading Astrological Weather Charts **3.** Astrological Temperature Charts **4.** Astrological Air Movement Charts **5.** Astrological Moisture Charts **6.** Unusual Weather **7.** Tornadoes and Hurricanes

---

CS. 16, Stellar Healing

Astrological Predisposition, Diagnosis and Treatment of Disease

$14.95   6x9   320pp

Health is a valuable asset. The positions of the planets in the birthchart indicate the diseases toward which an individual is predisposed. *Stellar Healing* gives the birthchart and progressed constants of 160 diseases. It also sets forth what is probably the most effective of all methods of drugless healing, and indicates the specific Stellar Treatment. In addition, it shows how to calculate in terms of ASTRODYNES, HARMODYNES and DISCORDYNES the precise power and harmony of any planet, aspect, sign or house. ASTRODYNES are the unsurpassed mathematical formula for the measurement of astrological power.

1. Stellar Anatomy **2.** Basis of Stellar Diagnosis **3.** Principles of Stellar Healing **4.** Technique of Stellar Healing **5.** Stellar Healing in Practice **6.** Diagnosis and Treatment **7.** Abdominal Troubles - Bleeding **8.** Blindness - Coronary Thrombosis **9.** Cyst - Hay Fever **10.** Headache - Mumps **11.** Nervous Breakdown - Scarlet Fever **12.** Sciatica - Yellow Fever

CS. 17, Cosmic Alchemy

The Spiritual Guide to Universal Progression

$14.95   6x9   256pp

Man is not an isolated unit. Instead he is a member of world society, and should be an energetic worker in the realization of God's Great Evolutionary Plan. This course indicates how each person can become active in achieving the realization of this plan. In this progress there will be no more wars, poverty will be abolished, educational facilities and the widest access to information should be available to all. Cs. XVII shows exactly what spirituality is and the three general methods of gaining it; 1. viewing events from the standpoint of spiritual alchemy, 2. cultivating thoughts, feelings and actions that arise from the desire to benefit others, and 3. raising the vibratory rate through a heightened intellectual and emotional appreciation.

1. Conquest of War **2.** Abolition of Poverty **3.** Cosmic Politics **4.** Heredity and Environment **5.** How to Be Spiritual **6.** Spiritual Value of Education **7.** How to Appraise Spiritual Values **8.** Minor Aids to Spiritual Advancements **9.** Major Aids to Spiritual Advancements

---

CS. 18, Imponderable Forces

The Wholesome Pathway

$14.95   6x9   192pp

Cs. XVIII explains how much reliance should be placed on transits, minor progressed aspects, major progressed aspects and other astrological conditions, and the proper attitude toward such astrological weather. It indicates how sympathies and antipathies work and how much importance to attribute to birthstones, numbers, names and environmental vibrations. Since the greatest enemy of fear and superstition is thorough understanding, this course explains in detail ceremonial magic, sorcery and witchcraft, and how to protect oneself against black magic of any kind. It shows how to avoid the influence of suggestion and inversive propaganda. *Imponderable Forces* gives a comprehensive survey of the wholesome pathway, and how to follow it.

1. How to Act Under Adverse Progressed Aspects **2.** Sympathies and Antipathies **3.** Ceremonial Magic **4.** Sorcery and Witchcraft **5.** Ritual and Religion **6.** Press, Radio and Billboard **7.** The Wholesome Pathway.

CS. 19, Organic Alchemy

The Universal Law of Soul Progression

$14.95   6x9   192pp

To live in harmony with nature's laws we must understand them. Humans are not set apart from other living things, but all life forms come under one uniform, universal law. This course explains how soul progress occurs; its original polarity, as indicated by its astrological signature, is energized by its ego and conditioned through pleasure and pain. Nature uses pleasure and pain, not as reward or punishment, but to inform the organism whether is it successfully adapting to its environment. Cs. XIX gives information about the problems and habits of other life forms, why there is no unpardonable sin, how the cosmos is managed and an outline of the general cosmic plan.

1. The Ceaseless Surge of Life **2.** Every Life Form Manifests a Soul **3.** The Universal Law of Soul Progression **4.** The Uses of Pleasure and Pain **5.** The Universal Law of Compensation **6.** The Universal Moral Code **7.** Discerning God's Great Plan

CS. 20, The Next Life

A Guide to Living Conditions on the Inner Plane

$14.95   6x9   272pp

Life on earth is but one phase of existence. Physical life constitutes necessary schooling so that the soul can function effectively on a higher plane where it will be less restricted. By understanding the nature of the life to come, the individual is better prepared to live this life and the next. Course XX gives a great deal of information about the conditions to be met and the activities of life after physical death. It tells about the various levels of the inner plane world, about the three methods of birth into the next life, about the influence of desires there, of the effect of sorrowing for those who have passed to the next life and how they may be helped, of the work to be done there and how education is handled. *The Next Life* is not only interesting, but the information it contains will be a highly valuable guide to anyone when they pass from the physical.

1. Turning the Dial to Inner Planes **2.** Properties of Life on The Inner Plane **3.** Birth Into the Next Life **4.** Astrological Influences in the Next Life **5.** Occupations of the Next Life **6.** Education and Progress in the Next Life **7.** Earth Bound Souls and the Astral Hells **8.** Domestic Relations of the Next Life **9.** Social Contacts and Amusements in the Next Life **10.** Through Astral and Spiritual to Celestial

---

CS. 21, Personal Alchemy

The Neophyte's Path to Spiritual Attainment

$14.95   6x9   272pp

The student who has gained the knowledge contained in the first 20 Brotherhood of Light courses is apt to decide to develop himself and his powers to the very best advantage. Consequently, *Personal Alchemy* gives precise instructions on the steps such an individual should take, and the order in which he should take them.

1. Three Things Every Neophyte Should Know **2.** The First Three Habits a Neophyte Should Adopt **3.** Avenues to Illumination **4.** Spiritual Hindrance by Family and Friends **5.** Spiritual Trends in Personal Conduct **6.** How to Keep Mentally and Physically Fit **7.** What to Eat When Mercury or Uranus is Afflicted **8.** What to Eat When Sun, Moon or Pluto is Afflicted **9.** What to Eat When Saturn, Jupiter or Neptune is Afflicted **10.** What to Eat When Venus or Mars is Afflicted.

To Order Brotherhood of Light Books:

Qty	#	Item	Price	Amt

Please include shipping & handling charges:
$3.00 first item, $.50 for each additional item.

Subtotal	
Shipping	
TOTAL	

YES ! Please send me a free catalog.

Ship To: _____

Address _____

City_____

State & Zip Code _____

Telephone _____

For ☐ MasterCard ☐ Visa Orders Only:

Card No. _____ Exp Date _____

Card Holder Signature _____

Send your check or money order to:
The Church of Light,
2341 Coral Street, Los Angeles, CA 90031-2916
(213)226-0453

To Order Brotherhood of Light Books:

Qty	#	Item	Price	Amt

Please include shipping & handling charges:
$3.00 first item, $.50 for each additional item.

YES ! Please send me a free catalog.

Subtotal	
Shipping	
TOTAL	

Ship To: _____

Address _____

City _____

State & Zip Code _____

Telephone _____

For ☐ MasterCard ☐ Visa Orders Only:

Card No. _____ Exp Date _____

Card Holder Signature _____

Send your check or money order to:
The Church of Light,
2341 Coral Street, Los Angeles, CA 90031-2916
(213)226-0453